The Vegetarian Handbook

Edited by
Jane Bowler

The Vegetarian Society of the UK

D1333972

18th Edition

First published October 1990 by

The Vegetarian Society UK Ltd
Parkdale, Dunham Road,
Altrincham, Cheshire, WA14 4QG

© The Vegetarian Society UK Ltd

British Library Cataloguing in Publication Data

The Vegetarian Handbook

1. Vegetarianism

I. Bowler, Jane *1965–*   II. Vegetarian Society (UK)

613.262

ISBN   0–900774–33–9

Alll rights reserved. No part of his book may be reproduced, stored in a retrieval system or transmitted in any way or by any means without the prior permission of the publisher.

Cover illustration by Greg Walker

Typeset by David Geen
Millgate, Delph, Lancs.

Printed on recycled paper by
CBL Recycled Print Ltd
217 Springvale Industrial Estate
Cwmbran, Gwent

Contents

Foreword

by David Icke, spokesperson for The Green Party

The response to the outrages in the name of animal rights has served to confirm that, whenever you get two extremes, they are, in reality, basically the same in their view of life.

First of all you get the "You care more about animals than people" syndrome – the belief that somehow you can have one set of values for animals and another for people. To them, abusing animals is OK as long as you don't do it to people.

The reality is that you can't divide the values applied to animals and those applied to people – they are indivisible.

Any society that allows a pig to be tethered in a tiny stall for virtually its entire life in the name of economics will allow people to sleep in cardboard boxes in the name of economics.

Any society that thinks it acceptable to have chickens on wire mesh, five to a cage just 20 inches wide, will think the same about locking up people three to a cell for 23 hours a day, with a pan in the corner for a toilet.

Any system that allows at least 130,000 animals to be tortured and killed in the laboratories of the world every day will also allow a child to die of preventable disease somewhere in the world every two seconds.

Values are not transferable. Values are values and life is life is life.

Then you get the other extreme – though thankfully very small in number – those who say its wrong to abuse animals, but OK to bomb people.

Martin Luther King said "The unarmed truth is the most powerful voice in the universe"; and so it is — the *unarmed* truth. The truth doesn't need a bomb and a detonator, and the truths promoted by the animal welfare movement don't need them either, and nor do they want them.

Those who harm people should realise that they are just as misguided, just as worthy of our disgust, as those who cause harm and suffering to animals.

They think they are somehow superior to those they campaign violently against; but they are not. Anyone who campaigns with violence comes from the same direction, and for the sake of this great animal rights movement it's time they learned that lesson.

But let not the system that supports the horrors of the laboratories, the factory farms and the slaughterhouses, throw up its arms in mock morality because violence begets violence, always has and always will.

And I say this to the powers of the day: "If you want to stop violence then stop acting violently. If you want peace then act peaceably. And if you want human decency then start acting decently towards human beings."

They won't, of course, without our unremitting pressure, the pressure from that unarmed truth of which organisations like the Vegetarian Society are such a crucial part.

So, let the message be clear to both extremes. The wall of inhumanity is beginning to crack, and once that breach is wide enough it will fall very quickly.

The wall will fall through pressure of public opinion – not through the power of the bomb which turns that very public opinion against us.

And when it comes crashing down, the Vegetarian Society can rightly be proud of the part it played in the triumph of morality over immorality.

Introduction

by Jane Bowler, Editor

The Vegetarian Handbook has changed! It is still the essential reference book for all vegetarians, but now it is a good read too!

It's all here, whether you are teetering on the brink of going veggie or you are an old hand. There seem to be more arguments in favour of vegetarianism now than ever before. All the details about the cruelty suffered by farm animals, the illness and discomfort endured by meat-eaters, and the damage that is done on a global scale as a consequence of meat production, are set out here.

We're not raking over the facts for the sake of sensationalism. Vegetarians are the pioneers of a lifestyle which can make an enormous difference to the well-being of humans, animals and the whole planet. We have a duty to make meat-eaters see sense.

Hysterical preaching and confrontational anger never made anybody go vegetarian. But it is my belief that, faced with the facts, no thinking person would choose to eat meat. This book contains the facts, plus a large chapter on how vegetarians can help to spread the message by becoming actively involved in the movement.

There are more vegetarians now in Britain than ever before. We are a force to be reckoned with. The message of this book is – get involved!

All the staff at the Vegetarian Society (UK) Ltd have helped to make this book a success – especially Bronwen Humpreys, Jane Brophy, Juliet Gellatley and Lesley Wilkinson. I am also grateful for the contributions which have been made by Dr Robert Sharpe, Dr Gill Langley, Dr Erik Millstone and John Robins, all experts in their fields. Particular thanks go to David Icke, a tireless 'Green' campaigner and Patron of the Vegetarian Society, who has contributed a very positive and optimistic Foreword.

Pamela Daniels checked the proofs and straightened out my English; David Geen typeset the book and offered lots of helpful advice; Greg Walker designed the cover and drew the illustrations. The book is printed entirely on recycled paper by Karl Long and the team at CBL Recycled Print.

This book is dedicated to the man who made me coffee, tidied up my mess, chauffered me around, read the proofs without criticism, and could always be relied upon for sympathy. Thanks, Chris!

Personal stories

> *I asked some of the people who work at The Vegetarian Society what made them decide to become vegetarians – the idea being to show that the reasons can be very varied indeed. The reason that YOU decided to give up meat has as much validity as any of these personal stories.*

Pam Tinsley works in the Youth Education department. She answers letters and phone calls from children and parents, and visits schools to give talks on vegetarianism. She also helps to write *Greenscene,* our magazine for young vegetarians. Pam is a vegan. She writes: "The horrors of the meat industry were brought home to me when I was 10. A butcher who had been invited to my school arrived with half a pig, head and all. He cut off and cooked various parts and invited us to eat them. It was then I realised that I had been eating dead animals! I became vegetarian immediately, and now give school talks to promote vegetarianism."

Jane Brophy is our Research Officer. She has a qualification in nutrition and her experience from working at the House of Commons means that she is often called upon to speak to the press on behalf of the Society.

"Ever since I can remember I have hated butchers' shops and handling uncooked meat, but for a long time it didn't occur to me to become vegetarian. The process of becoming vegetarian began when I was looking for ways to change my own lifestyle to live in greater harmony with our planet. I was worried about global pollution and the unbalanced distribution of world resources. The wastefulness of meat eating, in terms of the energy, land and resources meat production requires, struck me as a powerful argument for vegetarianism. After a while my committment to vegetarianism was strengthened by linking together the issues of animal exploitation and the destruction of the planet. It seems to me that cruelty to animals reflects a deep malaise in the values of our society. Meat eating is not only cruel, it is also unhealthy and unnecessary."

Vee Longton, our receptionist, deals with hundreds of calls and letters every day. She writes: "One evening, as a bored teenager flipping TV channels, I came across a programme which looked at how aliens would see the 'civilised' human race. In one section, a cow was driven into a tunnel, shot, drained of blood, and skinned. This was shown in slow motion and in great detail. As the skin was peeled from the body, it suddenly clicked that my evening meal and the process I had been watching were one and the same thing. I haven't eaten meat since."

Pat McGlashan, our General Manager, experienced the death of an animal at first hand. She writes: "As a ten year old in New Zealand I watched a farmer kill a sheep. The worst bit was that he was talking to somebody and joking while he did it. I gave up eating sheep then, although it was some years before I became completely vegetarian."

Lynn Dimelow, a regular helper at Parkdale, has not forgotten the experience that made her think twice about her diet! "Fifteen years ago, I was on holiday and waiting for my dinner of tender Welsh lamb with mint sauce and all the trimmings. We were admiring the view through the windows and somebody sitting near us gushed 'Oh, look at the darling lambs!' We did so, just as the waiter placed our meal in front of us. Ugh! Complete loss of appetite – I have not touched anything killed since."

Shirley Donlan works as a clerk/typist for the Society, but recently she has had to spend a lot of time answering the phone which rings constantly at Parkdale. Her daughter Marianne is also vegetarian. Shirley writes: "When I was 17 I worked at a holiday home in Cornwall, and while I was working there I met somebody who was a vegetarian. Just after he went home, one of the gardeners shot a rabbit in the grounds, because it dared to mess up his garden. It was just outside my bedroom window, and I was horrified as it writhed about in agony for ages before it died. I never ate meat again, and by the end of that year I had given up fish as well."

Rabbits also played a part in the conversion of **Lesley Wilkinson**, who works in London as our ϒ Symbol Liaison Officer, and is responsible for most of the ϒ Symbols you see on the packaging of vegetarian foods. She writes: "At the age of 11 I went to stay with a penfriend in France. We had written to each other and I knew that like me she kept rabbits. I was horrified when I found out that the rabbits she had were kept crowded together in a shed and that we were expected to eat them! It made me realise where meat comes from, and I have not eaten any meat since that visit."

Christine Tilbury joined the staff at the Vegetarian Society as secretary to the General Manager, but after working for a while in our Youth Education Office she finally settled down as a full time tutor in our Cookery School. "When I was 19 a Beauty Without Cruelty leaflet came into my possession, and I read it with absolute horror! How could we do these horrendous things to animals? The leaflet opened my mind to animal abuse in general, and over a period of reading and study about the subject I gave up meat and then fish."

Greg Walker is a freelance designer who does a great deal of work for The Vegetarian Society. He created Space Sheep and Astro Pig, the daring vegetarian crusaders – you can read about their adventures in *Greenscene*. Greg also designed the covers for this book. "I'd been toying with the idea of being veggie for some time but had never quite 'got round' to it. Then during a trip to the South of France, I parked by the side of the road to rest. Seeing a very large shiny black beetle scrabbling across the pebbles I decided to put in a bit of target practice, to see how near I could get to it. My first palm-sized rock crushed the life out of it, and within about ten seconds I was violently ill. With that kind of karmic retribution I decided promptly that killing larger animals to eat would involve far more punishing consequences, and my first step towards vegetarianism was taken."

Linda Farmer, who took over from Christine as secretary to the General Manager, takes her karma just as seriously. "I went vegetarian because of my interest in Eastern religions and in Theosophy which teaches the unity and sanctity of all life. The further evolved a man is spiritually, the less is his desire to eat the flesh of his fellow creatures. The law of karma is that we should do unto our fellow creatures what we would have them do unto us."

Bronwen Humphreys is our Branch Liaison Officer, and was Editor of *The Vegetarian* magazine for many years. She has compiled many of the Vegetarian Society's information sheets, and a lot of her work has gone into this book.

"I first became a vegetarian in 1974. A close friend had converted some months earlier but I rebelled furiously against all attempts he made to win me over. To my shame, I trotted out all the old arguments against vegetarianism, and a few extra which I knew by virtue of my training in agriculture and laboratory research. Nothing was going to convert me, I thought.

Then we started getting news of the famine in Biafra. Back in those days, we weren't so used to seeing pictures of starving children. I remember very clearly one evening, I'd gone to bed early intending to read and taken a beef sandwich up to my room with me for supper. I was lying on my bed, half listening to my radio, eating my sandwich and reading, when a few phrases from the radio began to penetrate. It was a relief worker from Biafra. He was saying that the relief charities like Oxfam weren't short of money on this occasion, plenty had been donated by concerned folk in the West (myself included!). But they still hadn't been able to help the starving people in Biafra for the simple reason that no food was available. The European Common Market had bought up all surplus stocks of grain and soya beans that year to convert to cattle feed.

It suddenly dawned on me that I was eating my supper at the expense of starving babies. I put down the sandwich mid-bite and I have never eaten red meat since. It took me several more months to give up poultry, and about two years to give up fish completely – this as the animal welfare consideration began to penetrate my brain as well as the human rights consideration. Looking back, what appalls me now is that as an agriculture student I had all the information at my fingertips, but never made the connection. We were taught that grain and soya had to be imported, that animals had to suffer because there was no other way to feed the nation. I never questioned that until Biafra. The facts and figures didn't change, only my view of them."

Juliet Gellatley, the head of our Youth Education Department, previously worked for the National Anti-Vivisection Society. Juliet recently helped to produce a video to be shown in schools which shows the connection between animal rights and vegetarianism.

"A picture of insanity – that is what I thought when I walked into a battery hen shed at the age of 15. A friend's father was giving me a guided tour of his farm. His intention was that I would 'come to my senses' and realise that farm animals do not have such a bad life after all.

It had the opposite effect. Thousands of birds were crammed five to a cage in long rows several tiers high. Hens' heads bobbed madly in and out of their cages. The noise was unbelievable, the stench appalling. The hens had nothing to do in their tiny wire prisons, except peck at their food or each other. They could not stretch their wings, fly or exercise in any way. They could not scratch the earth for food, perch or even clean themselves. I was in the shed for about five minutes – that's all I could stand. I saw three dead birds in that time, and was told that two barrels of dead birds were removed every week. I was angry, outraged and upset. I decided that I could not support cruelty and exploitation of animals any longer. I became a vegetarian."

Rosemary Billings is our Cookery School Co-ordinator, and over the past year or two she has worked very hard to bring the school into the limelight that it deserves. "As a child in the Hertfordshire countryside I had felt that there was something very strange about eating animals. Why was their flesh disguised by names like beef and pork? I kept asking 'What animal is this from, Mummy?' – almost as if the animal had given me permission to takes its flesh. The question should have been 'What animal am I eating mummy? – And why?' I grew up next to a piggery where the pigs were at least allowed to roam (how often do we see free range pigs these days?). The pigs were my friends in the morning but at one o 'clock the rules changed as I ate my friends for lunch. This situation was very hard for me to grasp, and of course it was never explained. It was just what humans did – there was no other option. At the age of 14 I had had enough of this great 'cover-up' – I broke free and became the vegetarian that I am now. Fourteen years on, no other decision in my life has been so important or far-reaching for me – I suspect it will never be beaten as the 'best decision of my life'. The rearing and slaughter of animals for food is to me the most disturbing part of life. I sincerely believe that adopting the vegetarian diet and lifestyle is a major step towards world peace – it is the higher path for mankind to follow."

Adrian Steele came to work at The Vegetarian Society as a temp in the Membership Department, and he never left! His rapid conversion to vegetarianism, followed by his rapid conversion to veganism, amazed everybody who works with him. Well done, Adrian!

"I wasn't planning on becoming vegetarian, honest! You see, it started with the idea that I would do my bit for animals. Over the following year or so, I began to eat less and less meat, even though I knew next to nothing about vegetarianism. I gradually reached the point where I only ate meat when I wasn't at home. At that time, I was looking for a job that I could do to help either humans or animals.

I eventually discovered the Vegetarian Society, and wrote to them in the hope that they might have a vacancy. They did, but said I would have to be completely vegetarian when I started. To my complete surprise, this was easier done than said! At my girlfriend's house that Sunday, the meal was a traditional roast. I said that I didn't want too much as I was trying to give up meat – but I got a helping the same size as everybody else's. I started on the potatoes, wondering how much meat I should leave, so as not to cause offence. However, I began to feel mentally sick at the thought of being forced to eat the meat, and in the end I left it all. Veggie at last!

I wasn't planning on becoming vegan, honest! At the Vegetarian Society I read an awful lot about the cruelties of factory farming. However, I thought I'd never give up my beloved cows milk on my breakfast cereal, or honey in my herbal tea… Anyway, it started with eggs. It was BEFORE salmonella hit the headlines. I began to associate eggs with human abortions. The eggs in the fridge went in the bin. Within a few months I had become a dietary vegan. All I have to do now is to replace my motorcycle leathers. There are plenty of alternatives that are waterproof, but none that give adequate protection if you fall off. Perhaps one day I'll find something suitable."

Some of these stories are quite harrowing, and some people became vegetarians overnight. Others came to vegetarianism by a round-about route, and made the change more gradually.

Everybody's conversion is an important individual choice – the choice that can change your life completely.

How many vegetarians are there in the UK?

Every day more individuals decide to go vegetarian – those individual commitments add up to a movement, one which is gaining momentum, but just how many veggies are there? Nobody can be quite sure, but there have been surveys...

REALEAT survey This is a Gallup Poll carried out for Haldane Foods Ltd, on a more or less annual basis since 1984. The 1990 survey found that 43% of the population were cutting back on the amount of meat they eat. 3.7% of the adult population were vegetarian, and a further 6.3% avoided red meat. Women were found to still be more likely to avoid meat than men (12.8% as against 7.1%) and for the seventh year running, women in the 16–24 year age group were the most likely to eat little or no meat. The first survey in 1984 found that 2.1% of the adult population was vegetarian, showing a 76% increase in just 6 years! *Contact:* Realeat Survey office, 2 Trevelyan Gdns., London NW10.

Leatherhead Food Research Association survey A survey carried out in July 1990 suggested that 48% of the adult population was reducing its meat consumption, 3% were fully vegetarian, and a further 2% had cut out all meat but still ate fish. They predicted a rise to 6% of people fully vegetarian in the near future. For further information contact the Association on 0372 376761.

Mintel survey A survey carried out in 1989 found out that 12% of those questioned thought animal slaughter should be banned!

Extrapolating from the findings of a number of recent surveys we estimate a total of 2,200,000 vegetarians in the UK. These are the main divisions of this growing army...

- **Lacto-ovo-vegetarians** – include dairy products and eggs (free-range please!) as part of their diet. This is the diet most commonly thought of as vegetarian.
- **Lacto-vegetarians** – accept dairy products but *not* eggs.
- **Demi-vegetarians** – are not strictly vegetarian at all! This is the term used to describe people who still eat fish and sometimes poultry, but have given up red meat. Demi-vegetarianism is often a first step on the road to vegetarianism, but is sometimes adopted for health or medical reasons.
- **Vegans** – do not eat any animal products whatsoever. This includes meat, dairy products, eggs, and honey. Vegans also refuse to use animal products in the form of clothing, cosmetics, household cleaning products and so on.
- **Fruitarians** – only eat fruit as they believe that plants should not be killed for food. They will not dig up plants to eat the roots, or harvest them for leaves.

Famous vegetarians

> *Veggies are not all hand-knitted-sandal-wearing weirdos all obviously related to Neil in 'The Young Ones'. Some of us are quite normal, and lots of us are sort of famous...*

We know about these people mainly from press cuttings. Occasionally celebs claim to be vegetarian and then, in a later article, reveal that they eat fish, so although every effort is made to keep the list up-to-date, we can't be 100% certain of its accuracy.

Actors/film stars

Debbie Arnold
Rosanna Arquette
Bridgit Bardot
Angus Barnett
Alexandra Bastedo
Dirk Benedict (A-Team)
Sandra Berkin
Candice Bergen
Christopher Blake
Bobby Brown
Faith Brown
Nicola Bryant
Julie Christie
Michelle Collins
Billy Connolly
Peter Cushing
Amanda Dickinson
Jenny Donnison
Sheila Gish
Daryl Hannah
Nigel Hawthorne
Patricia Hayes
Penny Horner
Reina James
Louise Jameson
Cheryl Kennedy
Lindy Lawton
Jennie Linden
Rachel Lindsay
Virginia McKenna
Bill Maynard
Rue McLanahan
Spike Milligan
Hayley Mills
Derin Moore
Simon O'Brien

Hazel O'Connor
Maureen O'Farrell
Kate O'Mara
Anthony Perkins
River Phoenix
Pamela Power
Jacqueline Reddin
Linda Regan
Carol Royle
Jenny Seagrove
William Shatner
Martin Shaw
Brooke Shields
Rob Spendlove
David Thewlis
Rita Tushingham
Clint Walker
Sophie Ward
Tom Watt
Dennis Weaver
Lizzie Webb
Sinead O'Connor
Doris Pearson (Five Star)
Prince
Rebel MC
Marisa Robles
Sandi Shaw
Sinitta
Siouxsie Sioux
Jimmy Somerville
Michael Stipe (REM)
Tanita Tikaram
Jane Wiedlin (ex GO-GOs)
Paul Weller
Toyah Wilcox
Alan Wilder (Depêche Mode)
Womack & Womack
Yazz

TV personalities

Marian Chanter
  (Krypton Factor winner)
Phil Cool (comic)
Barbara Edwards (BBC tv first
woman weather forecaster)
Simon Hickson (Going Live)
Penny Junor (tv presenter)
Diane Kemp (Gardeners World)
Joe Longthorne (impressionist)
Don McLean (tv comic)
Anneka Rice
Michaela Strachan (tv presenter)
Trevor Williams (Going Live)
Victoria Wood (comedienne)

Sporting

Peter Burwash (tennis)
Andreas Cahling (body builder)
Joanna Conway (ice skater)
Sylvia Cranston (triathlete)
Di Edwards (runner, olympic
semi-finalist)
Katie Fitzgibbon
  (marathon runner)
Clare Francis (sailor)
Carol Gould (marathon runner)
Sammy Green (runner)
David Johnson (BAA coach)
Ivan Lendl (tennis)
Jack Maitland (triathlete and fell
runner)
Kirsty McDermott (runner)
Robert Millar (cyclist)
Jonathon Speelman (chess)

Historical vegetarians

Annie Besant
Blake
General William Booth
Fenner Brockway
The Buddha
St John Chrysostom
Clement of Alexandria
Sir Stafford Cripps
Diogenes
Edison
Emmerson
Benjamin Franklin
Gandhi
Goldsmith
Lamartine
Luther
Mahavira
Milton
Montaigne
Sir Isaac Pitman
Origen
Ovid
Plato
Plotinus
Plutarch
Pope
Pophyry
Pythagorus
Richard St Barbe Baker
Schopenhauer

Seneca
George Bernard Shaw
Shelley
Socrates
Swedenborg
Thoreau
Tolstoy
Leonardo da Vinci
Voltaire
Dr Barnes Wallis
Mary Webb (writer)
Wesley
Wordsworth
Zoroaster

Others

Paddy Ashdown (MP)
Tony Benn (MP)
Tony Blackburn (DJ)
Godfrey Bradman
   (executive chairman of
   Rosehaugh Group)
Christie Brinkley (model)
Brigid Brophy (writer)
Sarah Brown (cookery writer)
Victoria Cooper (model)
Heather Couper (astronomer)
Viscount Craigavon (House of Lords)
Patti Davis
   (President Reagan's daughter)
Lady Dowding

Rose Elliot (cookery writer &
astrologer)
Barry Fantoni (writer/cartoonist)
Uri Geller
Howard Goodall
Angie Hill (model)
Princess Sadrrudin Aga Khan
   (and her husband)
Carla Lane (BBC TV scriptwriter)
Sir Michael Lever
Gail McKenna (page 3 model)
Helen Page
   (*Cosmopolitan*/Nationwide
   Anglia Highflyer Award winner
   1989)
Rhonda Paisley
   (Ian Paisley's daughter)
Molly Parkin (author)
John Peel
T.B. Pitfield (composer)
Ruth Rendell (author)
Isaac Bashevis Singer (writer)
David Shilling (hat designer)
Freddie Starr
Christine Stone (model)
Albert Schweitzer
Matthew Taylor (MP)
Dave Lee Travis (DJ)
Tracy Ward
Bernard Weatherill (Speaker of the
   House of Commons)
Count Duckula
Ayesha (Rider Haggard's *She*)

Factory farming

> *One of the main reasons why people give up eating meat is quite simply that they are horrified and appalled by the practices of the industry ...*

Compiling this section has involved a great deal of help from organisations which work to improve the lot of animals used for food, most particularly Compassion in World Farming, who can supply a wide range of useful information sheets. The facts and figures have shocked me and they may shock you too. You should read them so that you know the facts and can explain them to anybody who asks.

Although as vegetarians we are helping to decrease the number of animals being treated in this way, we should not be complacent. We should consider changing our diet again to cut down on all factory farmed foods, and should join in the campaigns for better legislation and conditions for all farm animals.

The facts are grim, but we cannot neglect a very important argument in favour of vegetarianism – farm animals suffer in many ways during their lives, and are then subjected to the final indignity and horror of the slaughterhouse.

Pigs

Sows of breeding age are regularly immobilised and artificially inseminated. They spend the 16½ weeks of their pregnancy in a dry sow stall. They give birth in a farrowing crate. Three weeks after having given birth, sows are artificially inseminated again. They are meat machines.

Up to 60% of UK sows of breeding age are kept in dry sow stalls. The individual stalls are 2 feet wide with metal bars and concrete or slatted floors. The sows stay in these crates throughout their pregnancies. They cannor turn around. They cannot take more than one step backwards or forwards. Some are kept permanently chained to the floor, with straps around their bodies. In general, bedding is not provided. Lameness, sores and hip problems are common. Having made exhausting attempts to protest and escape, frustrated sows lapse into stereotypical behaviour such as gnawing the bars of their stalls. The sow is an intelligent, sociable animal, but she is deprived of company. She is by nature a clean animal but has no alternative but to lie in her own excrement.

1965 – Brambell Report to Parliament: "We recommend that pregnant sows should not be kept without daily exercise in quarters which do not permit them to turn around freely and in any event they should not be tethered indoors."

1981 – House of Commons Select Committee on Agriculture Report – "Every effort should be made to develop alternatives to sow stalls that are practicable and economically competitive."

1988 – Farm Animal Welfare Council Assessment of Pig Production Systems – "The government should do all it can to encourage the adoption of alternative systems ... and the improvement in husbandry skills needed to avoid welfare problems. As soon as it is satisfied that the necessary skills are available and that welfare problems have been eliminated ... it should introduce immediate legislation to phase out stalls and tethers."

The Dry Sow Stall is still legal.

When the sow is ready to give birth, she is transferred to a farrowing crate. Although it is her natural instinct to build a comfortable nest in which to give birth, she has to lie on a concrete or wooden floor. The sow suckles her piglets for two or three weeks, then they are taken from her and she is made pregnant again. The piglets would normally not be weaned until they are three months old. As the sow is not given any medication to stop her flow of milk, she becomes very sore.

Soon after birth, the piglets receive injections, their teeth are removed with pliers and their curly tails are cut off without anaesthetic. This is to stop them from being bitten off by other pigs in close confinement. The male pigs are castrated, again without anaesthetic.

Battery cages are now being developed for piglets. Piglets are kept in tiered cages, standing on wire mesh, in darkness. One problem with removing piglets from their mothers so soon after birth is that they do not receive enough of their mothers' milk to have a healthy immune system.

Once they are strong enough, the piglets are moved to fattening pens, crowded together on a bare floor without bedding. They are kept in darkness until they reach the required weight for slaughter.

Beef Cattle

Most bull calves are castrated. This can be done in their first week of life by putting a rubber band round the scrotum to cut off the blood supply. Legally, this does not require anaesthetic or the attention of a vet. Up to two months of age surgical castration of a bull can be carried out by any person – no qualifications are necessary and no anaesthetic is used. After this age, castration has to be done under anaesthetic by a vet.

Calves also have their horn buds removed during the first week of their lives, by chemical cauterisation. When they are a little older, other methods can be used such as a hot iron. The person who performs this operation needs no qualifications.

A limited number of lactating cows are kept with the calves to nurse them. A cow may suckle up to ten calves during the course of her lactation. Then, the calves are brought indoors to be fattened. Their feed may contain hay, root crops, silage, barley, fishmeal, and turkey and poultry manure. Since the uncovering of BSE it has come to light that cows may also be fed remnants of diseased sheep.

Fattening cattle are kept in covered yards with straw bedding, although there is now a trend to save money by dispensing with the bedding and having a slatted floor for waste disposal. Cows find it difficult to stand on this kind of surface so they lie down. In the USA the final stage of cattle fattening is carried out in feedlots – open air pens where cattle are kept very closely confined and fed high energy grain rations. Cattle are slaughtered between the ages of ten months and two years, depending on the system used.

Cows for beef are subject to selective breeding procedures and one breed routinely has to be born by Caesarian section as they are simply too large to be born naturally.

Dairy Cows

A dairy cow is expected to yield as much milk as possible, and to supply a healthy calf every year. As dairy cows are of a different breed to beef cattle, their calves are usually considered unsuitable for rearing as beef. The calves are taken away from their mothers within 12–24 hours of birth, after having had their first feed. Some go for slaughter immediately, to make the veal for veal and ham pies. Their stomachs yield the rennet that is necessary to make non-vegetarian cheeses. For their first few weeks, most calves are kept in individual pens not measuring more than 5 feet by 3 feet. They are fed colostrum, the special newborn calf milk produced by cows, which gives them the immunity they need. They are given milk after about 3 days, and weaned onto solids at about 3–6 weeks.

Dairy herd calves go to market at a few days old. Their immune systems will struggle to fight off infections rife at the markets. There is no legal limit to the number of times a calf can be presented for sale at market. Journeys are frightening and hazardous. Ten per cent of calves die before they reach six months old. Many of the unwanted male calves will be exported live to Europe where they are reared for veal. Their unnaturally white flesh is then exported back into Britain.

Veal calves have been the subject of intense debate over recent years and the system in which they are reared should change soon. Soft white veal meat for the luxury market is obtained by restricting the movement of the calf by confining it in an individual wooden crate and feeding it a liquid diet deliberately deficient in iron. The calves are chained for up to 16 weeks. By the time they reach the required weight, they may not be able to walk or stand. This is an extremely cruel practice, and most British farmers now rear veal calves in a more humane way.

Sixty per cent of dairy cows are artificially inseminated. They give birth to their first calf around the age of 2 years. The calf is taken away almost immediately. The 1965 Brambell Report to the government states that "separating the calf from the mother shortly after birth undoubtedly inflicts anguish on both. Cattle are highly intelligent, and attachment between mother and calf is particularly strong."

The cow is milked to capacity, sometimes giving up to 10 times as much milk as would normally be demanded by her calf. While she is being milked she is made pregnant again and she will continue to be milked until a few weeks before her next calf is born. This is an extremely unnatural practice which is very demanding on the cow's body. Though dairy cows may spend summer grazing outdoors before being brought in for the winter, some are kept inside all the time, in individual pens. Dirty floors can cause foot infections and it is estimated that about 25% of cows suffer from lameness in any one year. Inflammation of the udder, mastitis, is caused by dirty conditions and milking equipment. The infection affects about one third of all cows every year and is routinely treated with antibiotic injections into the udder.

Dairy cows are subject to genetic engineering and growth hormones. Embryos from genetically superior cows, whose milk yield is known to be good, are flushed out of the cow and implanted into another cow. Calves which are unnaturally big have to be born with the help of a winch or surgery.

In spite of the fact that farmers already produce more milk than can be used, scientists have developed a drug called Bovine Somatotrophin which increases milk yield by up to 40%. Tests are still going on to find out how this works. It is thought that nutrients are directed away from the body tissues of the cow to make milk. Unless the cow eats a great deal, she is producing milk off her own back. There is evidence to suggest that BST has adverse effects on the health of cows. The milk from these cows is going into the UK's national pool of milk, but there is no way of knowing which farms are producing BST milk, and who might be drinking it. There is no information about any possible side effects. Compassion In World Farming have compiled a great deal of information about BST and campaign against its use.

Dairy cows have short lives. The regime is hard and cows' bodies become burnt out. They may be slaughtered because they have an infection, or because their milk yield is low. They may be slaughtered because they have failed to become pregnant at the right time. Often they are slaughtered when pregnant. This means extra profit. The unborn calf's meat is particularly tender. Most old dairy cow meat ends up in processed foods such as burgers.

Humans are the only species to drink the milk of another animal. Yet the milk produced by all lactating mammals is intended for babies only. Cows' milk is designed for baby calves, and many humans find it difficult to digest. Although milk is high in calcium and protein, these are amply provided by a healthy vegetarian diet, and milk is very high in saturated fats which contribute to heart disease. To produce milk, cows have to have calves, and if the milk is given to humans, the calf has to be removed. There are healthy and humane alternatives to milk.

Sheep

Sheep are thought to be one of the earliest domesticated animals. They are kept for meat, wool, skins and milk, with different products being valued more highly in different parts of the world.

Most sheep are still kept in the open air, eating a fairly natural diet, with social contact. Most are reared by their own mothers or by a foster mother.

But 4 million sheep die each year from the effects of cold, hunger, sickness, from pregnancy complications or from injury. One million lambs die from exposure within a few days of birth. Around 5,000 sheep a year are killed by dogs. And all sheep have to face the slaughterhouse; some also have to go through rough handling at markets and live export.

Nature never intended sheep to produce so much wool that it has to be sheared off every year. Man has manipulated the genetic make-up of sheep to make them produce so much wool. Because the British prefer the taste of lamb to the taste of mutton, the sheep have short lives, and can arrive at the slaughterhouse between the ages of 10 weeks and 15 months. Breeding ewes are manipulated into producing more lambs by controlling the amount of light they receive and dosing them with hormones to bring them into heat out of season. This also allows the farmer to have all his lambs born at the same time.

As multiple births and out-of-season births become more common, sheep are being reared indoors as a ewe is unable to cope with more than one or two lambs in cold weather. Many of the lambs that die of exposure have been born too early in the year. This is the result of farmers aiming to cash in on the lucrative sales of lamb at Easter.

Frogs' legs

Frogs' legs, no longer just an anti-French joke, are now a delicacy amongst the British. The main markets for frogs' legs are the EC and the United States. India has ceased to supply the market and has banned the killing of frogs, but other suppliers have not been persuaded to stop this lucrative practice.

Some 300 million frogs are killed every year to supply this 'delicacy'. The decrease in the frog population has led to an increase in insects and in insect-borne disease in countries such as Taiwan and Bangladesh.

Although some frogs are farmed, most are caught by hand by villagers who dazzle them with torches. Bags of up to 300 live frogs are taken by village bus or bike to processing centres. Many frogs will be dead by the time they arrive, some may already be putrifying in the heat.

The live frogs are picked up in two hands. They are pushed onto a large curved knife. They are cut in half. The unwanted head halves are thrown onto the floor, where they can take up to an hour to die.

The legs are packed in ice made from water that is not considered suitable for drinking, and sent to factories. Sacks of frogs' legs and ice are tipped onto the floor and local women are paid to pull off the skins. The legs are trimmed and packed in ice again for export.

The decimation of the frog population had such a severe effect on the ecological balance in India that killing frogs for their legs was banned. The trade in frogs' legs now looks set to have a similar effect in Bangladesh. The upset in the natural balance causes an upsurge in disease, and insects are then dealt with using pesticides which may be improperly used and highly dangerous. A report by the Taiwan Bureau of Disease Control shows that frogs' legs are often diseased, and can carry typhoid.

Several top class chefs have recently announced their intention to stop using frogs' legs.

Chicken

Poultry is popular. It is considered to be healthier than red meat by the British public. There has been a great deal of publicity recently about the possible health risks of eating beef. It is surprising that when the salmonella in eggs headlines appeared, few people seemed to make the connection between salmonella in eggs and salmonella in chickens.

Chickens that are reared for meat are known as broiler chickens. They are reared intensively in broiler houses. These are huge windowless sheds, housing up to 10,000 birds in one building. The chickens are allowed to roam on the floor, but as they grow there is less room to move. The wood shavings on the floor become so sodden with excrement that the chickens can suffer burns and ulcerated feet. The broiler sheds are ridden with disease and are favourite haunts for rats and flies.

Between 20 and 30 million birds die in the sheds every year, before they ever reach the slaughterhouse. One worker told the *Lincolnshire Free Press* (5.10.87) that it was his job to pick up dead birds:

"This has to be done every day because of the heat and the way the birds are packed in so tight. When you pick up a dead bird it is quite common for them to be putrid that they are just bags of bone and fluid."

The chickens die from heat stress and dehydration, from heart failure, liver failure and kidney failure. Infectious diseases spread like wildfire through a broiler house. Many chickens which survive their 7 week ordeal die on the way to the slaughterhouse as a result of the way in which they are caught, handled and transported.

Almost all table chickens are intensively reared. They are fed growth promoting hormones so that at 7 weeks of age they are large enough to be slaughtered. The unnatural speed of their growth means that their feet and legs are often deformed. The fact that chicken feed contains unwanted parts of dead chickens including feathers, heads and guts, means that chickens reared in this way are especially prone to disease. Estimates of the number of chickens infected with salmonella range from 80 to 100%. Good cooking kills salmonella, but not all chicken is properly cooked. Chicken pieces can be the salvaged parts of diseased or injured birds.

"If cutting up raw chicken, sterilise the knife and all surfaces the chicken has touched with boiling water."

Advice of Veterinary Inspector, reported in *The Guardian* 3.4.87.

- In 1981 it was estimated that **400 million birds are subjected to broiler systems in the UK alone.**
- In 1981 7 million birds were slaughtered every week.
- In 1987 10 million birds were slaughtered every week.
- Up to 10,000 poultry an hour are killed in Britain's largest slaughterhouse, and there are plans for a factory to kill one million birds every week.

Turkeys

During the run up to Christmas, millions of turkeys are massacred to play their part in the coming celebrations. Figures given by MAFF state that 33½ million turkeys were slaughtered in the UK during 1988.

Before the 1950s turkey production seems to have been on a very small scale, perhaps because farmers believed turkeys were delicate, fussy, difficult to rear and so hardly worth the trouble. The advent of controlled environments has changed the scene dramatically. Whereas formerly a farm might have had a few turkeys laying 'under the hedge' for the Christmas market, thousands are now kept indoors in regulated conditions for the whole of their lives. The turkey hen naturally produces eggs only in summer, but that meant the resulting young birds were too large for the table by Christmas. Now controlled lighting is used to enable eggs to be produced at a time convenient for the farmer rather than the turkey, and turkeys are slaughtered in large numbers all year round.

In many animals and birds, the breeding cycle is 'triggered' by the number of hours of daylight received. By prolonging the light hours artificially, the birds can be induced to lay out of their normal season. Turkeys have also been bred selectively for higher egg production. Turkeys are not very fertile naturally, so artificial insemination is widely practised. The eggs are hatched in incubators so the females are denied any chance to fulfill their instincts.

Many of the young birds or 'poults' are reared in large, windowless sheds where they are placed as day-old chicks. The floors are covered with wood shavings and the temperature carefully regulated. Up to 15,000 may be kept together. Food and water are supplied by automatic hoppers. At first they have a reasonable amount of room to move around but as they grow, this freedom diminishes, although overcrowding does not appear to be as bad as in a chicken broiler house. The Brambell Committee recommended 4 square feet per bird over 12 weeks of age and CIWF reports that Britain's largest turkey producers allow 3.5 square feet per bird over 16 weeks. The birds are fed a high protein diet based on grain and soya so they gain weight quickly. Females are slaughtered at between 13 and 18 weeks to provide oven-ready birds. Males are slaughtered at 24 weeks and go for processed meats such as turkey 'ham' and sausages. About 7% die before they reach slaughter weight, mainly from heart attacks induced by the unnaturally rapid gain in weight.

Birds that are ready for slaughter are often transported at night, taken from the warm, artificially lit sheds where they have spent their whole lives, shoved into crates and loaded onto lorries with no protection from the December cold, the jolts and noises of traffic. At the slaughterhouse or 'processing plant' as it is euphemistically called, they are taken from the crates and hung upside down by leg shackles on a conveyor belt, fully conscious at this stage. It may take up to 6 minutes before they reach the stunner – an electrified water bath. If a bird lifts its head at this stage, it may escape stunning altogether. After stunning, the birds pass by an automatic knife that cuts their throats and there is a back-up man whose job is to finish off any which missed the knife or which received only a partial cut. From there, they travel over a bleeding tank, are dipped into a scalding tank then enter a feather plucking machine. It is possible, through human and mechanical error, for some birds to reach the scalding tank still alive and fully conscious. There must surely be a less barbaric way of commencing Christmas celebrations.

Eggs

Approximately 90% of Britain's flock of laying hens are kept in battery cages. A standard battery cage measures 18 inches by 20 inches. It is normal practice to put five hens in each cage (although there have been cases of up to nine hens packed into one cage). The average wing span of a hen is 30 inches. In such a cage a hen cannot spread its wings or even move about freely.

The cages are arranged in tiers in windowless sheds. Artificial lighting, maintained for up to 17 hours a day, promotes egg laying. A battery shed may house anything from 3,000 to 30,000 birds. Feeding, watering, and ventilation are automated, and the floors of the cages consist of a sloping wire mesh that allows excrement to escape. When an egg is laid, it rolls away onto a conveyor belt. The mesh and the slope of the floors mean that the hens' feet are frequently deformed.

Hens are put into these cages at the age of 18 weeks. Male chicks will have been killed at one day old, by gassing or crushing. Battery hens stay in the cages until they are 76 weeks old. Then they go for slaughter, having produced on average around 300 eggs. Exhausted battery hens are processed into soups, pastes, stock cubes, baby food or pet food.

It can take an hour for a hen to lay an egg. It is against her nature to lay 'in public', the equivalent of you or I having to defecate in public. She tries to hold back the egg for as long as possible. When the egg is laid, the hen's egg vent is reddened. The other hens in the cage may peck at this sore area and this can lead to cannibalism. The weaker birds are unable to avoid the dominant birds as they normally would.

Instead of giving the hens more room, the farmer's answer is to cut their beaks off when they are still small chicks. A single unqualified worker may mutilate 1,000 or more birds in one day. In 1964 a government welfare body stated that this causes "severe pain". Nothing has been done. The pain from this practice may be permanent. De-beaking can lead to profuse bleeding, inability to feed or drink, and death from shock.

Hens can lose feathers and rub their skin raw on the bars of the cage when they feed. They can lose all the feathers off their backs from being pecked by other hens. The hens peck each other because of the overcrowded conditions and their frustration at not being able to fulfil any of their natural instincts. Natural instincts would include exploring, dustbathing, searching for food, grooming, preening, perching and establishing a natural pecking order. These instincts cannot be bred out of a battery chicken – battery chickens that have been released soon revert back to the same behaviour as free range hens.

Two million birds die in these cages every year, before they even reach the slaughterhouse. If they do survive, they are taken to a special slaughterhouse that specialises in dealing with tough old chickens. The nearest slaughterhouse of this kind might be a long distance from the factory farm. Hens that have never experienced any temperature apart from 70° Farenheit, are loaded into crates on a lorry – around 5,000 per lorry load. They are driven through all kinds of weather, often at night, to the slaughter- house. If they arrive in the late afternoon they may legally be left on the lorry to be unloaded by the next shift of workers in the morning.

A national opinion poll conducted in 1983 showed that only 13% of the public found the battery cage system acceptable. 82% said that if cages were used, they should be large enough to allow the hens to stretch their wings.

There are alternatives to battery cages that would give hens a better deal. The term 'free range' is a loose one, but generally means hens have free access to grass during the day, at a stocking rate of about 100 per acre, and sheds to provide shelter for the eggs and security at night. But the term 'free range' can be abused and in some so-called free range systems the birds are kept at a stocking density as high as in battery cages and never get to take advantage of their access to outdoors because they can't fight their way through the crowd to the doors!

The 'straw yard' system utilises a large weatherproof building with deep straw litter on the floor and the south side open to light and air. Perches and nesting boxes should be provided and the birds need at least three square feet of floor space each.

The 'aviary system' has a hen house with several levels of slatted floor to which the hens have access by ladder, and access to a grass run. The runs have to be alternated to keep the ground fresh. This system is relatively intensive and egg collection can be automated, but it still allows the birds some freedom of movement and a choice of environment. When buying eggs, don't be misled by advertising slogans like 'Farm Fresh'. If you spot examples of dishonest advertising like this, complain to the Advertising Standards Authority.

These alternative systems allow the hen a better life, but vegetarians should remember that they are not perfect. Unless their owner is also a vegetarian, hens are likely to be slaughtered for the table as soon as their egg production begins to wane, though this is more likely to be done on the farm so they will not suffer the stresses of crating and transport and auto- mated slaughter.

Free range, aviary and deep litter systems can all be abused by overcrowding, insufficient care and attention, and inadequate protection from predators. Grass runs that are not properly managed and rotated become infected with disease and parasites.

The Kill

The annual kill in the UK comprises 4 million cows and calves, 15.5 million sheep and lambs, 16 million pigs, and 550 million poultry. This slaughter yields 1.3 million tons of beef and veal, 435,000 tons of mutton and lamb, 800,000 tons of pork, 265,000 tons of offal and 1 million tons of poultry meat.

The average Briton eats more than his or her own weight in meat every year. In a lifetime, he or she is likely to have consumed 7 or 8 cattle, 36 sheep, 36 pigs, 750 poultry birds, a few dozen rabbits plus some other game and part of a deer.

Farm animals are neglected. Over 6 million livestock die every year before they are old enough to be sent for slaughter. They receive something like 20 times less veterinary attention than the average pet.

There are approximately 900 slaughterhouses in the UK and most are privately owned – only 24 are owned by local authorities and only 93 are export approved for the EC. Only export approved abattoirs have a resident veterinary surgeon. There are fewer slaughterhouses than there used to be – this means that animals routinely have to be transported long distances before they are killed.

Stunning methods

The Slaughterhouses Act 1974 says that all animals should be stunned prior to slaughter "to render them instantaneously insensible to pain until death supervenes." There is an exclusion for animals slaughtered to feed Jewish and Muslim communities as long as the killing is done by a licensed competent person.

The Captive Bolt method is used for cattle, some calves and some sheep. A 3½ inch bolt propelled by compressed air or a blank cartridge penetrates the animal's brain. It is a very effective method of stunning, unless the animal moves its head or the bolt is placed incorrectly, as frequently happens.

Electrical stunning is used for pigs, most sheep and some calves. An electrical current is passed through the animal's head using charged metal tongs. The disadvantages of this method are that sometimes the current is not held for long enough. A shock lasting 3–4 seconds is enough to immobilise an animal but not to render it insensible. Sometimes stunned sheep slip out of the tongs as soon as the current begins, thus they do not receive an adequate dose. Animals that are stunned may only be insensible for 20 seconds. The time between stunning and having the throat cut can be anything from 5 to 82 seconds. This means that thousands of sheep and pigs are conscious when their throats are cut.

Some abattoirs use high voltage electrical stunning in conjunction with a water spray for better conductivity. Research is going on into a different method of electrical stunning which involves sending a current from the head to the back legs of the animal – this causes heart failure as well as anaesthetising the brain.

The concussion stunner is another form of captive bolt which does not actually penetrate the skull. These are expensive, cumbersome and difficult to operate so are unpopular.

90% of Danish pigs are stunned by carbon dioxide gas. Some British slaughterhouses use this method, but the pigs struggle violently and go into convulsions.

Some bulls and horses are killed outright with a bullet. This is a considered to be potentially dangerous to the operator.

Slaughtering

After stunning, the animal is shackled by one hind leg to a conveyor and moved to the bleeding area. The arteries in its throat are cut and it bleeds on the floor. Brain failure follows. The time this takes depends on how efficiently the cut was made.

Until recently it was thought that the animal had to be alive, and its heart had to be beating, to achieve a good 'bleed out.' This has now been found not to be the case, and it is possible that in the future animals will be killed instead of stunned before they are bled out.

Tenderising

Meat can be tenderised by administering more electric shocks to the flesh of the animal between stunning and 'sticking'. The other method of tenderising the meat is to give the animal a massive injection of papain enzyme into the jugular vein about 20 minutes before slaughter.

Compassion in World Farming campaigns against this practice which it believes causes pain and distress to the animals.

Slaughterhouse conditions
Many animals are in a highly stressed state on arrival at the slaughterhouse because of transport conditions. Abattoir staff may use electrical prods randomly to get the animals into crowded pens which are noisy and sometimes without water. Muscular exhaustion and stress can affect the quality of the meat.

Poultry slaughter
Birds are shackled upside down to a moving conveyor belt. They are stunned by having their heads immersed in an electrical water bath. The stunned birds then go on to automatic knives which cut their throats. They bleed out. Then they go to the scalding tank.

But this mechanised process has failures. Some birds lift their heads to avoid the electrified water tank, and go through the knives without having been stunned. Some birds which are not of a uniform size are cut by the knives in the breast or in the head. It is possible that as many as 15% of birds enter the scalding tank still alive.

Manual back-up of each process, in which a man will check that birds have been stunned and properly cut, is now advised, but it is not a legal requirement.

Every year 40 million day-old chicks are slaughtered. They are the males, which are genetically unsuitable for meat production and cannot produce eggs. They are useless to the industry. There is no legislation on how the chicks should be killed – obviously they are too tiny to be treated on a large mechanised conveyor belt system like grown birds.

Sometimes they are gassed with carbon dioxide. Sometimes they are suffocated in sacks or containers. Densely packed chicks die within 2 or 3 minutes, but the chicks at the top can live for over an hour.

Sometimes they are drowned, in cages or nets. Boiling water is sometimes used. Finally, live chicks can be fed into a mechanical mill and crushed to death.

Ritual slaughter
If animals are being killed for the Jewish or Muslim community, they need not be stunned before killing, as long as the killing ritual is carried out by qualified practitioners of the faith. In 1985 the following figures were issued by the Farm Animal Welfare Council:

- **54,700 cattle ritually slaughtered by the Jewish method,**
- **36,500 by the Muslim method.**
- **28,000 sheep and goats ritually slaughtered by the Jewish method,**
- **1,531,000 by the Muslim method.**
- **2,340,000 poultry slaughtered by the Jewish method,**
- **9,100,000 by the Muslim method.**

Jews believe that originally man was vegetarian and that he has been allowed to eat meat only since the time of the Flood. Jews may eat beef, veal, sheep meat and poultry.

Cattle are placed in pens which turn them upside down. Their throats are cut with an extremely sharp blade. When they have bled out, the fore quarters are taken for meat, but the hind quarters are not used. Poultry have their throats cut, and are then placed head down into bleeding cones.

This method of slaughter was originally conceived in order to reduce the suffering of an animal as much as possible. But Orthodox Jews are convinced that no new methods can improve on the laws laid down by Moses, and consequently they reject new ideas about stunning animals before they are slaughtered.

Islamic slaughter requires that the animal must be spared as much pain as possible and that the meat should contain as little blood as possible. Muslims are allowed to eat meat from ordinary butchers when Halal meat is not available. There is debate within the Muslim community over whether stunning could be acceptable for ritually killed animals.

The information used to compile this chapter has been taken from many animal welfare organisations, most notably Compassion in World Farming. Their address and the addresses of other organisations are listed below.

INFORMATION

Alternatives to Factory Farming
  Paul Cartmell

British Society of Animal Production,
  PO Box 3, Penicuik, Midlothian, EH26 0RZ

Campaign Against Farm Animal Abuse(C.A.F.A.A.)
  P. O. Box 45, Birmingham, B5 5TW, (021) 440 2445 (24 hrs)
  To highlight and campaign against the cruelty inflicted on farm animals
  and to end all forms of factory farming. Promotion of the Vegetarian Diet.

Chickens' Lib,
  PO Box 2, Holmfirth, Huddersfield, HD7 1QT, (0484) 683158 and 861814
  Campaigning for total abolition of the battery cage system for laying hens
  and for improved conditions for broiler (table) chickens. Produces videos,
  fact sheets, leaflets, posters, etc. SAE for membership details.

Compassion In World Farming (CIWF),
  20 Lavant Street, Petersfield, Hampshire, GU32 3EW. (0730) 68863 and 64208
  Campaigns against factory farming. Has a network of local groups who take the
  campaign to the public. Takes a lead in political lobbying in UK and Europe.
  Publishes *Agscene*.

Farm Animal Welfare Council,
  Government Buildings, Hook Rise South, Tolworth, Surbiton, Surrey, KT6 7NF

The Farm and Food Society
  4 Willifield Way, London, NW11 7XT, (081) 455 0634
  For farming humane to animals, wholesome for consumers and fair
  to farmers. Works by informed pressure, education, consultation, co-operation.
  Welcomes new members — min. annual sub £4 includes lively newsletter.

The Free Range Institute
  P. O. Box 2, Newton, Powys SY16 1 22

The Free Range Egg Association (FREGG)
  37 Tanza Road, London, NW3 2UA. (071) 435 2596
  FREGG is a voluntary society whose aim is to encourage the production
  of genuine free range eggs. Advice is given on the production and marketing
  of such eggs. Where possible (mainly in the South East) farms are inspected
  and a list is issued annually of approved farms and the shops they supply.

The Humane Slaughter Association,
  34 Blanche Lane, South Mimms, Potters Bar, Herts, EN6 3PA

Universities Federation For Animal Welfare,
  8 Hamilton Close, South Mimms, Potters Bar, Herts, EN6 3QD

Fish – a special case?

The average meat-eater (and many who call themselves 'vegetarian') consumes half a ton of fish in a lifetime. Countless children's teas of fish fingers taught us that fish was good for us. Fish currently bears the seal of nutritional approval, particularly in view of its low fat content in comparison to red meat. The public is being encouraged to eat more of it and to incorporate it into a healthy lifestyle.

It is easy to identify with the smooth-skinned pig, whose hot breath sets him firmly in our familiar element. We can be tormented by visions of his intelligent face as he goes to slaughter, vocal and perturbed. But what of the cod, or the crab; beady-eyed inhabitants of an alien environment?

Lying on the fishmonger's slab, however, with glassy eyes and bloody gills, its flesh already exuding the rancid smell of decay, a fish is the victim of the same deadly process as the chicken which hangs in the butcher's window. It is strange that while many 'vegetarians' will avert their eyes from the limp, white carcasses of the latter, they will gladly consume the body of the former and enjoy a meal of Bombay Duck while recoiling in horror from their companion's Chicken Kiev.

If we choose to continue eating fish or seafood, we may defend ourselves by arguing that the first are cold-blooded and the second are invertebrates but this doesn't let us off the hook. The ability to feel pain is simply a device to escape from danger, or to encourage immobility of a wounded part as an aid to healing. And, like all vertebrates, the fish nervous system consists of a brain, a single nerve cord along the back (the spinal cord) and nerves. Nerves from the sensory organs enter the spine, making connections with the motor nerves and forming circuits which allow the fish to withdraw part of the body if pain is felt. Invertebrates, like the crab and the lobster, possess nervous systems which operate in a very similar manner. Although they do not have complex brains, their 'nerve ganglions' receive signals from the nerve cells in their bodies and allow them to move away from painful stimuli. In the case of the crab, these nerve centres are situated at either end of the body. Lobsters have many nerve centres which lie in a chain along the middle of the body and the same is true of their relatives, shrimps and prawns. Yet we toss them to horrible deaths in boiling water, where they suffer for a minimum of 15 seconds before they die.

But fish also die slowly and unstunned, from suffocation. They are hauled in from the sea in their wriggling thousands and left to asphyxiate in our thin atmosphere. Some fish, like trout, are caught by means of a line and fight furiously for their lives with a hook impaled through their sensitive lips.

Modern fishing fleets trawl with fine-gauge nets, catching everything in their way, including inedible and endangered species. Many people have recently decided to stop buying tuna, because tuna and dolphins tend to swim together and the nets used to catch tuna inevitably catch and kill dolphins. Dolphins are sea mammals – they need to surface for oxygen, and if they are caught underwater in nets they drown. Dolphins are popular creatures, but sadly fish seem to be regarded as a kind of vegetable by some 'vegetarians' who eat fish. Fish are living creatures and they do feel pain.

The pollution of our seas is directly absorbed by fish. As well as raw sewage, the seas are now polluted with chemicals used in industry and agriculture. Polychlorinated Biphenyls (PCBs), amongst the most poisonous chemicals ever used by man, have worked their way into the sea and so into the fish, where they can become part of the food chain.

Many marine mammals are now facing extinction, as the contamination becomes more widespread. Dead dolphins washed up around the world have been found to have high PCB levels in their blubber and livers, and humans who eat fish are also accumulating this poison.

Direct exposure to PCBs causes irritation, rashes, numbness, liver damage, clinical hepatitis, hypertension and strokes. PCBs also affect reproduction, causing infertility, spontaneous abortions and birth defects, and they can reduce the ability of the immune system to fight infection.

Sophisticated marine equipment has doubled and trebled catches in the past thirty years. Nations engage in verbal hostility to protect their fishing rights and wage war on animals like dolphins and seals who eat fish as their natural diet. Yet 50% of the world's catch is not used to feed humans – instead it is processed into fish meal and fed to livestock animals. We catch and kill animals to feed other animals to fatten them for slaughter ... a pointless cycle.

Fish are subject to factory farming methods too. The following article originally appeared in *Greenscene,* the Vegetarian Society's magazine for young vegetarians.

They're only fish!

by John F. Robins, Animal Concern (Scotland)

They're only fish! That's how many people think about the salmon farming industry. OK so they are packed into floating cages. OK, so they are denied their natural instinct to swim thousands of miles migrating between their breeding rivers and feeding grounds. OK, so they are injected with anti-biotics, treated with pesticides and hauled out of their natural environment into our alien world several times before they are finally killed by a knife or blow to the head. So what, they're only fish! The fact is that they are not 'only' fish. They are sentient animals which can feel pain and suffer from stress and deprivation. Only last year there was a successful prosecution in Germany against anglers who caused suffering to fish. You only have to look at the thankfully receding practice of giving out goldfish for prizes at fairgrounds to realise fish can suffer.

300 farms

There are now about 300 coastal salmon farms around Scotland and the Scottish isles. The industry sprung from experimental work carried out by university laboratories, notably Stirling, and has grown from a handful of small units to its present size in about two decades. Scottish farms produced 18,000 tonnes of salmon in 1988 and, in keeping with the rapid and controlled expansion of the industry, production is estimated to top 50,000 tonnes in 1991.

About £25 million pounds of public money has already gone in direct grants to establish salmon farms. Much of the industry is owned by multi-national companies. Unilever and Volvo cars are amongst those with stakes in the industry.

Cramped

In the cages, the salmon, depending on their size, swim around in their hundreds or thousands in a space about the size of a large sitting room. Six fish of about seven pounds each in weight share around one cubic metre of space. One way to tell the difference between a wild or farmed salmon is to pick up the fish by holding it at the base of the tail. Wild salmon, having swum thousands of miles, have a thick 'wrist' of muscle by which you can hold them. Salmon reared in cages have had no real exercise, develop little muscle tissue and will slip through your grasp. There are other obvious differences between farmed and fresh salmon. Through their diet wild salmon naturally develop pink flesh. Farmed fish have grey flesh. Although this makes no difference to the quality or taste of the salmon the farmers feed the fish expensive colouring agents before they kill them to make them cosmetically attractive to customers. This changes the flesh from grey to pink. Bulk buyers can even choose the shade of salmon they want and the farmers feed the right amount of dye to achieve the required hue. One of these pinking agents, Canthaxanthin, has been reported by the World Health Organisation to have been found as crystals in the eyes of people who consumed large amounts. Although recently banned from direct use in food for human consumption it is still allowed as an additive in food for battery hens (to give eggs yellow yolks) and farmed salmon.

Chemicals

Pinking agents are the most obvious but far from the only additives used in fish farming. In the wild, salmon are infected with sea lice. When they enter fresh water the lice die and fall off. This natural process is denied farmed salmon and, because they are packed together in cages, sea lice infestation can reach epidemic proportions. Nuvan, a pesticide which contains Dichlorvos (known to be dangerous to fish as well as humans), is used to clean the lice off the salmon. It is widely known that Nuvan is often used carelessly, causing pollution and damage to the fish. Even when used correctly it is not known just what effect the pollutant Nuvan has on animals or the environment. Despite numerous calls for it to be banned it is still the most commonly used chemical in fish farming even though it is at the top of the toxic list of the Department of the Environment's literature on the Input of Dangerous Substances to Water. The industry has reacted to public fears over Nuvan's safety: they have changed the name to Aquaguard! Sounds nicer but it's the same nasty stuff. Farmed salmon are also injected with antibiotics and treated with fungicides. Like any other intensive farming system the animals suffer through being confined, stressed and manipulated. Instead of improving the system to prevent problems the abusers look to their cohorts in the vivisection and agrochemical industries to suppress and camouflage the symptoms.

Slaughter

Salmon farming also has a tremendously destructive effect on wildlife. In 1987 a conference in Oban was shown photographs of herons, diving ducks, cormorants, shags and seals which had been killed at salmon farms. Animal Concern has received evidence of eight seals shot in a seven week period at one farm, seven seal pups shot on one afternoon at another and incidents of farmers travelling up to three miles to shoot seals. One conservation group openly surveyed farmers and from the replies received estimated that they would shoot 1,000 seals a year. From talking with farmers without revealing my identity to them and from eyewitness reports I would say 3,000 would be nearer the mark. On 1st August 1989, following an Animal Concern investigation, Skye fish farm manager Dane Reeve was fined £200 for shooting seals with a shotgun. Had he used a rifle, like other fish farmers, he would have committed no offence. In addition thousands more die at the hands of salmon netsmen and salmon angling authorities. It is more difficult to estimate the number of wildfowl killed but as they are more numerous and are more frequently tangled and drowned in nets the figure is likely to be high. It has also been suggested that rare otters have been killed by fish farmers. The sad fact is that anything which could possibly prey on salmon or salmon fry is an enemy of the fish farmer. It is a sick fact of economics that it is cheaper to shoot predators than spend time and money on non-lethal methods of keeping them away. While the industry has a million-pound budget to sell its produce, it has set aside just £3,556 to investigate non-lethal predator control.

Plastic

Another nasty by-product of fish farming is the physical waste created on site. Under the cages, excrement and uneaten food pellets build up, causing the ecosystem of the sea bed to suffocate. Even if the farms were removed it would take years for the sea bed to recover in some areas. The plastic sacks in which the food pellets are delivered also cause problems. On one short stretch of coastline beside a farm I picked up over 20 sacks. The farmer had also collected sacks and burned them on the beach releasing toxic fumes and leaving large areas looking like moonscapes.

What is in the food sacks also raised cause for alarm. In the February 1989 issue of *Fish Farm International* one manufacturer of a food pellet production plant stated that the following were all suitable for turning into food pellets: "...poultry and meat slaughterhouse wastes including feathers; incubator and broken eggs; reject cheese and other dairy produce ... and a host of other reject materials including manure." In the same magazine Professor Allen J. Matty of the Nutrition Unit, Institute of Aquaculture, University of Stirling, stated: "Animal by-products such as meat waste, blood, bone meal or poultry by-products or feather meal are... incorporated into compounded complete diets." Although it is believed that, because they are 'cold blooded', salmon cannot become infected with salmonella surely it is a mistake to allow such materials to be used in food pellets. After all, it was not until such things had been fed to cattle and poultry for many years that the danger of BSE or 'Mad Cow' disease and salmonella became apparent.

Salmon are starved for two weeks prior to slaughter, and it is seriously being suggested that, to stop fish reaching sexual maturity and dropping in value, they should be fed on alternate weeks during crucial periods of their life cycle. When you remember what they are fed it's hard to decide whether that's cruelty or a favour.

Workers

Although it may be difficult to feel sympathy for those who work in the intensive farming industry, it should be recognised that some of the employers are just as likely to exploit their staff as they do the salmon, wildlife and environment. There have been numerous cases, including an instance where a propeller fell off a boat, of workers having to be rescued from cages. Animal Concern has had contact with one employee who had to wait until a colleague resigned before a lifejacket became available. Another worker found that the provided accommodation consisted of a blanket on a bothy floor. There have been difficulties with vaccination of salmon. Workers on undulating cages have to inject thousands of wet, living fish using pistol grip syringe guns. Self inoculation is a serious problem and several workers have been hospitalised because of this.

Legislation

One of the big problems is that there has never been a serious attempt to establish proper coordinated legislation to control the fish farming industry and to limit its damage to the environment. The Crown Estate Commissioners, The National Farmers Union of Scotland (Fish Farming Section), various Regional and Local Councils, Water Purification Boards and the Health and Safety Executive have all had direct contact with the industry. Although different bits and pieces of existing legislation affect parts of the industry, most of the control is left to voluntary codes of conduct which are not worth the paper they are written on. In parts of the USA fish farming is subject to strict legislative control. Cages must be sited in a minimum of 60 metres of water with a half knot current to avoid sea bed destruction, and killing of wildlife is illegal. Basic legislation of this nature is long overdue.

Cost

One of the main controls over any industry is consumer pressure. To exert that pressure the consumer must have the facts to allow proper evaluation. If the price is all that counts then the consumer will welcome farmed salmon. If detrimental impact on the environment and wildlife, the scientific and agrochemical background and the factory farming features of the industry are all taken into account, perhaps the consumer will decide that the cost is too high.

Vegetarianism for health

Health has always figured largely amongst the reasons why individuals give up meat. In recent months – with Mad Cow Disease and stories of unfit meat getting into the shops – many people have realised with sudden urgency what veggies have always known – that meat-eating is really very bad for you as well as for the animals.

Vegetarians are healthier than meat eaters. The facts speak for themselves.

A study carried out in 1986 (Jill Davies/John Dickerson) concluded that lifelong vegetarians visit hospital 22% less often than meat eaters, and that vegetarians spend a similarly reduced time in hospital when they do have to be admitted. If the difference in time spent in hospital by these people is converted into economic terms, using the average cost for treatment as an in-patient, the lifelong vegetarians cost the National Health Service £12,340 compared with the omnivores' £58,062. Since vegetarians clearly cost less the health services less, one wonders why the Health Service does not encourage more people to become vegetarians!

The NACNE report of 1983 was commissioned by the government to draw up recommendations for a healthy diet in Britain. The vegetarian diet falls closely into line with the recommendations of the NACNE report:

- **A vegetarian diet tends to be lower in total fat particularly in saturated fat which is generally associated with animal sources (including dairy products) and proportionately higher in poly-unsaturated fats.**
- **Vegetarian diets easily reach the recommended levels of fibre intake.**
- **Vegetarian diets tend to contain less salt and sugar.**
- **A vegetarian diet contains adequate protein but with a greater amount from vegetable sources, as recommended by NACNE.**

Heart disease

Coronary heart disease is the single largest killer in Britain, claiming 180,000 lives every year. Yet it is almost entirely preventable. It is usually caused by fatty deposits (mainly cholesterol) building up in the lining of the coronary arteries, restricting blood flow. This is called atherosclerosis. If the blood flow to the heart muscle is cut off, the muscle dies. This is a heart attack.

The risk of suffering from heart disease is related to blood cholesterol levels. The medical consensus linking meat, dairy products and eggs to heart disease is virtually unanimous. These products are the chief source of saturated fat, and along with fish they are the only source of cholesterol. Vegetarians have on average a 20% lower blood cholesterol level than meat eaters and hence a reduced risk of heart disease.

According to *Diet For A New America*, by John Robbins, the only plant foods with a significantly high level of saturated fats are coconuts, palm kernel oil and chocolate.

Carnivorous animals have an almost unlimited ability to deal with satu-rated fats and cholesterol – even force-feeding laboratory dogs with butter fat failed to produce atherosclerosis. Natural herbivores cannot deal with saturated fats and cholesterol in this way. Man is subject to a build-up of deposits in the artery walls due to his unnatural consumption of animal fat.

Vegetarians also have lower levels of low density lipoprotein (LDL) – high levels of LDL are a particular risk factor in coronary heart disease.

Although other factors, such as lack of exercise and smoking, do contrib-ute to the disease, saturated fat and cholesterol are the main culprits. Numerous studies have illustrated this, and medical bodies all over the world, including the British Medical Association, agree that as the frequency of meat and poultry consumption increases, so does the risk of death from heart disease. Also, in 1984, the US Federal Government announced the results of the broadest and most extensive research project in medical history. It proved that people already at risk from heart disease can lower their cholesterol levels by cutting down on animal fats, and by doing so they can reduce their risk of having a heart attack by one third.

Cholesterol is essential to human life. It is needed for hormone and vitamin D production, and it helps metabolise fats. However, cholesterol is not needed in our diets because every cell in our body can manufacture it. A vegetarian diet cuts down heart disease by more than 30%. And a vegan diet, which excludes dairy products, cuts the risk by a massive 90%.

Blood pressure (Hypertension)

An editorial review, published in the *Journal of Hypertension* in 1984, asserted that vegetarians have lower blood pressure than meat eaters.

Similarly, an article in the *British Medical Journal* in 1986, reported that vegetarian diets have been shown to reduce blood pressure in controlled intervention studies.

Cancer

We live our lives surrounded by carcinogens that are difficult to avoid – there are hazards in the air we breathe, the water we drink and the clothes we wear but we *do* have some control over what we put into our bodies and vegetarians have a tremendous advantage.

Colon cancer Colon cancer has been linked to a lack of dietary fibre and excess animal fats, and vegetarian diets are associated with a lower incidence of colon cancer. There is not a single population in the world with a high meat intake that does not have a high rate of colon cancer. The National Cancer Institute in the USA has specifically related it to an increase in beef, pork, and chicken consumption.

A recent study published in the *American Journal of Clinical Nutrition* in 1989 demonstrated the reduction of acidic lipids (which are believed to play a part in the development of colon cancer) in people who switch from a meat-based to a vegetarian diet. After 3 months on the vegetarian diet levels of the acidic lipids were reduced by 75%.

The less fibre in a person's diet, the greater the incidence of colon cancer. Fibre is only found in plants – there is no fibre in meat or dairy products. Fibre acts like a broom in the intestines, sweeping things along. Without it, waste gets blocked up, giving the colon more time to absorb the poisons that the body is trying to eliminate. Meat itself produces carcinogenic substances in the colon. To deal with this, meat eaters produce bile acids in their intestines. One such acid, deoxycholic acid, is converted by bacteria into a powerful carcinogen.

Breast cancer At the National Cancer Research Institute in Tokyo as many as 122,000 people have been monitored for decades. Dr Takeshi Hirayama concludes that women who consume meat daily have an almost four times greater risk of getting breast cancer than those who little or no meat. The risk also increases with the levels of eggs, butter and cheese consumed.

Girls who eat meat start menstruation earlier than vegetarian girls. Early onset of menstruation has been linked with greater risk of breast cancer. As animal fat consumption rises, menstrual periods become heavier, longer, further apart and more painful, with greater pre-menstrual difficulties.

Cervical cancer and ovarian cancer have been shown to be most common amongst women whose diets are high in animal fat. Ovarian cancer is noticeably affected by egg consumption – a 20 year study of the links between ovarian cancer and diet published in the *Journal of the American Medical Association* in 1985 reported that "Women who ate eggs three or more days each week had a three times greater risk of fatal ovarian cancer than did women who ate eggs less than one day per week."

Prostate cancer By the age of 60, 40% of American men are suffering the discomfort of an enlarged prostate. This can be a fore-runner of cancer. Autopsies on American men have shown that by the time they reach old age, close to a quarter of men have developed latent cancer of the prostate. A study carried out by the University of Lorna Linda in California over a period of 20 years showed that men who consume large amounts of meat, eggs, cheese and milk have a 3.6 times greater chance of developing prostate cancer than those who ate little or none of these foods.

Atherosclerosis can cause restriction of the blood flow to reproductive organs, which can cause impotence.

Osteoporosis

Osteoporosis is the clinical term for the bone loss commonly suffered by elderly women. Technically, to qualify for the term, a woman will have lost 50–75% of the original bone material from her skeleton. The bones become weak and prone to fractures, posture deteriorates as the skeleton cannot hold up the body, and the results are back pain and pressure on internal organs. Osteoporosis is caused by excess dietary protein. The greater the excess intake of protein, the greater the loss of calcium, along with minerals such as magnesium, zinc and iron, from the body. A vegetarian diet is less likely to contain excess protein than a meat based diet.

Osteoporosis is also aggravated by the consumption of acid-forming foods, such as meat, eggs and fish. The body must maintain the blood at an alkaline pH. If we consume acid-forming foods, the body compensates by withdrawing calcium from the bones to boost the alkalinity of the blood.

Kidney stones

The calcium taken from our bones serves the purpose of boosting the alkalinity of the blood. When the body has finished with it, the calcium travels to the kidneys where the body tries to excrete it in the urine. This is hard work and can cause extra strain on the kidneys. High levels of calcium in the kidneys can crystalise into kidney stones – an extremely painful condition.

Fibre

Lack of fibre can contribute to diverticular disease, constipation, haemorrhoids and varicose veins. Fibre can help in the treatment of these conditions and is also helpful in the treatment of diabetes.

A vegetarian diet is also thought to be protective against the following conditions: gout, peptic ulcers, obesity, hypoglycaemia, gallstones, appendicitis, hiatus hernia. Most of these diseases are related to diets containing high levels of saturated fats and low levels of fibre.

Other health risks may be associated with the use of growth-promoters and antibiotics in meat production, with the use of nitrites in meat processing, and BSE.

Vegetarians can find that their health is improved because they are more in tune with their bodies and take personal responsibility for their own health, using holistic alternative techniques like relaxation and natural remedies rather than invasive medical options.

This material has been compiled from the work of Jane Brophy (SRD), from an article by Juliet Gellatley first published in *Green Magazine,* and with reference to John Robbins' book *Diet for a New America* which is highly recommended.

How now mad cow?

Obscene farming practices have led to the outbreak of a new and deadly disease that has killed over 18,000 cattle in Britain. But no one knows what type of agent causes B.S.E., or what the risk is to humans. Juliet Gellatley, the Vegetarian Society's Head of Youth Education writes:

Mad cow disease is killing over 300 cattle a week. The European Community, USA, Soviet Union, Australia, Austria, Israel, Finland and Sweden have various boycotts on British beef, and twenty local authorities in England and Wales have stopped serving it in their schools. But John Gummer, Minister of Agriculture, insists: "British beef is perfectly safe. It is not a public health risk and can be eaten with complete confidence." The government's record, however, on protecting the consumer from the meat and farming industries is terrible. There is a question that must be answered – is Gummer talking 'bull'?

The government, the Ministry of Agriculture, Fisheries and Food (MAFF) and the Department of Health all claim that either there is no risk at all to humans from beef, or that it is very remote. Nobody knows enough about the disease though, to be able to measure such a risk. Mad cow disease or BSE (bovine spongiform encephalopathy) belongs to a group of nervous diseases all caused by similar agents. These agents are a mysterious entity. They have never been seen and their chemical make-up is unknown. Not destroyed by cooking or irradiation, they could be an unusual type of virus, but then again they may just be a protein, sometimes called a 'prion'.

Whatever these agents are, they cause some devastating diseases: scrapie in sheeps and goats, TME (transmissible milk encephalopathy) in farmed mink, chronic wasting disease in deer, and two human diseases, kuru and CJD (Creutzfeldt Jakob disease).

Mad cow disease is unique to Britain. It appeared out of the blue in 1985, and has killed over 18,000 cows. It takes several years for symptoms to develop, but when they do the disease progresses rapidly. Sick cows become nervous and irritable; they lose co-ordination of their limbs and may become violent. Their brain is irreversibly damaged and turns into a spongy mass. The disease is always fatal.

The ludicrous practice of feeding cows – natural herbivores – with sheep brains infected with scrapie is thought to have caused the disease. Although this practice is common in other countries, they – unlike Britain – have to heat the brains to a temperature high enough to kill the agent. This temperature is not reached in ordinary cooking.

According to Professor Richard Lacey, clinical microbiologist at Leeds University, once the scrapie agent was eaten by the cow, it changed itself – it changed or mutated to cause a new disease. And if the agent has changed itself *once* to infect cows, what will stop it changing *again* when eaten by humans to infect them in turn?

The government's response is to state that the agent is not dangerous to people because they are different from sheep and cows. But there are many diseases that affect both humans and cows: salmonella and listeria poisoning, tuberculosis, brucellosis and cowpox. Also, if the agent is not expected to cross to people because they are different from cows, it is even less likely to cross to carnivores. But this has already happened. Mink have been fed sheep brains on fur farms in North America and have developed a disease identical to scrapie. And if rhesus monkeys are fed sheep with scrapie they do not contract the disease; but if the sheep are fed to mink, and the mink in turn to the monkeys, this time the monkeys are infected. This shows that the scrapie agent has somehow changed, in the mink, to be able to infect the monkey (a primate, like ourselves). It *is* possible then that the scrapie agent could also have changed in the cow, enabling it to infect people. This makes the government's argument that BSE will not infect us, because we have not contracted scrapie from sheep, (even though they have been infected for the last 250 years) a nonsense.

Mr Gummer's retort to this is that even if people could catch mad cow disease, they won't, because he has taken all the precautions necessary to stop infected cows being eaten. He states: "First, we destroy any animal which is found to have BSE. Secondly, any cattle entering the slaughter-house have the offals (brain, spleen, spinal cord, thymus, tonsils and intestines) which could harbour the agent, removed... Thirdly, almost two years ago we stopped the feeding of ruminant protein to cows and other ruminants. We thus cut off what is considered to be the source of infection." (In other words he stopped forcing cows and sheep to eat one another). At first glance they may seem fine words, even if they were put into practice three or four years after he knew about the disease, but examined a little closer many flaws – in fact large whopping gaps – appear.

There is no test for BSE in live cows. It is only known that a cow has the disease when symptoms appear, and as this takes several years, many cows are being slaughtered before having time to show that they are infected. The government claims that 87 cows suspected of having BSE turned up at slaughterhouses in 1989. Yet vet Martin Cooke told ITV's *World In Action* that there were 50 cases at his abattoir alone. Mr Cooke said: "The official figures are a serious underestimate. BSE cows are not being picked out at the slaughterhouse. I work at one of the few slaughterhouses where vets are always present – 90% only have meat inspectors with no veterinary training. How can they be expected to pick up BSE cows when most healthy ones show signs like the symptoms of the disease (such as anxiety and fear) when they're taken to an abattoir anyway?"

So some farmers are unaware that they are sending diseased cattle for slaughter, but others have been more unscrupulous. When the government decided to pay farmers the full price (instead of half price) for their sick cows, the number of BSE cases shot from 270 to 469 a week. Food Minister, David Maclean's predictable response is that even if BSE cows are reaching the slaughterhouse, this doesn't matter because the offal is cut out of every cow and this is the final preventative measure. But this is not the case. Instead of discarding the whole head, some meat suppliers are splitting them open with mechanical saws to remove the brain. Others are putting a steel nozzle attached to a hose into a hole at the front of the head. Water is then forced into the skull at high pressure and the brain gushes out of the chopped neck. Both methods spread the infection over the head which is sold to the public.

MAFF over-ruled environmental health officer David Shepherd's efforts in Truro, Cornwall, to stop the saw being used in abattoirs. MAFF stated that if any saws were smeared with brain tissue then they should be washed. Mr Shepherd retorted that "Anyone who accepts this suggestion doesn't understand the first thing about food hygiene. One of the main rules is that you never put water near red meat in a slaughter environment as it can spread the infection further." David Statham, environmental health officer, points out that when a cow's carcass is split, bits of the central nervous system are splattered over the meat, which is sold to the public.

It is thought that the BSE agent is confined to the nervous system, but almost all organs, glands and muscles (the bit we call 'meat') contain nerves. So even with the offal ban, nervous tissue that may harbour the agent is being consumed by beef eaters. Professor Lacey said: "The risk is one of degree. Meat for human consumption must contain nervous tissue since it is impossible to remove all the nerves from it."

Worse still, the offal from calves born after July 19 1988 is not included in the ban. The government argues that no ban is needed because these animals have not been fed on dead sheep or cows. But as sheep pass on scrapie to their lambs, it is likely that cows will also have transmitted BSE to their young. If this turns out to be the case, meat eaters may be regularly eating infected products.

Although ground-up cows and sheep are no longer fed to one another, they are still fed to pigs and poultry, and put in pet food. (Is this the cause of the recent outbreak of 'mad cat disease'?) Experiments have shown time and time again that the scrapie agent can pass to other herbivores, omnivores and carnivores and yet MAFF insist that because pigs and birds are not herbivores, they will not be infected. However, MAFF have been proved wrong again – pigs *have* now been infected in experimental conditions. Dr Gareth Roberts, a neuropathologist at the Royal Post-Graduate Medical School, has predicted that pigs on farms will be next to succumb. "My guess is that in a year or so, we are going to start mad pig disease," he said. MAFF and the farming industry have still not learnt their lesson. Both are giving way to pressure from the rendering plants which process 170 million tonnes of animal remains each year. John Field, chairperson of the UK Renderers Association revealed to the *Meat Trades Journal*: "We can only make a profit from bovine (cow) offals if we can include them in blood and bone meal for pigs and poultry". James Robertson of Forth Meat Supplies, added that if farmers insist that some parts of an animal are not used, then the large amounts of unused offal "could very quickly choke the slaughter industry."

BSE is already choking beef farmers. Bans from abroad are severely threatening their £450 million export trade in cattle, and sales of beef in Britain have slumped by a third.

The BSE agent has a long incubation period, so we won't know for ten or more years whether people are infected. "The worse scenario", said Professor Lacey, "will be that perhaps 5% of the population – say two million people – will gradually go mad. And they will need 6–8 million people looking after them." The BSE-like disease that already infects humans – CJD – causes loss of co-ordination and the senses as the brain is destroyed. There is no cure.

Mad cow disease was created by the obscene agricultural industries who are now paying the price for continually abusing animals with their intensive farming methods. It is about time Gummer stopped talking 'bull' (if that is possible) and protected the public rather than industry. All cattle from infected herds – around six million – should not be used for food or any other products – or for breeding. And if people really do care about their health, and the poor animals inflicted with the diseases, they should stop supporting the industries that cause all the damage, and go vegetarian.

Food poisoning

Food poisoning has been in the news a lot during the past year – and it's no surprise that meat is usually the culprit. Vegetarians can use the information on food poisoning caused by meat to back up their claims that vegetarianism is a more healthy way of life. There are some related issues, however, such as contamination of dairy products, and high residues of toxic chemicals on fruit and vegetables, which can directly affect vegetarian consumers.

Because new dangerous substances seem to be exposed almost every week, it would be very difficult to anticipate what the big food scare will be when you read this. It is not so hard to predict that whatever it is, it is likely to have been caused by intensive farming methods (in which unsaleable parts of diseased animals are processed into cheap animal feed, and animals are crowded together in filthy conditions), or by efforts to make greater profits by saving money (by adulterating food to make it seem better value for money, cutting corners on food storage conditions, stretching sell-by dates).

By becoming vegetarian you will already have made a great step towards protecting yourself from the modern epidemic of food poisoning. There are a few simple measures that you should take to minimalise the risk still further.

- **Keep your fridge at 4 degrees centigrade or less, and your freezer at less than –18 degrees centigrade. Invest in a fridge thermometer.**
- **Be sensible about reheating foods, and don't try to save money by finishing up scraps that have seen better days.**
- **Don't buy dented tins – they may have a tiny hole in them.**
- **Keep food preparation areas and your fridge clean, using a cruelty-free cleaner.**
- **Buy free range eggs, and if they are dirty, wash the shells before you crack them.**
- **Don't buy foods which you suspect have not been stored properly, for example sandwiches from warm counters where flies are able to reach the food.**
- **Abroad, drink only bottled water, and avoid ice cubes, washed salads, and dairy produce.**
- **If you do see something suspicious, report it to your local environmental health inspector.**
- **If you are unfortunate enough to get food poisoning from food that you have been served in a restaurant or hotel, complain!**

The Food Commission believes that as many as 2 million people suffer from food poisoning every year, though only a minority of cases is reported or even identified. About 50 people a year die as a result of food poisoning – babies and the elderly are particularly at risk.

Keep an eye on the newspapers and TV. Watch out for reports of suspicious foods – as soon as anything you eat comes under suspicion, act immediately to avoid the risk until you feel confident that the food you eat is safe.

Here are a few names which have been in the news recently, with brief explanations.

Salmonella – the most frequent cause of food poisoning – 90% of reported outbreaks are due to this bacteria. It can cause severe stomach upsets, gastroenteritis, vomiting and septicaemia. It is most commonly found in chicken, (one statistic is that 80% of frozen chickens are contaminated), eggs and intensively farmed salmon. Duck meat and eggs, tinned meat and fish, and cream products such as cakes and pudding, can also harbour salmonella. Proper cooking kills the bacteria.

Campylobacter – similar effect to salmonella, usually from poultry.

Botulism – rare, but deadly, the bacterium clostridium botulinum affects the nervous system, causing confusion and paralysis. Found in canned foods. Again, the bacteria is destroyed by cooking.

Listeria – found in ready packed salads, unpasteurised soft cheeses, sandwiches that are not kept properly chilled, and preservative-free chilled foods which have not been stored properly. Listeria is particularly dangerous to babies, as it can cause bacterial meningitis. It has been known to cause miscarriages and still births.

Staphylococcus – bacterium carried by humans which lurks in noses, boils and cuts. The bacterium is common but easily destroyed in cooking. Cases of illness caused by staphylococcus tend to be from uncooked foods such as sandwiches.

Clostridium perfringens – the second most common source of food poisoning after salmonella, tends to affect people in large numbers because it rears its ugly head in conditions of poor storage temperature control, such as canteens. Mostly found in beef and meat pies, and has been known to cause problems amongst workers on North Sea Oil rigs.

Bacillus cereus – harmless in small numbers, this organism breeds in mass-produced foods such as the rice from Chinese take-aways and is resilient to all forms of cooking. Incidentally, some people suffer reactions such as dizziness and nausea after eating Chinese food which has been prepared using too much monosodium glutamate.

Salmonella seftenber – bacterium which grows in the nozzles of tubes used to insert jelly into pies after cooking. The jelly is made with gelatine, from waste slaughterhouse products.

Aflatoxins – moulds that contaminate dried figs, peanuts, and grain, said to cause liver cancer.

Alar – commercial name for the chemical Daminozide, used by farmers to improve yield, colour and shelf life of apples, said to cause cancer. Wash all fruit and vegetables before use.

Mineral hydrocarbons – Previously used to prevent dried fruits such as currants and prunes from sticking together, also on citrus fruit as a wax coating, on some sweets as a glazing agent, and on the rind of some hard cheeses. The use of these products has now been ended due to doubts over their safety.

BST – Hormone used in cattle to improve milk yield, possible dangerous effects not yet fully researched.

Infected fruit – fruit which is imported from countries with poor sanitary facilities may become infected if it falls on the ground before it is harvested.

Red Kidney beans – must be cooked thoroughly to destroy toxins in the skins which can otherwise cause vomiting and diarrhoea.

Food poisoning, food adulteration and food additives are the subject of a number of books which make fascinating reading. It is said that during the Industrial Revolution, bread was adulterated with sawdust, and sugar was mixed with sand. Nowadays, some unscrupulous manufacturers continue to take advantage of loose laws to make a profit through unnecessary adulteration, whether it be by using water to bulk out products, using cheap slaughterhouse products in place of more expensive ingredients, or using artificial and potentially dangerous chemicals to make products seem more attractive. You owe it to yourself to find out more.

A vegetarian world?

> **"What would happen to the animals — if everyone became a vegetarian, all the farm animals would die out!"**
>
> **"Wouldn't we become dependent on imported foods?"**
>
> **So, OK I become veggie, get healthier and feel better about animals — it isn't exactly going to save the world, though, ... is it?"**

by Bronwen Humphreys,
Branch Liaison Officer and Editor of *Members' Forum*

I expect that most readers have come across these common objections to vegetarianism. The first one first — it *is* true that if the population of this country adopted a mostly vegetarian diet, the number of farm animals around would dwindle considerably. Some breeds might well become extinct altogether. The real problem is deciding whether this would be 'a good thing'.

The possibility that the British will convert to vegetarianism overnight is very remote, so we are never going to be faced with the problem of having to feed and care for thousands and thousands of redundant animals without warning — as some objectors may suggest. A much more likely prospect is that demand for meat, milk and eggs will fall gradually, so farmers simply will not breed so many replacements, and instead will start looking for alternative, more profitable crops. (Remember, no matter what economists might argue about the costs of food production, any particular product is only profitable if someone is willing to buy it.)

Many of us fall into the trap of thinking that the preservation of a breed or species must be a good thing in itself, regardless of the cost to individual animals within that species.

But we are talking about a very different situation to the preservation of native wild animals in their natural environment. We are talking about a situation where many of the animals are not native, where none are wild and few have any vestige of a chance of ever living a natural life in a natural environment. Above all, we are talking about a situation where the preservation of the breed is carried out at a high cost to individuals in that breed, in terms of pain, fear, loss of liberty, loss of natural environment, social deprivation, sexual manipulation, mutilation and assault.

The very concept of 'breed' is an artificial construct. A 'breed' is something humans have made, changing or fixing natural genetic features to build up a uniform population with characteristics that benefit the human manipulators rather than the animals themselves. Just one example is the very heavy fleece of modern sheep, developed so that humans can have wool for clothes and furnishings. Wild sheep don't need to be sheared every year. If they couldn't survive with the fleece nature gave them, they would soon become extinct. Farm sheep have to be sheared before the weather gets too hot or they would suffer from heat stroke and the fleece attracts parasites that make dipping necessary.

Yet, when considering the artificiality of a 'breed', we must never forget that the individuals within a breed are not mere units, but living, sensitive creatures, as capable of feeling fear, pain and deprivation as we are.

In his book *The Animals Report,* Richard North questions the morality of keeping animals in zoos in order to preserve a greater number of species from the consequences of human encroachment on their habitats. He postulates that if we have nothing better to offer them an artificial environment, with little hope of ever being able to restore the species to its niche in the world's ecology, then it would be more humane to let them quietly die out. If we insist on preserving them in the face of such odds, it's because humans don't want to lose out on something, not because we are considering the best course to take to prevent suffering to individual animals.

Such a view is even more valid when applied to farm animals, because for the most part we do not even pretend we can offer them a natural life. We breed them in the full knowledge that their lives will be, at the least, distorted and unnatural, at the worst, filled with pain and fear, and we do it solely because there's profit in the business. Don't be confused here by the issue of factory farming. Free range animals may be considerably better off than animals kept in crates, batteries, feedlots and other forms of intensive production, but they are not living a natural life, not by a long score. A modern farm field isn't a natural environment, it doesn't contain a natural population of plants and animals. A group of cows grazing together in a field may look aesthetically pleasing, but it is not a natural herd, it doesn't have a natural balance of gender, age and social relationships.

Unfortunately, humans seem to like preserving things for aesthetic reasons. We like to save trees and old buildings and ancient customs because it gives us some kind of pleasure or personal fulfilment to experience them. But when the thing in question is a living, sensitive animal, should we really put our own desires before its welfare? The fact remains that all animals originally evolved with senses, skills and patterns of behaviour designed to help them survive in a particular environment. The senses, skills and behaviour patterns don't go away just because the animal is placed in an artificial environment where they are no longer needed. Frustrating these senses, skills and behaviour patterns can be just as much an act of cruelty as beating or starving an animal. The pig in the narrow stall evolved to search for its food in woodland, rooting amongst the leaf mould on the forest floor. The fact that it is well fed and fat in its concrete and metal stall, doesn't mean it is happy. If you had a child and looked after all its physical needs perfectly, but kept it locked up in a white room with no windows, no toys, no chance to develop fully, you'd soon be apprehended by the Welfare Departments.

Perhaps we should be honest and admit that if we can't be bothered to preserve natural habitats, there's no real point in trying to preserve the animals that should be living there.

Very few people question that it is an act of kindness to put an animal painlessly to death if it is injured beyond hope of a pain-free future; or that it is better to neuter our pets than to allow thousands of unwanted litters to be born. But mention that it might be better for a breeding sow in a farrowing crate if she had never been born, and you will be met with chants of "Any life is better than no life". Is it really? Would you honestly like to be that child, fat and bored in its blank white room? Humans have an odd way of finding justification for activities that bring them pleasure, or profit, or both.

So, if we are to be consistent and follow our humane principles to their logical conclusion, will we end up with a countryside that is uniformly uninteresting, a vast expanse of cabbage patch with nary a bird or beetle in sight? That is what some of the most steadfast objectors would have you believe!

Personally, I'm a lot more optimistic than that. I think that a largely vegetarian population would encourage a greater variety of crops to be grown. Instead of the monoculture of cereals, mostly to feed farm animals, a demand would be created for new kinds of fruit, vegetables and salads, so it would be profitable to replant orchards and nut groves, and smallholders and market-gardeners would be encouraged. We might see a return to the sort of countryside depicted in story books, a chequerboard of small fields of varied crops divided by hedges and interspersed with plantations of trees. Such a change in itself would encourage wildlife.

You should also remember that animals are wasteful converters of food stuffs. They eat a lot more than they give back as meat, milk or eggs. It is said that a meat eater needs five times as much land as a vegetarian to provide his food (including food for all the animals he eats). With research continually going on to find new crops and improve old ones, the balance could tip even further in favour of vegetarianism, so a huge conversion to the vegetarian diet could release quite a lot of land from food growing.

Crop yields have improved so much that we are producing more cereals than we need. Farmers are now being paid to set aside land and not farm it. The Countryside Commission has recently announced plans for planting major new forests in several areas of Britain.

With more space, we could introduce parks where hardy British breeds could live in almost complete freedom, like the historic white cattle at Chillingham today. Meat-eaters argue that no one would allow these animals to live untrammelled on good land unless there was money to be made from their meat, milk and eggs. But there is even now a resurgence of interest in the countryside. Stately homes keep flocks and herds of the old British breeds that on commercial farms have been completely ousted by foreign introductions like Friesians and Charolais. With more and more people spending most of their lives in cities, the countryside has become a major leisure industry. People want to see animals and wildlife, trees and flowers.

With less land being used for farming, there would be space for more wildlife reservations where genuinely wild British species of plants and animals could flourish. It might be more humane to let those species we have bred to such an extreme state of distortion that they can no longer fend for themselves in a natural environment, die out. Instead, we could encourage the countries where the original wild ancestors of those species still live, to set aside reservation where they can live freely in their natural environment, while we ourselves look after our genuinely British animals and birds. It really boils down to how much humans care. Farming isn't the only way to 'preserve' various breeds. There is room for animals if we are prepared to let them have it.

No, I'm not afraid that a vegetarian future will lead to a boring, sterile countryside. I believe it would be a lot more interesting than the one we have at present.

Vegetarian Britain – *how would we fare?*

Many people express the worry that if Britain became a largely vegetarian country, we would become increasingly dependent on imports of food from Third World countries – imports that might be depriving the native inhabitants of much needed food. This is a difficult question to answer. A wide range of crops can be grown in Britain, but what *can* be grown, and what *is* grown, are two different matters. Economic demand, government policies and EC regulations, all determine what may be grown – not just climate and soil conditions.

It is also difficult to say to what extent importing food from Third World countries *does* deprive the inhabitants. Again, many political and economic factors influence the picture. Some governments are so deeply in debt that their need for foreign currency outweighs their concern for the health of their citizens. Wheat was exported from Ethiopia even during the height of the famine. Crops like coffee, tea, sugar, may be grown at the expense of food for home consumption because these can be sold to richer countries. Avoiding such products doesn't necessarily help the poor farmers in Third World countries. "With all cash crops, the evil lies in the way the rich world consumes too much, pays too little for it and ruins the environment to get it. " (Ann Cullen, *New Internationalist* , June 1986.)

Oxfam Trading and Traidcraft are organisations which import such products but cut out all middlemen so that the producers (the farmers who actually do the work) receive a fair price. Although the range of products is still small, we should certainly do our best to try to encourage such ethical trading. Finding out which big-name companies have a poor record on human rights, and urging them to reform, will probably have more effect on this issue than our decision to become a vegetarian.

Why meat-eating is destroying the planet

by Juliet Gellatley, Head of Youth Education, VSUK

Destruction of the rainforests

We need the rainforests. They are vital sources of oxygen. They moderate our climates, prevent floods and protect against soil erosion. Forests recycle and clean our water. They are the home of half of all animal and plant species on earth. They are a source of beauty and inspiration – an ancient life-giving wilderness. And yet they are being destroyed ... for meat.

A hectare of rainforests supports 800,000kg of plants and animals forever or 200kg of beef a year (1,600 hamburgers), for just 7 years. Once lost, these forests will never grow again.

Tropical rainforests store their nutrients in their trees and plants, and not in the soil. When they are cleared, the grazing land produced is so poor that little vegetation grows and the land is turned into a lifeless dustbowl.

Forests also control the run-off from rivers. Typically 95% of rain reaching the ground is trapped in the soil by the elaborate network of roots in the forest floor, and then released slowly into the atmosphere. When the trees are destroyed, the soil dries and cracks in the hot sun, and water rushes off the land. Because the soil is baked hard, water cannot seep through to underground reservoirs. So droughts alternate with devastating floods, killing millions of people and animals.

Not only are individual animals killed by deforestation, but one species of animal or plant is lost every hour. Also, trees are like the lungs of the planet, soaking up carbon dioxide and producing the oxygen we breathe. And yet an area of rainforest the size of Britain is destroyed each week, most of it to make way for cattle ranching.

Almost all the beef produced in Central America is sold (as a means of repaying foreign loans) to the USA for hamburgers. In countries such as Brazil in South America, rainforests are also cut down to grow soya beans – not for Brazil's own people, but for export to the UK, and the rest of the European Community where 90% of the beans are processed for animal feed … Cheap meat doesn't come cheap at all.

The Greenhouse Effect

Deforestation and the increase in cattle kept for meat are also changing the climate on a global scale.

The earth is wrapped in a blanket of protective gases, the most important one being carbon dioxide. It lets sunlight through while trapping infra-red heat, keeping the earth warm enough for life to exist. But because the atmosphere is being polluted with carbon dioxide and other gases, too much heat is being kept in. This insulating effect – or 'Greenhouse Effect' – is causing a rise in world temperature and is one of the worst threats to the environment.

Destroying the rainforests contributes to the Greenhouse Effect in two ways:

(1) Trees soak up carbon dioxide, so by burning and felling them we are destroying one of our most vital defences against the Greenhouse Effect.

(2) The burning of the forests sends huge amounts of carbon dioxide into the atmosphere, making the Greenhouse Effect even worse. Forest burning in Brazil was responsible for $1/5$ of Greenhouse gases released in 1988; and $4/5$ of these forests were burnt to make way for cattle ranching.

The cattle themselves are also increasing the Greenhouse Effect. They produce 100 million tons of methane – another harmful Greenhouse gas – each year. The methane is caused by bacteria in the cows' digestive system breaking down cellulose from the grass that they eat. The gas is belched out of both ends of the animal.

Each molecule of methane warms the earth 20 times as much as each molecule of carbon dioxide, and is responsible for almost $1/5$ of the Greenhouse Effect. One of the main reasons for this build up of methane is the staggering number of cows (1.3 billion) bred and slaughtered in the world for food each year.

Water Isn't Everywhere

Water is a gift we take for granted in the West. But our supply of water is disappearing at a terrifying rate. The source of this ominous trend can be traced to meat eating.

Farm animals are responsible for consuming 80% of the world's water supplies. It can take up to a hundred times more water to produce a pound of meat than it does a pound of wheat. And to produce a day's food for one meat-eater takes over 4,000 gallons of water; for a vegetarian 1,200 gallons; and for a vegan only 300 gallons.

Meat eating is taking its toll. Water tables are dropping and wells are going dry throughout the western world.

Water Pollution

A meat diet not only wastes water, but pollutes much of what is left. The factory farming of animals is probably the major source of water pollution in the UK. Waste from about 600 million animals is ending up in our water. This is extremely significant because the quantity of waste is so immense.

A typical battery egg factory with 60,000 hens produces 165,000 pounds of excrement every week. A small farm of 2,000 pigs produces four tons of manure and five tons of urine in one day. In many western European countries so many animals are raised that more than three tons of liquid manure exists for every citizen. There is simply too much dung to return to the land.

In Holland liquid manure is stored in large tanks and then dumped. Ammonia evaporates from the manure and causes acid rain. A third of the dying forest in Holland is attributable to this process.

Animal waste contains nitrates, antibiotics, hormones, parasites, heavy metals and pesticides. In the Netherlands, it is estimated that nitrate levels are so high that within 10–20 years there will be no water available for drinking. It will have to be imported.

In Britain manure is also devastating the soil – partly because of the excess ammonia and partly because the slurry from factory farming is too thin for the soil to absorb in large amounts. As a result, the slurry has seeped into our water-table.

Also, the dumping of wastes into our rivers has caused algae overgrowth and oxygen depletion, killing thousands of fish.

Meat production wastes and pollutes. Going vegetarian does more to conserve and clean up our nation's water than any other single action.

Famine

Western greed for meat actually causes famine in the Third World. 15 million children die slowly from malnutrition every year.

We feed animals with plant protein to create meat protein. But animals are wasteful. Only about 10% of the plant protein they consume is converted into meat. The rest is wasted.

It takes 3 pounds of grain to make one pound of poultry, or 10 pounds of grain to produce one pound of intensively reared beef. Over half the world's grain production is fed to livestock being reared for slaughter, instead of to people.

It makes far more sense to use plant protein to feed humans directly. By using land resources to grow plants instead of using them to support animals, the world can easily produce enough food to solve the World Food problem.

Western consumption of food is far higher than Eastern consumption of food. This is not because Westerners eat so much more than Easterners, but because Westerners waste food by feeding it to animals. To satisfy ourselves with a meat based diet we have to use most of our food to feed animals.

A lot of useful arable land is used either for grazing or for covered factory farms. To make up for the loss of arable production, we take arable crops from the East.

The Third World is crippled by debt. Instead of using land to grow crops to feed its population, it is forced to grow crops that can be sold to the West to help cover its debts. The good land in the Third World is owned by profiteering farmers and multinational companies which produce cash crops for the West. Small farmers are forced to try to grow crops on poor soil which quickly becomes exhausted.

Did you know that during the Ethiopian famine the West was importing grain from Ethiopia to feed cattle?

In theory this country alone could grow enough plant protein to sustain 250 million people. But farmers will always produce meat at the expense of plant protein while there is profit to be made. By rejecting meat you are helping to make the meat industry less profitable, and stimulating the demand for plant based foods.

Who we are...
and what we do!

The Vegetarian Society is central to the vegetarian movement in Britain. By joining us you can help to spread a message which is vital for animals, humans and the whole planet!

We are

- The main voice for vegetarians in Britain. Our membership is currently 16,000 and steadily increasing.

- One of the longest established societies working for vegetarianism and animal rights worldwide. We have been in continuous existence since our founding in 1847 and have an unbroken tradition of working for vegetarianism, healthy nutrition and animal rights.

- The National Headquarters of an organisation with branches and affiliated groups all over the country. We encourage new groups to start up in areas not already covered, and we keep all branches and groups in touch by a regular campaigning newsletter, *The Mailing*. Branches and groups organise local campaigns, meetings, lectures and social events in their own areas – full details are given in the Diary section of the VSUK Forum. By joining a branch or group you can play an active part in our work – we hope you will.

We have a team of full-time enthusiastic staff who are dedicated to the promotion of your views and the development of a healthier and humane society. We answer thousands and thousands of enquiries every year and send out about 50,000 sets of introductory literature. Members of the Society receive regular copies of *The Vegetarian* magazine with the *VSUK Forum* supplement, a copy of *The Vegetarian Handbook* and a membership card that entitles them to claim discount at over 260 establishments.

What we do

- Campaign:

    Through television, newspapers and radio... spreading the message of vegetarianism throughout Britain. We organise peaceful protests like the annual Smithfield Demonstration; have stalls at major events like the Living Without Cruelty Exhibition; we are co-organisers of the MEATOUT campaign. Next Smithfield Gala Dinner is 1st December 1990, the MEATOUT demonstration takes place on 2nd December.

- Promote vegetarianism by:

    Giving talks and cookery demonstrations to local groups, women's groups, youth clubs etc.

    Running a full-time Cookery School with courses on vegetarian cookery and nutrition for the general public and professional caterers. Students who successfully complete the four Foundation courses are awarded the Cordon Vert Diploma© Our Cookery School Consultant, Roselyne Masselin, frequently advises caterers and manufacturers on how to provide food for vegetarians. For more information see the central section of this book.

    Giving advice about nutrition and vegetarianism to the government and its agencies, caterers and food manufacturers. Promoting the use of our ϒsymbol on products that are completely vegetarian thereby ensuring a standard definition of 'vegetarian' and also making vegetarian goods much easier for shoppers to identify.

- Educate:

    We publish *The Vegetarian Handbook, The Vegetarian Travel Guide, Vegetarian Nutrition, Vegetarian Cuisine* and a variety of leaflets, booklets and information sheets. We are co-publishers of *The Vegetarian* magazine. We sell a wide range of books on vegetarianism and related subjects. We can help groups find a speaker; we have a library of videos available on loan.

    We have a Youth Education Department that organises the SCREAM! (Schools Campaign for Reaction Against Meat) and CHOICE (the right to choose a healthy vegetarian meal at school) campaigns; publishes *Greenscene*, a magazine for under-18s, and other leaflets and promotional items for young people; has produced and sells a video about vegetarianism suitable for use in secondary schools; gives talks to schools, and answers queries from children and teenagers. Under-18s can become junior members of the Society and receive *Greenscene* regularly.

- Research:

    Our Research Section sponsors scientific research into subjects related to vegetarianism, e.g. comparative health studies, agricultural projects and medical research that strengthens the arguments in favour of vegetarianism — all without animal experimentation. The Research Section has a separate membership and subscription rate.

Our office is open Monday to Friday, 9.00am–5.00pm. Cookery courses are run most weeks but must be booked in advance (send SAE for details). Our archive library is available for students who wish to browse but please arrange an appointment in advance (no library material may be taken off the premises but photocopying facilities are available at reasonable cost). We have a mail order book and merchandise service.

The Vegetarian Society of the United Kingdom Ltd.
Parkdale, Dunham Road, Altrincham, Cheshire, WA14 4QG.
Tel: (061) 928 0793 Fax: (061) 926 9182

WHY NOT JOIN US AND GET IN ON THE ACTION?

This is your invitation to become a member of the Vegetarian Society of the United Kingdom. Simply fill in the form and post it (or a photocopy of it!) to: The Membership Secretary, VSUK, Parkdale, Dunham Road, Altrincham, Cheshire WA14 4QG.

Please tick either: *or:*

☐ I wish to become a MEMBER of the Vegetarian Society of the United Kingdom Ltd. I declare that while I am a member I will not knowingly consume the flesh of animals (meat, fish or fowl) as food.

☐ I wish to become an ASSOCIATE of the Vegetarian Society of the United Kingdom Ltd. While I cannot yet practise vegetarianism I agree with its principles and would like to help the work of the Society.

I enclose payment as follows (please tick)

	Normal	Reduced
One person membership	£16 ☐	£10 ☐
Family membership	£20 ☐	£14 ☐
Life membership	£250 ☐	£180 ☐
(reduced rate for Senior Citizens)		
Junior membership	£4 ☐	

Reasons for reductions:
Senior Citizen   ☐
Unemployed or receiving income support ☐
Full-time student   ☐

I would also like to support the work of the
Research Section – subscription   £4 ☐

I would like to help your work generally and
enclose a donation of £ _____

Please make cheques payable to VSUK Ltd, or charge to Mastercard/Visa
Card number: ☐☐☐☐ ☐☐☐☐ ☐☐☐☐ ☐☐☐☐

Name on card: _____   Expiry: _____
Name & Address: _____

_____

_____   Postcode: _____
Signature: _____

(In the case of family membership please give names and, if under 18, dates of birth on a separate sheet)

For younger people

by Juliet Gellatley

Factory farming, animal slaughter, battery hen units, BSE, rainforest destruction, Greenhouse gases: these are just a few of the horrific factors that have made over 1.4 million of under–16s turn veggie. Judging by the thousands of letters we receive each week at the Youth Education Department, over 90% of you find it morally unacceptable to slaughter animals. You want to educate your parents, friends and family to a vegetarian lifestyle.

Many you are leading the fight against animal cruelty, writing contributions to *Greenscene* magazine – the only magazine for young vegetarians – and helping our campaigns by giving out leaflets and petitions.

Campaigns
SCREAM!!

You may have helped make our SCREAM!! (School Campaign for Reaction Against Meat) our most successful campaign so far. Over 500,000 information packs have been sent out. SCREAM!! has already educated many young people about the horrors of factory farming and slaughterhouses. The meat industry is big business – profits come before animal welfare. You are helping to make people aware of the horrific conditions endured by animals in factory farms, by handing out leaflets, putting up posters and talking to people. If you haven't already done so, send for your SCREAM!! pack today! It contains a leaflet, a badge, and a poster. The more y<u>ou</u> campaign the more y<u>ou</u> can achieve for animals.

Environment campaign

It is not only animals that suffer because of the meat industry – the environment and developing countries are affected too.

Our new environment campaign says 'meat production is inefficient – and causes pollution too!'

Fifteen million children die from malnutrition each year. Throughout the world millions of people are deprived of food because the agricultural land which could grow what they need is used to grow food for cattle.

In Britain, nine out of ten acres of land are used to feed cattle. Even so, we still import cattle food from abroad. To be so dependent on food imports to support a meat-based diet is immoral especially of you consider that Britain's own agricultural land could sustain a 250 million population on a vegetarian diet.

The amount of pollution caused by animals is reflected in the damage to the environment. Water is contaminated with slurry, methane produced by cattle is one of the major contributors to the Greenhouse effect and ammonia evaporating from manure is a cause of acid rain.

Fast-food chains are destroying the beautiful and precious rainforests at an alarming rate. Vast areas are cleared for cattle ranching and after only seven years the land becomes a lifeless dustbowl. Burning the forest produces another major Greenhouse gas – carbon dioxide. Help us to stop this suicidal destruction – join us in our environment campaign.

CHOICE! campaign

Can you get vegetarian meals at your school? The CHOICE! campaign, which was launched in 1988, aims to encourage schools to provide a healthy and varied selection of vegetarian meals.

In North Yorkshire and Solihull schools an estimated 20% of meals sold are vegetarian. These include all your favourites such as pizzas, pancakes, macaroni cheese and soya burgers and bangers – all quick, easy, cheap and nutritious foods. Many schools have already realised the moral and economic sense of serving vegetarian meals.

If you wish, as a veggie to be catered for, or to improve your choice of veggie meals, you have the right to petition at school – so send for our CHOICE! pack now. Put up those posters and fill in those petition forms!

The *4-week Menu Planner* for vegetarian catering and the *Nutritional Guidelines* booklet have been distributed to schools by half of the Local Education Authorities in the UK.

Health and diet

All foods contain nutrients that your body uses to keep fit and healthy. Because you are growing people, your parents may worry that you are not getting enough nutrients on a vegetarian diet, however you can assure them that a well-balanced vegetarian diet contains all the nutrients the body needs. There is nothing in meat, fish or poultry that cannot be obtained from vegetable sources. Five basic food groups provide everything you need; select from cereals, beans and nuts, dairy produce, fruit, and vegetables.

Eating meat is unhealthy, as animals are pumped with antibiotics and growth-promoting chemicals and some of these drugs stay in their flesh. Meat is the cause of 80 per cent of all food poisoning in the UK. A great many diseases are associated with meat-eating – high blood pressure, heart disease, kidney stones and some cancers. Meat cannot be a natural food for humans if it contributes to so many diseases.

School talks

Many of you will already have been visited by us in your school. You may have seen our *Food Without Fear* video which deals with the conditions in which animals are reared and slaughtered and examines the health, environment and Third World issues surrounding meat production. It has proved highly effective and can be shown to 14 year olds upwards. The video can be hired or bought by schools for £9. 99.

We provide, free of charge, as much literature as is required. For your teachers, we have the primary and secondary school teachers' packs. The former contains our *Space Sheep* and *Astro Pig* leaflets – which are designed for younger veggies and provide information about factory farming, nutrition and veggie recipes.

The Primary School Teacher's Notes are packed with ideas as is the *Youth Groups' Campaigning Book*. The secondary school teachers' pack examines four main areas of concern central to vegetarianism; Animal Rights, The Environment, The Developing World, Health and Nutrition. The pack contains ideas for class activities such as art work, debates, and role playing. It also has lists of resource materials and a reference section.

Encourage your teachers to send for a pack or write off yourself for one, it will be a great aid in Geography, Religious Studies, English and Home Economics classes.

Pointless dissection – Your right to refuse

GCSE and A level biology courses sometimes require students and school children to carry out dissections. The dissections are viewed as routine – they have been carried out thousands of times and the results will reveal no new information. There is no good reason why animal biology cannot be learned in the same way as human biology – from videos, slides, books and diagrams. Nobody would expect children to help dissect a human body!

Many schools practise vivisection as well as dissection – ie, they carry out experiments on live animals. To do this, the school should have a licence from the Home Office.

Most children do not want to cut up an animal, or even touch a dead animal. They hate the idea that an animal has been killed specifically for them. But often they feel intimidated by teachers or less sensitive friends. Dissection teaches a child nothing except that the lives of laboratory animals are cheap.

Two organisations, the British Union Against Vivisection and Animal Aid, run campaigns to help young people say "No!" to dissection. Contact them for leaflets and information.

National survey of young vegetarians

You and your teachers can help with the first ever national survey of 'Vegetarianism amongst under 18 year olds'. It is to be conducted by Bradford University. It will be aimed at you, not your parents, and will discover the number of under 18 year olds who are veggie and the reasons why.

Regional differences in numbers of veggies and any attitude differences between males and females will also be recorded. We also want to find out the attitudes of non-vegetarians. It will be of great interest to us to know how you feel about animal slaughter, factory farming, pollution caused by meat production, what organisations you are involved in, which magazines you read and what influences and pressures you feel from friends and family.

We will use this information to help us in our campaigning work and in designing literature; so that we can be more effective in saving animals and the planet. The results will be available in early 1991.

Membership and youth contacts

We run two clubs – 'The Green Gang' for under 12's and 'Club V1' (Veggies 1st) for 12–18 year olds. It only costs £4 to join and membership offers such a lot. You will be entitled to free copies of *Greenscene* magazine which is packed full of articles, competitions, recipes, fun pages, poems, book reviews, readers' letters and interviews with the famous! A membership card will entitle you to discounts in health stores, and members will receive, on request, free leaflets, posters, badges, and stickers.

If you want to become more active you can become a 'Youth Contact' and promote youth campaigns and vegetarianism to other young people in your area/school. We have over 100 'Youth Contact's already who give out leaflets, posters and set up stalls and raise funds. As a 'Youth Contact' you may work on your own or set up a group, and you can campaign on animal welfare, the environment, and other issues that are important to you. The Youth Education Department will help and a Youth Groups campaigning book is available free.

Leaflets, badges and stickers

There is a lot of information available to help you. There are leaflets on nutrition, factory farming, the Third World and yummy recipe leaflets. There are also CHOICE! and SCREAM!! leaflets, badges, posters and lots of stickers.

For younger veggies a sticker is available saying "I'm a vegetarian, no meat please!" It will help you to explain to people that you have made a choice not to eat animals. It will be of particular help when being served school meals.

INFORMATION

THE FOLLOWING IS A LIST OF FREE LEAFLETS AND STICKERS AVAILABLE FROM THE VEGETARIAN SOCIETY.

Why vegetarianism is growing
Livestock farming isn't just killing animals
If you saw what goes on in an abattoir
Things that vegetarians avoid ... heart disease etc.
Missing from your diet ... cholesterol etc
The Fish Leaflet
Vegetarian recipes (2 leaflets)

THE ABOVE LEAFLETS CAN BE ORDERED INDIVIDUALLY OR AS A SET OF EIGHT

SPACE SHEEP & ASTRO PIG....

Talk about nutrition
Talk about factory farming
Very easy veggie recipes
The SCREAM!! Pack
　　　which contains
　　　A petition form
　　　A badge
　　　A poster
　　　A leaflet

The CHOICE Pack
which contains
Stickers
A petition form
A leaflet
Campaigning info sheets
A poster

FOR ALL THE THINGS FOR YOUNGER PEOPLE PLEASE JUST PHONE AND ASK...
WE ARE VERY FRIENDLY AND APPROACHABLE... ASK FOR JULIET, PAM, FERGUS OR JO!

ALSO AVAILABLE
Results of school meals questionnaire to vegetarian secondary school children
Results of school meals questionnaire to catering managers at LEAs
4-Week Menu Planner
(and recipe book) for schools (£3. 50)
Vegetarian Nutritional Guidelines for school children (£1. 00)
Vegetarian Meals Sold Here (sticky on front/back) (50p)
Menu Board – stand up, write-on wipe-off counter top board with wording 'Vegetarian Dish of the Day' (£7. 50)
GO FOR IT – First steps in the Veggy Direction.

Research Section

The Research Section came into being in 1974, incorporating the earlier Vegetarian Nutritional Research Centre. The Section exists to promote, sponsor and assist in research projects, in order to establish the scientific foundation for the vegetarian diet and way of life, and to show economists, ecologists, agriculturalists and scientists how vegetarianism provides the solution to the worsening world food situation.

The projects largely deal with nutrition and food production. The findings of the research are made available through the normal scientific channels, through the Society's magazine and through lectures. Members of the Section receive detailed annual reports of the progess of the projects.

The Section also publishes, at intervals, an Information Bulletin, which consists of extracts from a variety of sources, including the latest issues of scientific journals, and gives up-to-date information on advances in nutritional research and other topics of interest to vegetarians.

With a growing proportion of the world's increasing population aspiring to the western diet, intensive livestock production is increasing, with more of the poorest people going hungry. People are now beginning to question the ethics of feeding livestock while the people of the Third World starve: they are wondering about the advisability of consuming large quantities of meat and perhaps even feeling a twinge of conscience. We must be able to present well researched alternatives if progress is to be made.

The Research Section initiates and supports investigations relevant to the wide scope of the VSUK's *Green Plan* for farming, food, health and the land. It administers funds for such enterprises, using the donations it receives mainly for these purposes. Its interests range from educational concerns over children's perception of animals, farming and food, to methods of husbandry in poor countries, and the economic effects of the EC's policies, as well as surveillance of all aspects of farming at home, nutrition, and additives and residues in food.

The section does not support any project involving experiments on animals. Its epidemiological efforts represent one of the best ways of replacing them.

The Section counters ill-founded criticism of vegetarian and vegan practises and can furnish evidence for the advantages of vegetarian living.

Collaboration with researchers at universities, polytechnics and hospitals strengthens the VSUK's influence and enables it to draw on their expertise. The Section is also involved in service to the Society's publicity efforts and in the work of other campaigning groups, such as the Food Commission, the Food Additives Campaign Team, the National Food Alliance and the Parliamentary Food and Health Forum. Its information and experience have been sought by consumer organisations and Government departments, as well as by journalists and producers of programmes on radio and television.

The Section's investigations extend to what happens on farms, in livestock markets and slaughterhouses, in knackers' and fellmongers' yards, in rendering plants and tanneries. The research takes into account practices in the rest of the EC and the USA, as well as trends in trade and consumption. It furnishes material for campaigners for animal welfare, and in particular for submissions and comment addressed to the Government-appointed Farm Animal Welfare Council. The Section's evidence has illuminated many murky areas in the meat trade. Biotechnology will command increasing attention as it is applied to food production and the rearing of animals.

As 1992 approaches, and with it harmonisation within the EC, the Research Section's testimony on the manufacture and labelling of feeds and foods, and the appropriate surveillance and control, takes on a wider significance. The use of growth-boosters and other drugs ('farmerceuticals') in rearing animals and of pesticides ('agrochemicals') will require broader scrutiny. Controversial practices such as the irradiation of food are 'hot' topics for assessment. The Section is being increasingly called upon for comment in articles and interviews intended for readers and audiences in other EC countries and in the USA.

Much of the Research Section's work is done by volunteers. The Section is dependent on donations and membership income to finance its work. Contributions and applications for membership should be sent to: The Research Section, c/o VSUK Ltd.

Spreading the vegetarian message

If you are a vegetarian for health reasons, then you may wonder why 'spreading the word' has been given such prominence here. If you are a vegetarian for ethical reasons, the chances are that you are already keen to try to convert other people.

The motto of the vegetarian movement is 'Live and Let Live'. Shouldn't we keep our convictions to ourselves, and let other people simply continue to live life in the way that they see fit? Of course we should – up to a point. No amount of preaching, angry confrontation or hysteria is likely to persuade a person to become a vegetarian. Have another look at the reasons given by some Vegetarian Society staff for their decision to go vegetarian – do you notice a single person who decided to change their diet because somebody else TOLD them to?

The change to a vegetarian diet is an important step. Sometimes it can take months, even years, for a person to cut out all meat and all fish from their diet. It is impossible to stay vegetarian if you do not feel satisfied and happy about the food that you eat. This is one reason why every vegetarian has to make the choice for him or her self.

Converting people to a vegetarian diet, or even to a demi-vegetarian diet, cannot be done by preaching. It simply contradicts human nature to suggest that mature adults will happily do what they are told without question. The vegetarian movement has suffered untold damage from over-zealous veggies who pour scorn on everybody who doesn't share their beliefs. The 'crank' image that we have all come to know and hate will only be reinforced by ill-timed and unconsidered attacks on meat-eaters.

This is not to say that we should not try to spread vegetarianism. Members of environmental groups campaign to help spread awareness about our environment. Members of animal protection groups campaign to persuade people to help protect animals. Committed vegetarians should go out of their way to reinforce the message that a vegetarian diet is a healthy diet, a humane diet, an environmentally-friendly diet, an interesting and easy diet. The best way to make other people sympathetic towards vegetarianism must be to show by your own example that vegetarians are not cranks, but happy, healthy people who have chosen to renounce meat on very sound grounds.

The preceding section dealt with some very good arguments in favour of the vegetarian diet. It is for these same reasons that we should try to persuade others to give up meat. Spread the word; for the sake of the animals imprisoned in factory farms; for the sake of our environment, poisoned by the effects of factory farming; and for the sake of the thousands of people suffering famine to sell *their* grain to feed *our* cattle. If you really care about your friends and family, and you truly believe that the vegetarian diet is a more healthy diet than a traditional meat diet, try to explain your convictions to them – for the sake of THEIR health.

If you are convinced that there are sound reasons for adopting a vegetarian diet, and you are convinced that you have made the right decision by deciding to become a vegetarian, then spread the good news!

Join the Vegetarian Society

Membership of The Vegetarian Society costs £16 for one year. There is a membership form included at the front of this book, which give junior membership, associate membership, and concessionary membership rates. We can send more membership forms to you on request.

We are a charity, and depend upon your support. With the money that you give us, we print thousands of leaflets giving support and advice to everybody who is a vegetarian or considering a vegetarian diet. We run campaigns to make it easier to get a vegetarian choice in schools. We publish the *Travel Guide* to help vegetarians to find good meals and accommodation in this country and abroad. We produce merchandise that helps to spread our vegetarian message. We run our Cookery School, teaching beginners, and company chefs, and restaurant owners, to produce great vegetarian food. We give support and advice to groups and branches all over the country; and we keep a register of speakers who can visit groups. We run a lending library of video tapes and slide shows. We work closely with food manufacturers to convince them that by making small alterations to the ingredients they use, they can use the Vegetarian Society's ⋎ symbol on their packaging and attract vegetarian consumers. In this way we help to increase the variety of foods available on the market which are truly suitable for vegetarians. We also have a Research Section which investigates areas of special interest to vegetarians – such as the development of new vegetarian foods. By becoming a member of The Vegetarian Society, you can help us to continue our work in all of these important areas.

Membership Card

What do *you* get, apart from the satisfaction of knowing that you are supporting our work? When you become a member, you will receive a membership card which entitles you to discounts at health food shops, hotels and guesthouses, restaurants and other establishments all over the country. A list is printed at the end of the book. New establishments are being added all the time – phone us for an update.

Take full advantage of the discounts that are available to you – shopkeepers will be impressed at the number of vegetarians using their facilities, and may increase their stocks of vegetarian items. Other customers may be interested to see your membership card, and ask how they can get the discounts too.

Free Handbook

When you become a member, you will receive your copy of this book – FREE.

Show your *Handbook* to friends and relatives – it is a handy directory for everybody who is interested in the vegetarian way of life. Tell them that Vegetarian Society members get this book FREE! If you have already bought this book, and don't need another free copy, give your free copy to a vegetarian friend or perhaps to a school library.

Magazines by post

When you become a member, you will receive copies of *The Vegetarian* magazine by post for a year. This magazine is full of interesting news, interviews with vegetarian personalities, lots of recipe ideas, information about new products, and travel news – along with a useful classified section, itself an up-to-date directory of guesthouses and restaurants.

When you have finished with your copies of *The Vegetarian,* take them to a doctor's surgery waiting room or a library where they can be enjoyed by other people. A casual read could turn into a lifetime of committment!

Members Forum

When you become a member, you will also receive *Members Forum,* a special newsletter full of news about local group activities and the recent activities of The Vegetarian Society.

Joining The Vegetarian Society helps *us* to spread the word. It can help *you* to spread the word too.

There is a special section on our membership form for supporters of our Research Section. By becoming a supporter, you will help the Research Section to continue its important work of encouraging and subsidising useful vegetarian projects. You will receive bulletins about the work that you are helping to sponsor.

Join the local branch

There is a list near the end of the book of local contacts and branches – we can advise you of any new ones in your area – just phone us. There are new branches springing up all the time. Bronwen Humphreys is our Branch Liaison Officer, and she can send you information about how to set up a new branch if there is not already one in your area.

Local groups

The Vegetarian Society has a country-wide network of local branches and affiliated groups, which play a very important role in our work. When we campaign at national level, we rely on the local groups to put forward the local angle in their own area. They can do this in various ways; by holding public meetings, publishing local newsletters, speaking to the local press and radio, distributing leaflets and so on. But that's not all they do! Obviously, each group chooses its own activities. Some concentrate more on one aspect than another, but generally the local groups support local vegetarians with help and advice. They might campaign for better vegetarian catering in schools, hospitals, restaurants etc. They hold social events, so no-one need ever feel isolated as a vegetarian. These include rambles, outings, meals at restaurants, parties, trips to the theatre and veggie barbecues. They have stalls at exhibitions, festivals and fêtes. They hold meetings, often with guest speakers talking about a whole range of 'Green' topics. They organise cookery demonstrations and 'taste-ins'. They sell our books and merchandise, and raise funds for our national campaigns. Events are advertised regularly in the *VSUK Forum*.

If you join the Society, you will automatically be assigned to your local group and be sent their address. You don't have to be a VSUK member to join in group activities, just go along and introduce yourself. If you don't know the address, send a SAE to Parkdale and we will send you an up-to-date list of local contacts.

We keep the groups informed of national campaigns and provide a forum for them to discuss their problems, describe their achievements and generally make comments and suggestions, by producing an internal newsletter called the *Branch Mailing*.

If there is no group in your area but you would like to start one, please write to our Branch Liaison Officer at Parkdale for a Start Up Pack, which is crammed full of ideas and information about getting a group off the ground. You might decide to become either a Branch or an Affiliated Group, which ever seems to suit your circumstances best. A Branch is an integral part of the Society, and becoming a Branch commits a group to certain formal obligations. An Affiliated Group is linked to us much more informally, but both branches and affiliated groups are entitled to a range of benefits, like insurance cover and grants, that don't apply to independent groups.

If you are keen to promote vegetarianism, but find that there are too few people in your area to form a group, you can still, make a valuable contribution to our work by setting up a vegetarian information centre. Should this idea appeal to you, get in touch with the Branch Liaison Officer.

Some of our branches have a long tradition, dating back to the early days of the VSUK, others were formed only a few months ago. Whichever category they fall into, you can be sure of meeting like-minded people if you go along to their events, so please give them your support.

Joining your local group, or setting up a new local group, can really help you feel a part of the growing vegetarian voice. There are many things which can be done more effectively by a group of like-minded people working together than by an individual. Being part of a group need not be all hard campaigning work though! Meetings can be in local vegetarian restaurants, or you might arrange group visits or activities. It's a chance to meet the people in your area who are vegetarians. Bronwen can help with suggestions for activities, and there are lots of ideas listed here too. All branches receive the *Branch Mailing* – this is a very informative and lively paper compiled by Bronwen, with input and reports, success stories and appeals for help, from groups all over the country. Each branch can learn from the experience of others, and it is a good forum for the exchange of ideas.

Become an expert vegetarian cook

If you are a keen cook, and you have enjoyed making the transition to vegetarian cookery, you can use your talent to help other people, and enjoy yourself at the same time. The ideal way to start is to do a cookery course at The Vegetarian Society.

The Vegetarian Society's Cookery School has really taken off in the last few years. Courses are now scheduled every week, and during some weekends too. Based at 'Parkdale' in Altrincham, Cheshire, we are very well located for all transport links, including easy access to both Manchester City and Manchester Airport. 'Parkdale' provides overnight accommodation, and we have lovely grounds.

Not only is our location an advantage for our students, but the fact that we offer such good tuition in vegetarian cookery means that people will travel from all over the country, and even from overseas. The variety of the courses attracts a diverse range of people.

We are seeing an increasing number of professional chefs and cooks who come to learn how to cater for their growing numbers of vegetarian customers. We also welcome beginners in cooking and the occasional hardened meat-eater! The courses are packed with information and practical work but the social side of the courses are not ignored, many a friendship has been made over the preparation table!

We run week long courses – a set of four leading to the coveted Cordon Vert Diploma© – as well as day courses, weekend courses and evening classes for locals. Why not come along for a day or a weekend – then you may decide to sign up for our Foundation One course, the essential base on which you can then build up to Foundation Four, and your own Cordon Vert Diploma© By doing some of our courses you can learn a great deal about food preparation and vegetarian cuisine.

The course content is continually being revised and up-dated so that we remain the prime source of information on vegetarian trends in the UK, if not the world. Our team of staff in both the Cookery School and the office and campaigning sections means that we stay one step ahead of the growth in the meat/fish-free diet and lifestyle.

If you feel you would like to become involved in some way then write or phone today for a Cookery School brochure. Not all our students are studying for the Cordon Vert Diploma© but if you would like to try your hand then do give us a call. It may change your life – for the better!

There may also be some other courses being run in your area – full time BTEC courses or just evening classes. There is a short list of courses at the end of the book, and your local library may know of others.

When you feel confident, you can use your skills to offer to do a cookery demonstration. Start by inviting some friends over for an afternoon in the kitchen followed by an evening meal, and make your dinner parties really special events. Make sure you are ready to share your recipes! Perhaps you could combine your parties with home sales of cruelty-free cosmetics and perfumes, or goods to support the Third World, such as those supplied by Traidcraft. At the very least, you could pass round a merchandise catalogue from an organisation such as Lynx (the organisation which campaigns against fur, and is also well known for producing some great fashionable T shirts), Greenpeace, or of course the Vegetarian Society – see if you can arrange a bulk order. This is a very easy and pleasant way to raise funds for charity. Your guests might also be interested to see a copy of The Vegetarian Society's list of cookery books which are available by mail order.

You could offer to do cookery demonstrations at local fairs and events, setting up your own stall. Don't forget to phone the Vegetarian Society first, to get a supply of Cookery School leaflets and perhaps some recipe leaflets to put out on the stall. Leon Lewis, a very well known vegetarian chef, travels the country doing cookery demonstrations. He has written a special leaflet called *Guidelines for Organisers of Cookery Demonstrations.* You can obtain a copy of the leaflet by writing to Leon at 132b London Road, Brentwood, Essex, CM14 4NS. You could give demonstrations to groups such as Girl Guides or Scouts, the local Women's Institute, mother & toddler groups, and perhaps schools and colleges. If you do not really feel confident about being able to teach other people about vegetarian food, why not just offer to set up a stall at your local fête to sell veggie burgers in a bun, or bring in some special vegetarian sausage rolls for the refreshment stall. You can help other vegetarians to find food at the event, and perhaps also convince a few meat-eaters that vegetarian food is freely available and tasty! One of the very best ways to impress non-vegetarians and make them re-assess their attitude towards their diet, is to make sure that there is always a tasty vegetarian alternative available – when they find themselves *choosing* vegetarian, they may decide to make it a habit!

If you become really proficient, come back to the Vegetarian Society for our cookery course called *Learning to Demonstrate.* This course is normally aimed at people who have completed their Cordon Vert Diploma.© When you reach this standard you may even be able to offer classes yourself. Contact your local college to see if they are interested in setting up some evening classes in vegetarian cooking.

Catering as a Business Idea

The Vegetarian Society's Cookery School also runs occasional weekend cookery courses for those people who are considering vegetarian catering as a business idea – with extra tuition in the other skills, such as book-keeping, which are necessary for running your business successfully. Try to use your own success to give publicity to The Vegetarian Society whenever you can. You never know how many people may make their first moves towards vegetarianism through your example, or because of a leaflet they have picked up from your stall.

If you decide to make cooking your speciality, perhaps eventually you may open your own vegetarian café or restaurant! Or perhaps you could have a regular stall at the local weekly market, selling hot and cold vegetarian food. You could contact your local health food shop to see if they are interested in selling your pasties and quiches from their chilled cabinet; or even look into making ready-made vegetarian frozen meals. It is, of course, essential to check that your kitchen and your working methods comply with regulations for health, hygiene and safety if you are considering cooking on a large scale. There is a list of organisations you might find helpful at the end of the book.

You could put a notice in the window of your health food shop to tell people that you are able to offer a vegetarian catering service for local events, meeting, weddings and so on. Always be sure to offer the very best service that you can – the aim is to impress people, not to put them off vegetarian food for life!

Speak your mind

Perhaps cooking is not your forté. But you still feel very strongly about your vegetarian diet and would like to help educate other people. Have you considered giving talks? The Vegetarian Society runs regular Speakers' Courses, hosted by our Chairman Mr Maxwell Lee, who is highly experienced and a leading light in the International Vegetarian Union. Learning to

speak in public may at first seem daunting, but a visit to our Headquarters in Altrincham is a great way to learn, amongst like-minded people, in a friendly atmosphere. There are also plenty of books on public speaking which may help – The Vegetarian Society stocks one called *Stand And Deliver* by Kenneth P Brown which can be ordered from our Merchandise Department and costs £2.50. There are even some self-hypnosis tapes on the market now, which may help to conquer the initial fears of public speaking! If you do decide to address an audience, try to make a good job of it – each member of the audience may be basing their opinion of vegetarianism on *you!*

All vegetarians who are in the public eye should bear in mind that they are seen as representatives of the vegetarian movement. It is important to show that vegetarians are fit and healthy. Like it or not, public opinion will judge you as much by your appearance and your behaviour as on your words. It pays to make an effort on special occasions!

Once you become confident, you can offer to do talks for local groups such as local branches of environmental groups, youth clubs, schools and women's groups. Make absolutely sure that you know your facts and take along some Vegetarian Society leaflets for people to pick up afterwards. If you would like to be 'on call' in your area to do talks, phone Linda Farmer at The Vegetarian Society. Linda is secretary to the General Manager and she holds an up-to-date list of people who are willing to speak to groups. We can send speakers all over the country.

As a first step, why not try to arrange for a speaker to visit a group that you belong to? This is a good way of finding out what is involved in giving talks, and you can educate your group at the same time.

The video

Last year, the Vegetarian Society's Youth Education Department raised enough money, through a fund-raising campaign, to finance the production of a brand new video about vegetarianism called *Food Without Fear*. Although the video was initially aimed at young people, it can be shown equally effectively to groups of almost any age. The video lasts 20 minutes, and you can buy it or hire it from The Vegetarian Society. You may choose to use it as a jumping-off point for a talk or a discussion – perhaps questions from the audience can be answered by two or three vegetarian 'experts'. Make sure you are familiar with all the arguments raised in the video before you show it. If you have any queries, phone The Vegetarian Society.

Made by award-winning Channel Four film makers Vanson–Wardle, *Food without Fear* is an entertaining, powerful and thought provoking programme on all the pressing issues concerning meat production.

Food Without Fear exposes the conditions in which animals are reared, and looks at the effect meat has on health, the environment and the Third World. It also gives careful consideration to the alternative lifestyle available, and explains how vegetarians can get all the nutrients they need.

Through the scepticism of Vas Blackwood ('Winston' from *The Lenny Henry Show*) and the considered arguments of Ishia Bennison (from *East*

Enders), it tackles the myths surrounding vegetarianism and sets the record straight.

Food Without Fear is a valuable and informative video. It may be used either on its own or with a presenter. It is a must for anyone interested in or concerned with the welfare of our planet and its inhabitants.

The Vegetarian Society has a library of informative animal welfare videos and slide shows which are available for hire. Linda Farmer and Shirley Donlan deal with this, and they can tell you which videos are available.

Be well informed

The perils of meat-eating, and food scandals in general, have been in the news a great deal this year. It pays to keep up to date with current affairs if you hope to persuade other people to go vegetarian. There is nothing more humiliating than trying to convince somebody that a vegetarian diet is a good diet, and being asked a question about which you know nothing. Read up on the subject, and become an expert in your field. The Vegetarian Society sells books by mail order and has a very extensive selection of useful books available. The list changes all the time – phone in for your updated copy.

INFORMATION

Why You Don't Need Meat
  Peter Cox
Living Without Cruelty
  Mark Gold
Compassion, The Ultimate Ethic
  Victoria Moran
Vegetarianism – The Philosophy Behind the Ethical Diet
  Daniel Domrowski ,Thorsons

Networking

You can also make sure that you are well-informed by taking part in activities arranged by other local groups, like the local branch of Friends of the Earth. By going to workshops on topics such as recycling, for example, you can meet other people who are knowledgeable in specialist areas, and you should become known in those circles as somebody who knows about vegetarianism.

And then you have the beginnings of a network! Networking seems to be a buzzword of the '90s. In the modern world we cannot ever hope to know all there is to know in every field – so we become experts in one particular area and offer our specialist knowledge to other people, who may be experts in other fields. The Vegetarian Society exists to educate people about the vegetarian diet, to encourage people to adopt a vegetarian diet, to give all the assistance it can to vegetarians by encouraging schools, restaurants and manufacturers to cater for vegetarians. We are vegetarian experts! Many vegetarians are also interested in trying to live a more 'green' lifestyle – being kind to our environment, and campaigning against the abuse of animals on farms and in laboratories. A later section of this book deals with related issues and gives useful addresses of organisations that can tell you more. The Vegetarian Society, also, can help by putting you in touch with specialist organisations.

By making yourself an expert, you can become a valuable part of a network in your local area, working hand in hand with people who are already specialists in, say, gardening, cookery, animal welfare etc. You will find that you can talk to them about vegetarianism *and* cookery, vegetarianism *and* gardening and so on. You will quickly build a large audience for the vegetarian message and get to know some interesting people. You may find that you can co-operate to run campaigns, share printing costs, or even get together to order foods and cruelty-free products, in bulk, from a wholesaler.

Running a stall

Keep your finger on the pulse of local events. What goes on in your town? There may be a regular open air market, craft fairs at a local stately home, a garden festival. If you are in touch with local special-interest groups, you will be able to find out in advance about any events they might be putting on. Every event of this kind can be an opportunity to spread the vegetarian message. You can arrange to have a stall.

Stalls can work in various ways, depending on the work and effort that you are prepared to put into them. You may simply contact The Vegetarian Society to get some leaflets and posters, and leave your stall for people to browse and help themselves. Or you might decide to mingle with the crowd and give out leaflets. At a large event, it can be useful to have one or two people walking around giving out leaflets and directing people to the stall.

You can get merchandise and books for resale at trade discount from Parkdale; also you can get a good selection of free leaflets, membership forms, Cookery School brochures etc. Some groups have also found it worthwhile stocking cruelty-free cosmetics, toiletries and household products (buy direct from the manufacturers at discount), and more unusual products like vegetarian 'chocolates' (most are actually carob-based) to show that you can live ethically without being dour and austere.

If you are on your own territory, it would be worthwhile having copies of your branch programme to give out (think ahead and get extra printed/ photocopied), and take names and addresses of people who seem genuinely interested, so that, later, you can canvass them to join your group. Have the name and address of your group prominently on display; there will be people who are too shy, or too busy, to come and talk at the time but they may make contact afterwards.

Things to do:

Make your stall look attractive; pile it high but neatly with merchandise. If you have some kind of back-drop, make an attractive display by pinning up posters, T-shirts, magazine covers etc. If there's no back-drop, a long table-cloth covering the front of the stall can be used to display things. If you are at an up-market event, a couple of potted plants add an extra touch.

Be interested in your stall. You can't expect the public to take an interest if you look bored or apathetic. Smile, talk to people, don't sit in the depths where people can't approach you easily. At least offer an info pack and membership form to passers-by – don't wait passively for them to come to you.

IT'S BEEN A VERY LONG DAY, OUR PATIENCE IS WEARING THIN AND WE'RE SICK TO DEATH OF SMILING AT PEOPLE AND SAYING WOULD YOU LIKE A VSUK INFORMATION PACK !!. JUST DON'T ASK ANY AWKWARD QUESTIONS IF YOU VALUE YOUR EXISTENCE !!

VSUK SMILE RETAINER

VSUK PATENT SMILE RETAINER

A Vegetarian Society stall can easily be combined with a stall selling vegetarian food. Perhaps one person could sell books and give out free recipe leaflets, while two or three others cooked and sell veggie burgers or cold vegetarian snacks. You could give out leaflets with the recipes on – if they are not your own, don't forget to credit the author and the book from which they are taken. It would be a good idea to have some copies of the book to sell.

A simple stall with leaflets and a few small items of merchandise can be combined with a stall belonging to another group. If you are friendly with a local animal welfare group, or perhaps a co-operative group which grows and sells organic vegetables, you could team up with them to share a stall.

At the end of a long hard day on your feet it can be hard to keep smiling, but the idea of running a stall is that people feel able to approach you, to look at what you are doing and have a friendly chat. There are a few points about running a stall which are just common sense. Wear one of the colourful T-shirts that you are selling! Make sure your stall is attractively laid out and that prices are clearly marked – some people will not buy unless they can see the price without having to ask. Be friendly and helpful – familiarise yourself with the books you are selling so that you can answer questions and make recommendations. If you are running a stall as a branch activity, why not take the time to write a paragraph about the day, as a contribution to The

Vegetarian Society's *Branch Mailing*. If you did well, do you know why? Perhaps other branches may be inspired to try something similar. If you did badly ... own up! Other branches can learn from your mistakes.

Running a stall can be a very pleasant way to spend a morning or an afternoon. Try to arrange for the stall to be run in shifts – this means that your enthusiasm should stay fresh! And you will have time to wander around the other stalls, invest in a couple of spider plants and a pot of home-made jam, and introduce yourself to stall-holders from other interesting groups.

Leafleting generally

The Vegetarian Society produces several leaflets which are suitable for giving out free to passers-by, in shopping centres, at stations and the like.

The best way to leaflet people successfully is to tie the activity in with a special event of some kind such as ...

Annual Events

Here are some dates on which there is either a national event your group could support, or a 'theme' which would give you a useful subject to organise a meeting around.

March – *Great British MEATOUT*. (dates vary)
The VSUK organises this event jointly with other animal welfare groups. We will keep you informed via the *Members Forum* and the *Branch Mailing*.

April 7 – *World Health Day*

April 24 – *World Day for Laboratory Animals*

July – *UK Natural Health Week*. (dates vary)
Information from: UK Natural Health Week Press Office, 7 Floral Street, London, WC2.

September – *Green Shopping Day/Week*. (dates vary.)
Information from: Sustainability, 49 Princes Place, London, W11 4QA.

October 1 – *World Vegetarian Day*

October 2 – *Gandhi's Birthday, World Farm Animals Day*

October 4 – *Feast Day of St Francis of Assissi*.
The nearest Sunday to this is the *World Day of Prayer for Animals*. Ask your local churches to join in. The Christian Consultative Council for the Welfare of Animals, 11 Dagmar Road, London, N4 4NY often organises something for this date, and publishes a booklet of suitable prayers.

October 16 – *World Food Day*
Aims to highlight Third World problems.

18-25 October – *One World Week*
Covers many areas that are of interest to vegetarians. The organisation also produces good handbooks etc of ideas for events and meetings. Information from: One World Week, PO Box 100, London, SE1 7RT. Tel: (071) 620 4444.

End of November or early December – *Smithfield Demo*.
The VSUK holds a regular, peaceful demonstration against animal farming to coincide with the Smithfield Show. Ring our Office nearer the time for details. Some groups organise a coach to attend this demo. If that is not feasible, perhaps you could arrange a local demo at your nearest abattoir.

Some seasonal ideas

Christmas – '*Save the Turkey*' (free leaflets from VSUK).
Contact local newspapers some weeks before Christmas, and try to interest them in a special feature on vegetarian Christmas food. Organise Christmas cooking demonstrations, taste-ins, and recipe-exchange evenings.

Easter –
A good time for events highlighting battery egg production and broiler chicken production. Information from Chickens Lib, 6 Pilling Lane, Skelmanthorpe, Huddersfield, W .Yorks. It's traditional not to eat meat on Good Friday, so you could try to persuade people to give up fish too, and have a completely vegetarian day.

Harvest –
   What about an alternative Harvest Festival (perhaps focussing on a harvest-less Third World) or … healthy eating events, and bread-making demos. The World Wide Fund for Nature publishes an alternative Harvest-Festival liturgy, the *Winchester Liturgy* (£1. 50 inc. p&p) from WWF, Panda House, Weyside Park, Catteshall Lane, Godalming, Surrey, GU7 1XR. Tel: (0483) 426444.

Use your consumer power

Manufacturers make only products that sell profitably. Products which are popular survive – those which do not sell are quickly withdrawn. Consumer support is vital. So …You can use your choice as a consumer to support good services and boycott poor ones. You have the power!

Supermarkets

If your supermarket launches a new vegetarian selection of frozen meals, or turns a set of shelves over to health food products, write to the manager and thank him. If you find that your favourite vegetarian food is no longer available from your supermarket, write to the manager and ask why. If you discover a new supermarket own-brand food product that you enjoy, why not suggest that the supermarket approaches The Vegetarian Society for the use of the Ⓥ symbol? The supermarket manager wants to attract customers, including vegetarian customers, and he is bound to make a special effort to please if he believes that there could be a new market open to him.

Restaurants

If you have a good vegetarian meal at a restaurant, make a special effort to encourage the chef and the owners by thanking them either in person or by letter. If, on the other hand, you are disappointed, try to offer constructive criticism – don't make your demands too difficult or the chef may decide not to bother!

   The Vegetarian Society produces a special leaflet aimed at chefs called *Catering For Vegetarians*. The leaflet explains very clearly what is meant by a vegetarian diet, and gives suggestions for menu-plans, and ideas for promoting a new vegetarian option on the menu. You or your branch could get together to leaflet all the cafés and restaurants in your area, and perhaps if you are working as a branch you could offer to give extra publicity to a restaurant which decides to offer a good vegetarian choice.

'Health Food' Shops

Support your local shop! They come in two basic varieties; 'wholefood shops' aim to provide wholesome food – vegetarian, naturally, and free from additives. The other kind, 'health food' stores, put more of an emphasis on remedies, herbal and otherwise.

   In this edition of *The Vegetarian Handbook* we are not including a list of shops. Last time, we listed all those which stocked *The Vegetarian* magazine. Now, *The Vegetarian* is available in shops and newsagents all over the country! If you are not sure where your nearest 'health food' shop is, check the *Yellow Pages*.

   If there is one particular shop in your area that you really enjoy visiting, why not introduce yourself to the owner and congratulate him on a job well done. By making a friendly contact there, you could even influence the owner's decision on what he should order from the health food wholesalers. The best shops are colourful information centres full of leaflets, small magazines and little cards advertising useful services. It can be a real treat to browse around these places. Support them by buying from them, and participate in the special services they have to offer. Don't be afraid to give your opinion, whether good or bad, on new products that are being sold – the shopkeeper will appreciate your feedback!

It is a measure of our success that the big chains, notably Sainsburys, are increasingly selling 'green' and vegetarian food. But try, if you can, to patronise the small shops too: they often stock a wider range than the supermarkets, and they deserve your support for pioneering new lines long before they are commercially attractive to the big people. For the small shops, vegetarians are not just part of their business, we *are* their business!

Some health food manufacturers actually boycott supermarkets because they sell meat and may have investments in dubious areas.

Your local shop could sell *The Vegetarian* magazine and *Greenscene,* our magazine for young vegetarians. It could offer a special discount for members of the Vegetarian Society, and display a poster to advertise this. It could hold stocks of our literature, Cookery School brochures and posters. If there is room, it could have a special section for Vegetarian Society merchandise. Why not suggest that the owner phones The Vegetarian Society and asks about these ideas? Vee Longton, our receptionist, can arrange to have literature sent. Rosemary Billings and Rosemary Stewardson can send Cookery School leaflets. Pat Bowker can tell you all about selling Vegetarian Society merchandise. Pam Tinsley, Fergus Duff and Juliet Gellatley, in our Youth Education Department, can tell you how to get stocks of *Greenscene.* They can also give you the number of the company in London which co-publishes *The Vegetarian* magazine with The Vegetarian Society. Bronwen Humphreys can give you advice on offering discounts, and she will make sure that the shop is given extra publicity through our newsletter *Members Forum* and our *Discounts List* which is sent out to all new members of The Vegetarian Society.

Support vegetarian businesses wherever you are

You can also give your support to local vegetarian cafés and restaurants – if they are good. Take your friends there and spread the word. Vegetarian guesthouses also need your support – check your copy of *The Vegetarian Travel Guide* to see if there is a good vegetarian guesthouse on your holiday route. Incidentally, if you do have a report to make, drop a postcard to the editor who may be able to include your comments in the next edition of the *Travel Guide*.

Support the ϒ Symbol

This is known as the 'vee' symbol. It is the trademark of The Vegetarian Society and you will find it in all colours and all sizes on food products and menus. Manufacturers can only use the symbol if they submit their products to The Vegetarian Society so that the ingredients used can be checked.

Looking out for the symbol is the very best way of being sure that the goods you buy are 100% suitable for your diet. Manufacturers pay – as a percentage of their sales – for the use of the symbol. By buying their goods you are helping the work of The Vegetarian Society. Also, if they find that sales are especially good they are more likely to apply to use the symbol on other products. The ϒ symbol helps you to choose vegetarian, and it helps The Vegetarian Society to continue its campaigns.

You can wear the ϒ symbol yourself! The Vegetarian Society's Merchandise Department sells all kinds of goods which help to spread the vege-

tarian message. You can become a walking advertisement for vegetarianism – whether you choose a T-shirt with a veggie slogan, or a subtle pair of silver ϒ symbol earrings. Send a SAE to our Merchandise Department for a catalogue. There are all kinds of goods, including a big new range of clothing and non-leather shoes. You can also support the Society by checking through your copy of our Merchandise catalogue when you want to buy a gift for a friend.

Act locally

Support our Campaigns

The major campaigning work presently going on at The Vegetarian Society is championed by our Youth Education Department. The head of the Department, Juliet Gellatley, was given a *Woman of the Future* award by *Cosmopolitan* magazine in recognition of her tireless work to spread the vegetarian message especially among young people.

The SCREAM campaign (School Campaign for Reaction Against Meat) has now been joined by a sister campaign – CHOICE. The CHOICE campaign works towards establishing a nutritious, balanced, vegetarian choice of school dinner in every school in Britain. It has already been a huge success. Many school children have sent for our packs of information and posters for display at their schools. In response to the new demand for catering-sized recipes for vegetarians we have produced a book of nutritionally-assessed options, geared towards tempting children and teenagers.

We mailed every school in the country and have had lots of press coverage... but does *your* local school know about the CHOICE campaign? Is it providing a vegetarian choice? You can help by checking with schools in your area, making sure that they have plenty of information about the campaign. Perhaps you could visit schools yourself – particularly if you are a parent. You could offer to give a school talk, chat to the cookery teacher, and perhaps suggest vegetarianism as a theme for a project. The Society can supply some good materials, suitable for a small display in the school hall or library. The Youth Education Department produces an information pack, *Guidelines for Teachers.*

Use the Press

You should never be afraid to use your local newspaper as a forum to publicise your views. Write letters to react to local and national events from a vegetarian viewpoint.

See if you can get the newspaper to publish reviews of local vegetarian restaurants, books on vegetarianism and vegetarian recipe books. You can write these yourself and send them in. The paper may be very pleased to have a new topic to cover. Payment is highly negotiable – often the thrill of seeing your name in print and the knowledge that some people might be persuaded to find out more about the vegetarian diet by trying out your recipe is payment enough. You could also send in your recipe ideas to 'alternative' magazines; perhaps there is a small magazine in your area. Or try the parish magazine – if they are impressed, they may offer you a regular column!

Compile a Guide or a recipe book

You can help local vegetarians and vegetarian visitors to your town or area by getting together with some vegetarian friends to compile a guide pamphlet. This is an ideal project for members to work on together.

Include good local restaurants and cafés, shops, sources of cruelty-free cosmetics, guesthouses, and possibly some information about local events.

Once you get involved in the research for the project, you might find some good eateries that you had never tried before. You might even be able to persuade some restaurants to include a vegetarian choice. Don't forget to include a local street map with all the establishments marked on it – this is bound to be very useful indeed for vegetarian visitors. It is up to you how far you go – you could include interesting craft workshops, alternative book and record shops, well-stocked greengrocers – if you think they will be of use to visitors. If it turns out to be a big project, you could canvass for advertising to help cover your costs.

When the pamphlet is finished, make sure all the establishments listed have a supply of copies to sell, and take plenty to the tourist information centres in your area. Other likely distribution points might be art galleries, theatres, cinemas and music venues. Give some to your library too, in fact why not organise a big display in the library and invite the press?

If you have begun to devise your own recipes, and you think that some of your ideas may be helpful to the people who are just beginning to learn how to cook vegetarian food, why not look into producing your own little booklet or leaflet of vegetarian recipes. Be sure not to infringe the copyright of another person. You could begin by offering some photocopied sheets to be sold for a few pence or given away by your health food shop. Later, perhaps, you could produce a simple booklet. Some of the money made could be directed to a relevant charity.

Host a Cookery Course

Is there a good venue for a cookery course or demonstration in your area? Rosemary Billings, our Cookery School Co-ordinator, would be interested to hear from you if you know of a suitable venue for one of our Cookery School Tutors to visit. Our Parkdale courses are always over-subscribed, so we are happy to arrange courses in other areas. For a cookery demonstration we require a large hall or a large kitchen. For a practical course, to teach a maximum of 20 people, we would need good kitchen facilities and possibly accommodation. We can teach our Foundation One course or tailor a course to suit your interests.

Ideas for Fundraising

Fundraising can be fun! There are quite a few ideas in this section – you can raise money by selling our merchandise, selling vegetarian snacks and running a stall. You can ask for a donation for talks and demonstrations. What about trying to get some sponsorship for an event – Juliet Gellatley the head of our Youth Education Department took her life into her hands when she parachuted out of an aeroplane to raise money for the *Food Without Fear* video. Other people have arranged sponsored walks, sponsored swims, sponsored diets and teams of marathon runners. Last year, The Cutting Rooms, a hairdressing and beauty salon which uses cruelty-free products, organised a hairdressing exhibition and fashion show and made a donation from their profits to The Vegetarian Society. If you can organise an event like this, or if you are prepared to make a personal effort and would like help with publicity and sponsorship, contact The Vegetarian Society. We will be able to give you a mention in the *Members Forum* and perhaps even in *The Vegetarian* magazine or *Greenscene*.

Conclusion

The message of this section of *The Vegetarian Handbook* is – "Spread the Word!" Vegetarianism is a healthy lifestyle which deserves to be extremely popular. By making the choice more well known, every vegetarian can help other people to take the plunge. You should be proud to be a veggie, and you should feel almost duty-bound to share your convictions. By doing so you can help other people to become healthier and happier – and you can help the animals too.

Open Day The next Vegetarian Society Open Day will be held in the grounds and offices at Parkdale on 14th July, 1991. Make a special note in your diary! Perhaps you know somebody who would like to have a stall. We will be having marquees for stalls ranging from animal rights groups to craftsmen. There will be organic wine and vegetarian food on sale. There should be live music and exhibitions of theatre and dancing. Come and meet us all!

Volunteers The Vegetarian Society can often find room for a volunteer – you might end up stuffing envelopes, mowing the lawn or helping out in the Cookery School. If you think this sounds like fun and you have some spare time, write in for information! Let us know when you are available, and make sure you include information about any special skills that you have.

Vegetarian nutrition

A balanced vegetarian diet is a perfectly healthy diet. This chapter explains the principles of vegetarian nutrition and has been compiled with the help of Jane Brophy, the Vegetarian Society's Research Officer, who is also a State Registered Dietitian with experience of working in hospitals.

Vegetarian diets, quite simply, do not include meat, fish, fowl, or any products derived from slaughtered animals. The following variations exist:

- **Lacto-ovo-vegetarians** – include dairy products and eggs (free-range please!) as part of their diet. This is the diet most commonly thought of as vegetarian.
- **Lacto-vegetarians** – accept dairy products but *not* eggs.
- **Demi-vegetarians** – are not strictly vegetarian at all! This is the term used to describe people who still eat fish and sometimes poultry, but have given up red meat. Demi-vegetarianism is often a first step on the road to vegetarianism, but is sometimes adopted for health or medical reasons.
- **Vegans** – do not eat any animal products whatsoever. This includes meat, dairy products, eggs, and honey. Vegans also refuse to use animal products in the form of clothing, cosmetics, household cleaning products and so on.
- **Fruitarians** – only eat fruit as they believe that plants should not be killed for food. They will not dig up plants to eat the roots, or harvest them for leaves.

This section on nutrition applies mainly to lacto-ovo-vegetarianism and lacto-vegetarianism, although it is recognised that for some people these two forms of vegetarianism are a step in the direction towards veganism. A healthy vegetarian diet should not merely substitute dairy products and eggs for meat and fish – a reduction in consumption of all animal foods is recommended.

Healthy Eating

The government lays down official guidelines on the amount of each nutrient that it considers is required for good health. The levels are based on the opinions of a panel of experts. The guidelines are known as **RDA**(s) – **Recommended Daily Amount**(s). They vary from country to country, and the World Health Organisation also produces a set of nutritional guidelines.

RDAs have an added margin of error to cater for the needs of 98% of the population and therefore it is possible that a particular individual may be consuming less than the RDA of a particular substance yet still be in good nutritional health.

A sensible vegetarian diet can easily reach the RDAs for all nutrients where there is a recommendation. Vegetarians should not need to take supplements in the form of pills if they include a wide variety of foods from the different food groups in their diet, unless they have an illness or a particular metabolic problem. People may take supplements as a matter of personal choice, for example if they feel that their nutrition is compromised by living in a very polluted city.

In 1983 the National Advisory Committee on Nutrition Education produced proposals for nutrition guidelines in Britain. The NACNE recommendations were as follows:

- Decrease total percentage of fat intake and increase intake of complex carbohydrates to compensate.
- Decrease intake of saturated fats and increase the proportion of polyunsaturated fats.
- Increase fibre.
- Decrease salt.
- Decrease sugar.
- Protein intake should not be altered, but a higher proportion of vegetable or plant protein should be consumed.

The NACNE recommendations reinforce the message that a vegetarian diet is a healthy diet.

Vegetarian diets tend to be lower in total fat and proportionately higher in complex carbohydrates.

The fat content of a vegetarian diet tends to be proportionately higher in polyunsaturated fats, which are associated with plant sources, and lower in saturated fats which are associated with animal foods including meat and dairy produce.

A vegetarian diet contains adequate protein, but with a higher amount from vegetable sources, as NACNE recommends.

Vegetarians can easily reach the recommended level of fibre intake, because all fibre comes from vegetable sources.

Vegetarians tend to eat more wholefoods and therefore their diet contains less sugar and salt.

However it is still possible to have an unhealthy vegetarian diet, if for example too high a proportion of dairy products (high in saturated fats) is consumed, or if you live on chips and chocolate.

You are what you eat

According to nutritionists Davidson & Passmore, the body of a man weighing 65kg (10 stone 3 pounds) is composed of the following:

• Water – 40kg • Protein – 11kg • Fat – 9kg • Minerals – 4kg • Carbohydrate – 1 kg •

Our dietary requirements reflect this. The diet can be divided into two area – macronutrients and micronutrients.
 Macronutrients required by the body are:

• Water • Carbohydrate and fibre • Protein • Fat •

The body's daily requirements of these substances are measured in milligrammes (mg – thousandths of a gram).
 Micronutrients required by the body are:

• Vitamins • Minerals • Trace Elements •

The body's daily requirements of these substances are measured in microgrammes (µg – millionths of a gram).
 Your diet directly affects your state of health – in extreme cases an improved diet can help alleviate symptoms of illness, whilst a poor diet can contribute to disease and increase vulnerability.

FOOD + OXYGEN = ENERGY + CARBON DIOXIDE + WATER

This equation represents the life process. Energy is vital to sustain life. We obtain energy from the food we eat and the air that we breathe.
 Energy is found in the following:

• Carbohydrate – 4 calories per gram • Fat – 9 calories per gram •
• Protein – 4 calories per gram • Alcohol – 7 calories per gram •

The body needs to be fed regularly to maintain blood sugar levels. It can store a limited amount of energy in the form of glycogen, which can be converted into glucose, the blood sugar.
 The number of calories of energy that a person needs to consume each day is known as the Metabolic rate. Metabolic rates vary according to the age, health, size and genetic make-up of a person as well as the level of activity being performed by that person. A small woman, for example, may require only around 1,500 calories per day, while a man with an active occupation may require 3,000 calories per day.

MACRONUTRIENTS: Carbohydrate and fibre
Carbohydrate is the main source of energy in the diet. There are three types of carbohydrate:

• Sugars • Complex carbohydrate or starch • Unavailable carbohydrate or dietary fibre •

Sugars
Monosaccharides

– glucose (blood sugar)
– fructose (plant sugar)
– galactose

Disaccharides
- sucrose (table sugar)
- lactose (milk sugar)
- maltose (germinated barley)

The body takes disaccarides and uses them to make monosaccharides.

Glucose + Fructose = Sucrose • Glucose + Galactose = Lactose • Glucose + Glucose = Maltose

Carbohydrate is not found in meat, fish, fowl, eggs or cheese. A small amount of lactose is found in milk – some people cannot digest this. The major source of carbohydrate is plant foods.

Starches
There are two kinds of starches – refined, such as white flour and rice, and unrefined such as brown flour and 'wholefoods'. It is best to eat wholefoods such as wholemeal bread and brown rice, as these contain more vitamins and minerals plus beneficial dietary fibre.

Fibre
The indigestible portion of our food which is essential in our diet. Fibre can be soluble or insoluble. Oat bran is an example of soluble fibre which is thought to help reduce cholesterol levels.

There is no fibre in animal foods. All forms of fibre come from plant foods. Vegetarian diets usually have a high fibre content. This helps protect against diverticular disease, heart disease, bowel cancer and varicose veins.

Protein
Protein is a very important nutrient because it makes up part of the structure of every cell in our bodies. Cells are constantly dying and being replaced, so a steady supply of protein is needed for good health. When we are growing and new tissue is still being made, protein is especially important, as it is for pregnant women who are also having to supply a growing baby as well as their own needs. Thousands of enzymes and some hormones in our bodies are proteins; keratin in our nails and hair is a protein, as is elastin in tendons and arteries and collagen in bones, skin and muscles.

People are rightly concerned about whether or not their diet contains enough protein. Being a vegetarian, however, doesn't mean you will go short of this vital nutrient.

What proteins are
Proteins are complex molecules made up of smaller units called amino acids. Amino acids in turn are made up of carbon, hydrogen, nitrogen, oxygen, and sulphur. There are twenty in all and some life forms, like plants and many bacteria, can synthesise them all from basic elements. Others, including animals and humans, can synthesise only some of them.

Humans need to have eight amino acids provided in the diet, these are called the essential amino acids and they are: methionine, tryptophan, theonine, valine, isoleucine, leucine, phenylalanine and lysine. Histidine is essential for children but adults can manage without it.

When you eat a food containing protein, your digestive system will break it down into the constituent amino acids, which are then reassembled into the particular proteins your body needs at the time. This gives rise to one of the things people find very worrying about proteins. Foods contain proteins which have amino acids in differing proportions; these may not necessarily be the same proportions that we need to synthesise our body proteins. The more nearly the proportions of amino acids match those we require, the more efficiently a protein food can be used, and so it is considered to be a better quality protein. You may well read that plant proteins are called 'Second Class' proteins. This means that their proportions of amino acids do not match our requirements as well as do those of animals. This gives rise to considerable worry that plant proteins are inadequate. Not all animal proteins are adequate either, gelatine is a very deficient protein.

This isn't really such a big problem as it sounds. When plant proteins are mixed together, the excess amino acids in one balance out any deficiencies in the other. For example, cereals are short of lysine, but have plenty of methionine; while pulses are short of methionine, but have plenty of lysine. Mix the two together as in beans on toast or peas and rice, and you get a well-balanced protein. In practise, we almost never eat a meal that consists of only one kind of protein. Even meat-eaters get protein from a variety of sources. It is very easy to make sure your meals have mixed proteins, some common examples are:

> Cereal + Milk = porridge
> Nuts + Cereals = nutloaf
> Pulses + Cereal = beans on toast
> Cereal + Cheese = cheese flan

You don't have to worry about all eight of the essential amino acids. Most of them are very abundant in the major protein foods. The two that are present in the smallest amounts are lysine and methionine. The amino acid in a protein that is in the shortest supply is the one that sets the biological value of the protein and is called the 'limiting amino acid'. We have explained above how pulses and cereals combine to prevent shortages of lysine and methionine in a vegetarian diet. The only other which might be in short supply is tryptophan. This is the limiting amino acid in maize, and people who use maize instead of wheat as their main cereal should be aware of this (eg people who need a gluten-free diet).

This ability of proteins to 'mix and match' is called 'complementarity' and two protein foods that balance each other, like pulses and cereals, are called 'complementary proteins'.

You should also remember that all the other components of a meal – the vegetables, salad and fruit – are contributing small amounts of amino acids to the total.

Some researchers believe that the body has a pool of amino acids, which can be used to make up any temporary deficiency so as long as your diet is well-balanced overall. You do not have to go to great pains to ensure that you have complementary proteins at every meal.

Modern vegetarian cookery authors are well aware of the need to mix proteins so if you invest in two or three cookery books, you will soon get a large repertoire of main course meals that incorporate complementary proteins.

Where do proteins come from?

Most foods contain some protein as it is needed by plants and other animals just as much as it is needed by humans. However, some foods are concentrated sources of protein and you should make sure that some of these concentrated sources are included in your diet every day. Vegetarian sources of protein are:

- Milk, cheese and other milk products
- Free range eggs
- Nuts – hazels, brazils, almonds, cashews, walnuts, pine kernels
- Seeds – sunflower, sesame, pumpkin
- Pulses – baked beans, butter beans, lentils, peas, peanuts, soya
- Cereals – bread, rice pasta, breakfast cereals

Cheese and eggs – should be used in moderation for although they are very good quality protein, they are high in saturated fat which could adversely affect your health. Never be tempted to simply substitute eggs or slices of cheese for meat when you become a vegetarian, make full use of the other sources of protein as well. A very small amount of grated cheese or skimmed milk powder added to cereals, pulses or nuts can increase the quality of the protein considerably and this is a good way to use them.

Seeds – if you have not been used to eating the above mentioned seeds, don't be put off even though it may seem strange. They are readily available in health food shops, have a pleasant nutty taste and can be a simple way of adding protein to a dish.

Soya – is such high quality protein that although a pulse, it can be considered the equivalent of cheese and eggs and has the advantage of having no saturated fat. Soya beans take a long time to cook and are not particularly appetising in themselves but fortunately there is now a huge variety of soya based foods available for vegetarians like tofu, tempeh, soya milk, soya ice cream, soya yogurt, soya dessert, TVP chunks and mince, burgers, rissoles and sausages. It is well worth looking out for them at your local health food shop.

How much do I need?

The minimum intake of protein per day to maintain health should be 45g for a man weighing 9½ stones, 38g for a woman weighing 8½ stones.

However, the Recommended Daily Amount(s) are higher than this to allow sufficient margin for error and to make sure that there is no risk of iron or vitamin deficiency which very low protein diets sometimes incur, so they are set at between 55 and 90g per day depending on your height and how active or sedentary your occupation is.

Children and adolescents need proportionally more protein, as they are using it for growth as well as maintenance so the RDA of protein for a child,

> at 1 year is 30g
> at 5 years is 45g
> at 12 is 58g for a girl, 70g for a boy
> at 17 is 58g for a girl, and 75g for a boy.

However, as protein foods aren't actually 100% protein, simply weighing your protein foods won't tell you if you are getting enough. It is probably more helpful to consider how much protein an average helping gives you.

For example,
> 3 slices of bread gives you 8g of protein
> one small tin of baked beans gives 8g
> 1 standard egg gives 7g
> 2 thick slices of cheddar gives 12g
> 1 medium potato gives 5g

2oz of almonds, cashews, sesame seeds or
sunflower seeds gives 10g
2oz of butter or haricot beans or lentils gives 10g
Half a pint of skimmed or soya milk gives 10g
2oz Shredded Wheat gives 5g

So during the day you might have:–

Breakfast – Shredded Wheat and milk = 15g protein
Lunch – 3 slices bread with cheese = 20g protein
Dinner – baked beans and two potatoes = 20g protein
Plus a half pint of milk taken throughout the day in
drinks gives another 10g ...

making 65g in all – well
into the allowance for women. As men tend to eat more, a larger portion of
breakfast cereal, an extra potato and a couple of extra slices of bread
would cover their greater needs. And don't forget, this is a very simplified
menu, it doesn't take into account the protein that will be provided by any
fruit, vegetables, salads or snacks you might eat during the day, it only lists
the main protein foods but it does show that it is not particularly difficult to
get enough protein on a vegetarian diet.

Fats, fish oils and cholesterol

The terms 'fats' and 'oils' are virtually interchangeable. Usually 'fat' is used
when the substance is solid at room temperature and 'oil' is used when it is
liquid at room temperature. You may also come across the term 'lipid' which
is applied to fats and oils alike, as well as some other, similar fatty substances found in the body.

Essential fatty acids

Fats and oils are made up of smaller units called 'fatty acids'. Some the body
can manufacture and some have to be provided in the diet. Those that the
body can't manufacture are called 'essential fatty acids'. There are only two
essential fatty acids for humans; linolenic acid and linoleic acid. These are
widely found in plant oils and so vegetarians have no problem getting all
they need. Good sources are sunflower oil, safflower oil and soyabean oil.

Saturated or unsaturated

Fats can be either saturated or unsaturated. This refers to the number of double-
bonds in the fat. Saturated fats have no double-bond, mono-unsaturated fats
have one double-bond and polyunsaturated fats have up to six double-
bonds. A double-bond is a site on the fat molecule which can take up an
atom of hydrogen. Saturated fats have more hydrogen and tend to be solid
at room temperatures. The process of adding hydrogen to an oil is sometimes called 'hardening' and is used during the manufacture of margarine.

Cholesterol

This is a different form of fat called a 'sterol'. It is found in all animal foods
but is absent from plant foods. Although cholesterol is essential to our body,
we can manufacture all our requirements. It is often present inappropriately
in lesions in the walls of arteries and this is associated with heart disease. A
high 'blood cholesterol level' is thought to increase the risk of heart disease.

People often think that too much cholesterol in the diet causes a raised blood cholesterol level. However, the blood cholesterol levels are more directly related to the amount of saturated fat compared with polyunsaturated fats in the diet.

The connection between saturated fat and cholesterol levels

Saturated fat, which tends to be associated with animal foods, including dairy produce and eggs, raises blood cholesterol levels.

Polyunsaturated fat, usually associated with plant oils, lowers blood cholesterol levels, although to a smaller degree than saturated fats raise blood cholesterol levels.

Mono-unsaturated fats such as olive oil have a neutral effect on blood cholesterol levels.

Nutritionists often speak of a P/S Ratio, which is the ratio of polyunsaturates in the diet.

Common oils and their degree of saturation

g/100g (less a little water!)

Oil	Sat	Mono	Poly
Butter	49	26	2
(Lard)	42	42	9
Hard vegetable marg.	30	38	10
Soft vegetable marg.	25	34	18
Polyunsaturated marg.	19	16	60
Coconut oil	85	7	2
Corn oil	16	29	49
Olive oil	14	70	11
Palm oil	19	42	8
Peanut oil	10	13	28
Safflower oil	14	24	72
Soya bean oil	13	32	57
Sunflower oil	14	11	50

(Lard is not vegetarian but included for comparison)

Disorders of blood fats

Hyperlipoproteinaemia (or hyperlipidaemia) is a condition where exceptionally high amounts of lipoproteins accumulate in the blood. Lipoproteins are the body's way of transporting fats and cholesterol around. People with this condition may also have particularly high blood cholesterol levels and their bodies do not regulate cholesterol in the normal way.

The term hyperlipidaemia covers a range of disorders and people affected need to be very careful with their diet. Depending upon the exact nature of their condition, they need to be careful with their intake of dietary fats and in some cases they would be asked to limit their intake of dietary cholesterol. If you have such a problem, your dietitian or doctor will be able to tell you precisely what to eat. The dietary advice should not be incompatible with a vegetarian diet and in fact, a well worked-out vegetarian diet is likely to be beneficial.

Healthy eating

The NACNE Report (1983) on Nutrition Guidelines in Britain recommended that people reduce the total amount of fat, in particular, saturated fat, in their diet. Unless a lot of cheese and other full-fat dairy produce or junk food is consumed, a vegetarian diet closely follows the NACNE recommendations.

Fish oils

There has been a lot of publicity recently about the benefits of consuming fish oil and it is sometimes stated that Eicosapentaenoic acid (EPA), a fatty acid found in large quantities in fish oil, is an essential fatty acid. It is not, as the body can manufacture it from the essential fatty acid linolenic acid. Good sources of linolenic acid are rapeseed oil and soyabean oil and linseed oil (flax oil).

Arachidonic acid

It used to be thought that arachidonic acid was an essential fatty acid, although now it has been discovered that it can be manufactured in the body from the essential fatty acid, linolenic acid. Arachidonic acid is used by the body to produce substances called prostaglandins, which have a vital role in blood clotting. The main sources of arachidonic acid are animal in origin (including eggs), so this is another reason for vegetarians to include in their diet a good source of essential fatty acids.

Points to remember

- Try to cut down on your total intake of fat if you have not done so already.
- Try to avoid consuming too much saturated fat, as in full fat dairy produce.
- Choose a good polyunsaturated fat, such as sunflower oil, corn oil, or soyabean oil to incorporate into your diet. These deteriorate to a certain extent on heating, so it is a good idea to include some raw oil in the diet, for example in a salad dressing. The effect of heat is to make a fat more saturated so don't keep on re-using the same fat for deep frying and be careful to store your oils in a cool, dark place as exposure to sunlight also causes some deterioration.
- Include some mono-unsaturated fat such as olive oil in your diet, as this is very stable on heating and is also thought to be beneficial.
- When buying margarines, look for the words 'high in polyunsaturates' on the label.

MICRONUTRIENTS: Vitamins

Vitamins are organic substances which the body requires in small amounts from the diet as it cannot manufacture them in sufficient quantities for itself.

Vitamins are Fat Soluble or Water Soluble.

<u>Fat Soluble</u>

1. Vitamin A or Renitol
   (carotene is the vegetable derivative)
2. Vitamin D_3 or Cholecalciferol
   (Ergocalciferol or Vitamin D_2
   is a vegetable source)
3. Vitamin E or Tocopherol
4. Vitamin K

<u>Water Soluble</u>

1. Vitamin C or Ascorbic Acid
2. Vitamin B_1 or Thiamin
3. Vitamin B_2 or Riboflavin
4. Vitamin B_3 or Nicotinic Acid (Niacin)
   and Nicotinamide (Niacinamide)
5. Vitamin B_6 or Pyridoxine
6. Vitamin B_{12} or Cyanocobalamin (Cobalamin)
7. Folate (Folic acid or Folacin)
8. Pantothenic Acid
9. Biotin

Vit A	Vit B$_1$	Vit B$_2$	Vit B$_3$	Vit B$_6$	Vit B$_{12}$
Carrots	Yeast extract	Almonds	Yeast extract	Bran	Eggs
Spinach	Brazil nuts	Cheese	Peanuts	Wholewheat	Cheese
Parsley	Peanuts	Wholewheat	Wholewheat	flour	Yeast extract
Butter	Bran	bread	bread	Yeast extract	Milk
Margarine	Oatmeal	Dried	Mushrooms	Hazelnuts	Yoghurt
Watercress	Flour	peaches	Broad beans	Bananas	Butter
Dried	Wholewheat	Mushrooms	Dates	Peanuts	Sosmix
apricots	bread	Broad beans		Currants	
Cheese	Peas	Dates			

Folic Acid	Vit C	Vit D	Vit E	Vit K
Yeast extract	Oranges	Eggs	Almost all	Green Veg.
Bran	Grapefruit	Cheese	Foods	
Spinach	Broccoli	Butter		
Broccoli	Spinach	Margarine		
Peanuts	Cabbage			
Almonds	Blackcurrants	*Sunlight*		
Hazelnuts	Parsley	*enables the*		
	Strawberries	*body to*		
		make Vit. D		
		in the skin		

Vitamin D intake may be a problem for vegans – however, as long as the body gets enough exposure to ordinary bright sunlight this should not be a problem. Vitamin D can be stored in the body. The young, elderly and house-bound are most at risk of deficiency, as are those with dark skins. Vitamin D can be taken in the form of supplemented margarines.

Vitamin B$_{12}$ Recommended daily intake (World Health Organisation 1987)

Adults: 1.0 µg • Pregnant Women: 1.4 µg • Lactating Women: 1.3 µg.
µg = microgram, i.e. one millionth of a gram

This vitamin (B$_{12}$) is made exclusively by micro-organisms, and is found mainly in animal-derived products, ie meat, dairy produce, eggs. It is scarce in the plant kingdom, which means that vegans should ensure they obtain adequate intakes.

Vegetarians will derive it from eggs, milk and cheese. Hard cheese is, weight for weight, as good a source as beef. However, note that the fermentation involved in making yoghurt destroys some of the vitamin, as does boiling of milk. each of the following provides an intake of 1 µg:

½ pint milk, or 2 oz cheese, or 1 egg.

Vegetarians regularly consuming less than these amounts are recommended to include some fortified foods in their diets on a regular basis.

Vegans have to deal with a conflict of opinion over sources of B$_{12}$. Bacteria in the large intestine can synthesise the vitamin. It is claimed that this synthesised vitamin can then be absorbed and used. However, this has never been verified; the bacterial activity occurs far down in the gut, possibly *too* far down for the vitamin to be absorbed.

Regarding dietary sources, it has been suggested that fermented soya products like tempeh and miso, and other fermented products used in macrobiotic diets like umeboshi plums, zenryu-fu and seitan are a source of B_{12}. However, recent analyses commissioned by the Research Section of the VSUK found these fermented foods to have no significant amounts of the vitamin. These results agree with analyses performed by other research workers. The only 'unfortified' plant food that appears promising is seaweed, both indigenous, eg in laverbread, and Japanese – Nori, Wakame, Kombu. Small amounts of the vitamin are sometimes found in vegetables. This is due to bacterial contamination.

Thus, potential sources for vegans are fortified foods, which are becoming more common, seaweeds and supplements. As only a small amount ($3.5\mu g$) can be absorbed at any one time, it is best to have a small but regular intake. Thus, we would advise regular consumption (at least three times a week) of fortified foods rather than the taking of supplements, as highly-concentrated sources may not be absorbed well. Just one ounce of Tastex or Barmene eaten over the course of a week will supply an adequate intake. Regular intake of the vitamin is crucially important for pregnant and lactating women, as B_{12} in breast milk is dependent on the mother's dietary intake.

Deficiency of B_{12} leads to a form of anaemia, and a type of neuropathy which starts with tingling and numbness in the hands and feet. An adult's body stores can last for $5 - 10$ years, so deficiency symptoms may be slow to appear. Vegans taking none of the sources mentioned should have their B_{12} levels checked yearly.

Minerals
Elemental Composition of a 75kg man   (Davies and Stewart 1987)

Element	Grams	
Oxygen	43,550	As protein, fat and carbohydrate
Carbon	12,590	
Hydrogen	6,580	
Nitrogen	1,815	
Calcium	1,700	
Phosphorus	680	
Potassium	250	
Chlorine	115	
Sulphur	100	
Sodium	70	
Magnesium	42	
Iron	6	
Zinc	2.5	
Fluorine	0.2–1.0	
Copper	0.05–0.12	

Less than 0.05grams (< 50mg)

Vanadium, Iodine, Manganese, Selenium, Silicon, Molybdenum, Chromium, Cobalt, Nickel.

Potassium and sodium are very important minerals which help our bodies to maintain theie fluid balance. Calcium, magnesium and phosphorus are also important; their role is linked with the formation of our bones. 'Trace elements' are minerals which we need in very small quantities – less than 100mg (0.1 gram) per day. The most important are iron and zinc, others are fluorine, copper, iodine, cobalt, chromium, manganese and selenium.

Potassium and sodium

Sodium and potassium regulate the water balance in the body. We generally consume far too much sodium in the form of sodium chloride, table salt. Salt is added to all prepared foods and so deficiency is unlikely. We are usually told to cut our salt intake by as much as ten or fifteen times, because the excess intake is simply excreted by the body and in the long term this can cause a strain on the kidneys and result in high blood pressure. Sodium deficiency is a possibility if the body has excreted a lot of salt in sweat – for example, in a hot climate or after strenuous physical exercise in hot weather.

Potassium is essential inside the body cells to regulate water. If a great deal of sodium is excreted by the body, valuable potassium may be lost at the same time. Potassium is hard to find in processed and overcooked foods, but can be obtained from almost all natural foods. Dried fruits and citrus juices are good sources. Potassium tablets can irritate the stomach wall, so it is important to cut down on sodium intake in order to help balance the work done in the body by sodium and potassium.

Calcium, magnesium and phosphorus

Calcium is the most abundant mineral in our bodies. Most of it is to be found making up our bones and teeth, but there is a little in the blood which affects blood clotting, nerve function and muscle contraction. Calcium works with phosphorus in bones, and with magnesium in muscles. The RDA is around 500 mg per day for an adult. This more than doubles for pregnant or lactating women. People who are recovering from illness or are bed-ridden may have to take care to obtain a good intake of calcium. Lacto-vegetarians will have adequate intake from their consumption of dairy products. Obtaining a good intake of calcium can occasionally be a problem for those on a vegan diet – but vegans can obtain their calcium from sesame seeds, almonds, spinach and soya flour. Both magnesium and phosphorus are plentiful in all kinds of foods, and deficiency is unlikely.

Iron

There should be no lack of iron in a well-balanced vegetarian diet. Foods containing iron include:

- Wholegrain cereals and flours – wheat, rye, millet, oatmeal
- Nuts – almonds, brazils, cashews, hazels
- Green vegetables – cabbage, watercress, spinach, broccoli, parsley
- Pulses – soya beans, chick peas, haricot beans (baked beans), lentils
- Dried fruits – apricots, prunes, raisins
- Seeds – pumpkin, sesame, sunflower
- Brewers and bakers yeasts, curry powder, textured soya protein, soya flour, black treacle, molasses, chocolate and cocoa, ginger.

The absorption of iron is facilitated by the consumption, in the same meal, of foods containing Vitamin C – citrus fruits (oranges, lemons, grapefruit), blackcurrants, cabbage, red and green peppers, Brussels sprouts, cauli-flower, parsley, salad cress, watercress, spinach. Tea reduces the absorption of iron; it is advisable not to drink tea with meals but to wait for at least an hour.

Women with heavy menstrual losses of blood may become anaemic. They need good dietary intakes of iron and should seek medical advice. They may benefit from taking the Pill.

Gastric secretions in the elderly are sometimes inadequate for the absorption of iron. Anaemia from this cause needs medical investigation and advice. Old people may loose blood because they become 'leaky', especially if they take drugs such as aspirin. They need good dietary sources of iron and should seek medical advice.

Zinc

Zinc is important in the absorption and function of some vitamins, especially the B group. It also plays a role in the production of prostaglandins (potent, short-lived substances effecting/controlling many body functions), in the immune system, the healing of wounds and in our sense of taste.

The 'average' adult human body contains 2.5g of zinc, most of which is found in the soft tissue and is particularly concentrated in the pancreas, eyes and the genitals of males.

There is no official RDA in the UK, but in the USA a daily intake of 15mg is recommended for adults. Pregnant or lactating women have additional requirements of 5mg and 10mg respectively, over and above the RDA.

It is, however, very difficult to give hard and fast guidelines as there are many factors which complicate the amount of zinc needed in the diet of a given individual. These factors include the type of diet, efficiency of absorption, age, sex, 'lifestyle', hormonal balance, emotional stability, smoking and the use of oral contraceptives. As far as vegetarians are concerned, useful sources of zinc are:

Zinc (mg per 100g)

Sesame Seeds	10.3
Cheddar Cheese	4.0
Almonds	3.1
Lentils	3.1
Haricot beans	2.8
Wholemeal bread	2.0
Brown rice	1.8

It is often said that zinc in a meat diet is more readily absorbed (ie has a higher bioavailability) than that from diets high in plant foods. This has been attributed to the binding effects that phytic acid and fibre may have on zinc. However, traditional bread baking, for example, destroys over 50% of the phytic acid, and cooking also reduces the binding effect of phytic acid and fibre on zinc. The mineral itself is not destroyed by high temperatures, although it may be leached out of boiled foods. Freezing will lower the amount of zinc in food.

Recent research, however has found that "the substitution of animal sources of zinc did not reduce zinc bioavailability or alter zinc utilisation". (Swanson, *et al* 1983) and "thus a diet high in *vegetable* protein, rather one high in *animal* protein is to be recommended with respect to bowel function, whereas it does not necessarily have a significant influence on mineral retention" (Van Dokkum, *et al* 1986).

The second point to bear in mind, with regard to zinc, is the high adaptability of the human body. As is the case with some other vitamins and minerals, its absorption tends to become more efficient when dietary intake is low. This is especially evident in lifelong vegetarians whose bodies seem to have adapted to lower zinc levels.

It is important to remember that the level of one particular vitamin or mineral should never be viewed in isolation, but within the context of the diet as a whole. There are several factors which may increase an individual's need for zinc. The amount of zinc required in the diet may be higher if the diet is high in cholesterol, sugar, copper, cadmium or lead, and also if a petrson is depressed. With respect to the latter, in situations of helplessness and hopelessness, it is the secretion of the hormone cortisol which blocks the action of zinc. Conversely, the requirement for zinc may be lower if the diet is high in Vitamin C, B_6 and essential fatty acids, as these act as co-factors in many of zinc's functions.

INFORMATION

The Z Factor
   Graham & Odent (1986) Thorsons
Swanson et Al (1983) *Amer. J. Clin. Nutr.*, 113; 2557 – 2567
Van Dokkum et al (1986) *Br. J. Nutr.*, 56; 341 – 348

Notes on supplements

A person who has a well balanced vegetarian diet should not need to take any supplements. However, supplements may be helpful at times when the body requires a higher intake of nutrients than usual. In highly polluted areas, undesirable intake of some poisonous trace elements can cause a reduction of the body's ability to make full use of the vitamins and minerals occuring in the diet. In this case, supplementation can be helpful.

Some drawbacks of using vitamin and mineral supplements are:

- Over-reliance on supplements instead of aiming for a properly balanced diet.
- The body may become temporarily dependent on artificially high levels of micronutrients.
- Discontinuation of supplements can cause a temporary low level of micronutrients in the body.
- Over-supplementation with a particular micronutrient may disturb the absorption rate of a different micronutrient. In some cases supplementation may not be as effective as it could be if a complementary micronutrient were also taken.
- Over-consumption of one micronutrient can disrupt the action or intake of another micronutrient. We cannot be sure if we have yet discovered all the micronutrients at work in the body, and it is possible therefore that over-supplementation with known nutrients could upset the activity of nutrients which have not yet been identified.

Conclusion

This table shows the main areas of nutrition that people may worry about

Nutrient	Principal sources	Advice
Protein	Soya protein, nuts, pulses, grains, milk, cheese, free range eggs and potatoes.	*Mix the proteins you eat to get a good balance, eg. cheese on wholemeal toast, macaroni cheese, cottage pie made with soya protein.*
Iron	Baked beans, wholemeal bread, dried fruit, cocoa, pulses, millet, nuts, molasses, leafy green vegetables, brewers and bakers yeast.	*A higher proportion of iron is absorbed if taken with vitamin C, so eat plenty of salads and fresh fruit. Women need more iron than men to replace that lost during menstruation.*
Calcium	Soya milk, milk, cheese, free range eggs, leafy green veg, wholemeal bread, sesame seeds and tahini, potatoes and also fortified flours.	*Growing children and nursing mothers require more than the normal daily amounts, so supplement your usual intake. Vitamin D helps to absorb calcium and is formed mainly by exposure to sunlight.*
Vitamin B_{12}	Milk, cheese and free range eggs, yeast extract. Many soya proteins are fortified, as are some soya milks.	*Vegetarians who use milk, cheese or eggs have no need to worry. It is recommended that vegans include a fortified food in their diet.*

All other vitamins, minerals and other nutrients are found in plentiful supply in a well balanced vegetarian diet.

Here is a checklist of foods that should be eaten every day to ensure that your diet is complete. Try to include something from each group if possible but don't worry if you miss one or two out now and then!

- Pulses, nuts and seeds – beans, lentils, sesame seeds, almonds, hazels
- Cereals – wheat (in wholemeal bread), rice, oats, millet, couscous, rye
- Dried fruits – apricots, peaches are especially high in iron
- Fresh fruits
- Salads and vegetables – especially dark green leafy veg like watercress, broccoli, cabbage and orange vegetables like carrots and tomatoes
- Soya products – soya protein, tofu, soya flour, soya milk (excellent, fat-free source of protein)
- Oils and vegetable fats
- Potatoes – to alternate with cereals.
- Yeast extracts – essential for vitamin B_{12} for vegans

"The unlimited capacity of the plant world to sustain man at his highest is a region yet unexplored by modern science... I submit that scientists have not yet explored the hidden possibilities of the innumerable seeds, leaves and fruits for giving the fullest possible nutrition to mankind."

Mahatma Gandhi 1944

INFORMATION

Vegetarian Nutrition
— Jack Lucas
Manual of Nutrition
— HMSO
Nutrition Tables
— HMSO
Minerals
— Miriam Polunin
Vitamin factfinder
— C Hunter
Thorsons Complete Guide to Vitamins and Minerals
— Leonard Mervyn

SOME RECIPE SHEETS AVAILABLE FROM THE VEGETARIAN SOCIETY
Meatless Means Delicious
Just for One
Very Easy Veggie Recipes
— Space Sheep & Astro Pig
Go For It
— First Steps in the Veggy Direction,
Christmas recipes
Budget Meatless Meals

Real food!

Staple foods

The following section deals with the foods which form a major part of a balanced vegetarian diet. The information has been compiled by Bronwen Humphreys.

Potatoes *(Solanum tuberosum)*

Potatoes originated in the Andes where they have been used for at least 2,000 years. They were brought to Europe in the second half of the 16th century and they are now a crop of world-wide importance. Under suitable conditions, potatoes yield a higher food-value per acre than any cereal crop and they have a great many uses including processing for crisps, flour, starch, dextrose, and alcohol. The plant is a perennial, but in practise is dug up to obtain the tubers, so it is replanted every year.

Potatoes got a bad press in the recent past as they were unfairly considered fattening. In fact they are a very useful and cheap source of nutrients. They supply Vitamin C, most B vitamins, protein and small amounts of iron and calcium. Some of the Vitamin C is destroyed in cooking. Nevertheless, potatoes remain one of the most important sources of Vitamin C in the British diet. New potatoes especially are a good source of Vitamin C. The amount of protein in potatoes isn't large, about 2g per 150g potato, but it is good quality protein and makes a significant contribution to the diet, because large amounts of potato tend to be eaten at one meal. Do try to avoid eating green potatoes or old potatoes that have begun to sprout as they may contain a toxin called solanine. As its Latin name suggests, the potato is related to Deadly Nightshade! However, there is no danger in eating normal potato tubers, which are a very useful food. Don't fry your potatoes, it is the added fat that makes them fattening; eat them boiled, mashed, baked, in stews or casseroles instead!

INFORMATION

The Potato Marketing Board,
50 Hans Crescent, Knightsbridge, London, SW1X ONB.

Leafy green vegetables

We eat a variety of leafy vegetables from various families. One of the most important is the *Brassica* family; cabbage, kale, Brussels sprouts, cauliflower, broccoli, calabrese and kohlrabi – although they look very different – are all descended from the wild cabbage *Brassica oleracea.* Various oriental greens like Pak Choi *(Brassica Chinensis)* and Pe Tsai *(Brassica Pekinensis)* are also available in this country. Other greens which feature in our diet include watercress *(Nasturtium officinale* and hybrids*)*, lettuce *(Lactuca sativa)* and spinach *(Spinacea oleracea).*

Leafy greens are particularly important in the diet because they supply Vitamin C, Vitamin A, Vitamin K, folic acid, iron, calcium and fibre.

Spinach is a good source of iron and calcium but unfortunately it seems to be largely unavailable because of the high levels of oxalic acid present in spinach. The iron in vegetarian foods isn't as easily absorbed as the iron in animal-derived foods, but consuming Vitamin C at the same meal improves absorption considerably.

The beauty of leafy green vegetables is that they contain Vitamin C and iron together in the same food! However, you should eat them raw or only very lightly cooked to avoid destroying the Vitamin C – but *don't* eat spinach raw!

There is some evidence to suggest that people who eat a lot of vegetables, particularly from the *Brassica* family, have a reduced risk of cancer.

INFORMATION

The Fresh Fruit and Vegetable Information Bureau,
Bury House, 126 -128 Cromwell Road, London, SW7 4ET.

Dried fruits

The most commonly available dried fruits are: dates *(Phoenix dactylifera)*, raisins, sultanas and currants, which are all from different varieties of grape *(Vitis vinifera)*, peaches *(Prunus Persica)*, apricots *(Prunus Armeniaca)*, prunes which are dried plums *(Prunus domestica)*, and figs *(Ficus carica)*.

Drying fruits removes the water, which not only makes them easy to store, but also concentrates the nutrients, making them a most useful source of vitamins and minerals. For example, 100g of dried apricots contains 4.8g protein, 3,600 μg Vitamin A, 4.1mg iron, 92mg calcium. Figs contain 3.6g protein, only 50 μg Vitamin A, but 4.2mg iron and a massive 280mg calcium. Dried peaches have 6.8mg iron. Currants have 1.8mg iron and 95mg calcium. Adding a handful of mixed dried fruit to your breakfast cereal or to a dessert is a very simple way of boosting iron and calcium intake.

However, you should remember that the drying process destroys most of the Vitamin C and thiamin in the fruits, so you should eat dried fruits in addition to, not instead of, fresh fruits.

per 100g	Vit A	Vit C	Iron	Calcium	
Watercress	3,000 µg	60 mg	1.6 mg	220 mg	
Lettuce	1,000 µg	15 mg	1.1 mg	23 mg	
Parsley	7,000 µg	150 mg	8 mg	330 mg	
Broccoli	2,500 µg	110 mg	1.5 mg	100 mg	
Green Cabbage	300 µg	60 mg	0.9 mg	75 mg	

Soya products

The soya bean is a pulse which has an unusually high content of good quality protein. By itself it is not very appetising and takes hours and hours to cook, but a lot of useful vegetarian foods have been made from soya and these products are very nutritious and easy to use. These products include:

Tofu Sometimes known as soya bean curd, it is made by crushing soaked and cooked soya beans into a paste, adding a curdling agent (usually calcium sulphate), then leaving in a press to set. It usually comes in two varieties, silken tofu which has been pressed only very lightly and which is soft and creamy, and firm tofu which is more like cheese and which is available in smoked and marinated varieties. All kinds of tofu are high in protein and also contain calcium, iron and B vitamins. It doesn't have much flavour of its own, so it is most suitable for recipes where it can provide protein, but where other ingredients will add flavour. Silken tofu is best for sweet dishes, dips and spreads. Firm tofu can be cut into chunks and added to sweet & sour dishes, stews and casseroles, or marinated in sauces to add flavour.

Tempeh Tempeh is made from soya beans that have been inoculated with a special fungus and left to ferment. Don't be put off by the black specks, they are similar in nature to the blue veins in some cheeses and do no harm. Unlike tofu, tempeh is chewy and has its own flavour. It is high in protein, free from gluten and salt and, unusually for a purely plant product, contains a small amount of Vitamin B_{12}.

TVP (Textured Vegetable Protein) TVP is basically a dried foam made from soya flour. The flour which is left behind after the oil has been extracted is mixed with water to form a dough, heated under pressure and then forced through a small nozzle. It expands as it comes out because of the fall in pressure and has a texture rather like a sponge. It is then cut into chunks or ground up to form mince. It is cheap to produce and stores well. It is often flavoured to resemble meat, but unflavoured versions can be purchased. There is also a type of spun protein that can be produced which resembles meat even more in its texture, but although used by the catering trade, it is not readily available in shops. A lot of vegetarians don't like these artificial meats because they resemble real meat so closely, but there is nothing objectionable about the way they are made, and they do provide a cheap source of protein that has the advantage of being low in fat too. TVP may often be incorporated into vegetarian burgers, sausages and the like, in which case some fat may be added, but the protein content is still high. It is probably best to buy unflavoured chunks or mince, and flavour them yourself – perhaps with herbs or yeast extract. They are usually sold dried and have to be rehydrated before use. The dried form keeps almost indefinitely – you can keep a packet in your pantry for emergencies.

Tamari, miso and shoyu Miso is made by fermenting soya beans and rice, barley or wheat together under pressure, for a couple of years until a thick paste has been formed. It is very nutritious, being rich in protein, minerals and some B vitamins, and is very strongly flavoured. A little can be used to give a savoury flavour to stews and casseroles. Tamari and shoyu are liquids formed during the production of miso and are the true 'soya sauces'. Do check the label, no additives should be included in real tamari and shoyu. Tamari has the advantage of being gluten-free, but is stronger than shoyu. They are sprinkled on foods after cooking to add flavour but use sparingly until you are sure you like the taste!

Soya milk/yoghurt A range of soya milks is available these days from supermarkets and health food stores. Whilst they make a convenient addition to the diet, it is important to realise that most are not nutritionally equal to dairy milk, usually being lower in calcium, Vitamin D and B_{12}. Some brands however, have been supplemented to bring them up to a similar level to dairy milk. Soya milk – except in specialised baby formulations – is not suitable as a sole food for young infants.

The recent scare that soya milks are unhealthily high in aluminium was unfounded. Ordinary soya milks have less aluminium than cows' milk.

INFORMATION

The Soya Milk Information Bureau,
   The Chestnuts, Fosse Way, Moreton Morrell, Warwick, CU35 9DE.
British Soya Milk Advisory Service,
   Bowles Well Gardens, Folkestone, Kent, CT19 6PQ.

Yeast extract

Yeast is a form of microscopic plant life which is a good source of protein and B vitamins. Common uses include brewing and baking. Yeast extract is hydrolised brewer's yeast with salt added. Although yeast itself does not produce vitamin B_{12}, many brands of yeast extract have had B_{12} added (check the label!) and this makes it one of the easiest ways a vegetarian or vegan can ensure a regular intake of B_{12}. Yeast extract can be used in a variety of ways – as a spread on toast or sandwiches, as a hot drink, or as a base for stocks, soups ,stews, gravies, casseroles etc. It really is a basic item for the vegetarian store-cupboard.

Pulses

Peas, beans and lentils are collectively called 'pulses'. They are the seeds of plants belonging to the family *Leguminosae,* which gets its name form the characteristic pod or 'legume' that protects the seeds while they are forming and ripening. With approximately 13,000 species, the family *Leguminosae* is the second largest in the plant kingdom and it is very important econ-omically. Different kinds of legumes provide us with food, medicines, oils, chemicals, animal forage, timber, dyes and ornamental garden plants. Legume products include: carob, senna, gum arabic, gum tragacanth, balsam, indigo and liquorice. Pulses are valuable because they contain a higher percentage of protein than most other plant foods, and because they can be produced without the use of nitrogen fertilisers. Legumes have characteristic nodules on the roots which contain nitrogen-fixing bacteria. These bacteria can take free nitrogen, which plants cannot make use of, and convert it into a nitrate, a form available to the plant, so pulses can in fact produce valuable protein crops on comparatively poor soils. Nitrogen is the element which gives protein its particularly important place in our diet. Humans and other animals can only use nitrogen after it has already been incorporated into protein. So ... we ultimately depend on plants to produce protein for us. Even people who eat meat depend on plants, because the sheep, cattle, pigs and poultry get *their* nitrogen by eating plants.

Origins Pulses have been used as food for thousands of years.

The lentil, *Lens esculenta*, was probably one of the first plants ever to be domesticated by humans, and has spread so widely, no-one knows where it first came from. Most pulses prefer warm climates but there are varieties which grow in temperate regions.

Beans are mostly the seeds of plants of the family *Phaeseolae*. Like lentils, they have been eaten since prehistoric times and are grown in many parts of the world. They can be eaten fresh or dried and come in a great number of varieties with a great range of colours and patterns of seed coat. Some examples are broad bean, lima bean, mung bean, runner beans.

The English pea or garden pea is *Pisum sativum*. This originated in Middle Asia in prehistoric times and is a legume that prefers cooler climates. Other legumes are called peas but are, in fact, different species eg chick pea, *Cicer arietinum*; pigeon pea, *Cajanus indicus*.

Finally, in spite of its name, the peanut is also a legume, not a nut. It is a native of South America, but is grown in India, China, West Africa and the USA as well. Legumes store very well when dried and are often considered to be 'poor man's food', but they are very nutritious and should not be despised.

Nutrition All pulses, except for soya beans, which we will consider separately, are very similar in nutritional content. They are rich in protein, carbohydate and fibre, and are also important sources of some B vitamins. Fresh pulses contain Vitamin C, but this declines after harvesting and virtually all is lost from dried pulses. Canned pulses however, lose only a little Vitamin C except for canned, processed peas which have been dried before canning! Canned garden peas usually contain only a little less Vitamin C than cooked fresh garden peas. Canning doesn't affect the protein content, eliminates the need for soaking, and considerably reduces the cooking time compared with dried pulses. Quite a few varieties are now available in cans in supermarkets.

Pulses are usually eaten for their high protein content, about 21–25%. They are a good source of the amino acid lysine, but are relatively lacking in the amino acid methionine, so they should be eaten with cereals – which are good sources of methionine but relatively poor sources of lysine – or dairy products. You will find that most main-course vegetarian recipes based on pulses take this need into account. Simple examples are: beans on toast, rice and lentils, and pea soup (with added oatmeal).

A typical nutritional breakdown is that for broad beans. 100g of dried broad beans contains: 25g protein, 1.2g fat, 51.8g carbohydrate, 6g fibre, 4.2 mg iron, 104 mg calcium.

Haricot beans, which are used to make baked beans, contain, per 100g dried beans: 21.4g protein, 1.6g fat, 45.5g carbohydrate, 25.4g fibre, 6.7mg iron, 180mg calcium; so you can see that the humble baked bean is a nutritious food, though you should try to look for brands without too much added salt and sugar.

The nutritional quality of the soya bean is superior to that of other pulses. It contains more protein, which in turn has more of the amino acid methionine – and from the point of view of protein utilisation, may be considered comparable to cheese. It is also a good source of iron and calcium.

The nutritional breakdown of soya is, per 100g of dried beans: 34.1g protein, 17.7g fat, 28.6g carbohydrate, 8.4 mg iron, 226 mg calcium.

Dried soya beans are a nuisance to prepare because they need a very long soaking and cooking time: 12 hours soaking, 4 hours boiling. A large number of convenience vegetarian foods, including tofu, tempeh and textured vegetable protein (TVP), are based on soya so you can take advantage of its nutritional properties without the tedium of a long preparation period.

Storage and cooking One advantage of dried pulses is that they will store very well for long periods if kept in a dry, airtight container. However, like most foods, it is best to eat them as fresh as possible! You can often save money by buying dried pulses in bulk, but only do this if you are really sure you are going to get through the quantity bought in a year or so. It is also wise to buy small quantities until you know which varieties you like. I can tell you from experience there is nothing more depressing than working your way through kilos of, say, pigeon peas long after you have discovered you don't really like them!

Most dried pulses, with the exception of red lentils and split peas, need soaking for several hours before they can be cooked. Some are still sold with a tablet of sodium bicarbonate which shortens the soaking time, but is also destroys B vitamins, and can be harmful if you are on a low-sodium diet for hypertension. Soaking times vary from four hours for aduki beans to twelve hours for soya beans. It is usually most convenient to put them to soak the evening before you are going to need them. Always discard the water they have been soaking in, rinse and cook in fresh water. This will help to reduce the flatulence some people suffer when eating pulses.

Warning Although they are a very nutritious food, some beans contain toxic substances called 'haemagglutinins', which are destroyed by heat. It is therefore very important that when cooking beans, the temperature actually reaches boiling point and stays there for at least ten minutes. After that, they can be simmered until soft. Canned beans are safe as they are heat-treated during processing. Temperatures in a pressure-cooker are also sufficiently high to render the beans safe, but slow-cookers do not reach high enough temperatures, so beans should always be boiled in a saucepan for the required ten minutes before being transferred to the slow-cooker. Don't buy soya flour unless it states 'heat-treated' on the label.

Some people suffer flatulence and/or indigestion when eating pulses. This can often be relieved by discarding the soaking water and rinsing as described above; very thorough cooking and the addition of aromatic herbs like dill or caraway to the beans while cooking. However, some people simply don't seem able to digest pulses properly and if the trouble is severe and persistent, they should be avoided. Typical cooking times are;

Aduki beans, black-eyed beans, marrowfat peas:	*1 hour conventional, 15 minutes pressure.*
Broad beans, butter beans, haricot beans, pinto beans:	*1.5 hours conventional, 20 minutes pressure.*
Chick peas:	*3 hours conventional, 40 minutes pressure.*
Soya beans:	*4 hours conventional, 50 minutes pressure.*

As beans and peas are all very similar nutritionally, with the exception of soya, they can be interchanged in most recipes if you want to experiment or have run out of one kind, as long as you take into account the different cooking times. If the beans are likely to need a lot longer to cook than the other ingredients, try pre-cooking them in a separate pan before adding to the other ingredients, or using canned beans.

INFORMATION

The Bean Information Bureau
c/o Paragon Communications, 142 Wardour Street, London, WlV 3AU.
Peanuts Information Service,
4 Bedford Square, London, WC1B 3RA.

Nuts

Nuts are a good source of protein and can be used in many ways. Raw, they can simply be ground in a coffee mill and sprinkled on a dish of salad – or cooked rice, pasta, millet, buckwheat, sweetcorn, mashed potato. Flaked nuts can be used in the same way, and finely-ground nuts can be added to a white sauce in much the same way as grated cheese.

The classic vegetarian savoury is a Nut Roast and all vegetarian cookery books will give a recipe for one. Roasts can be endlessly varied with different herbs and flavourings, and different combinations of nuts and cereals and the use of onions, mushrooms etc. Made up slightly more moist than the recipe suggests, a nut roast can be used as a sandwich spread, a filling for a pie or pastry or 'sausage' roll.

Nuts can be added to sweet dishes, cakes and biscuits. Nut butters are widely available and can be used as spreads or thickeners for soup.

Nutrition Nuts are very nutritious, providing protein and many essential vitamins and minerals and fibre. They combine well with cereals to form a balanced protein dish, and the classic nut roast recipe, with its many variations, makes use of this. Nuts are also high in carbohydrate and oils, so they really shouldn't be eaten as a snack between meals, but are better served as a main-course savoury.

Almonds *(Prunus dulcis)*

Probably originated in the Near East, but it now grows in Southern Europe, Western Asia, California, South Australia and South Africa. Almond oil is used for flavouring and for skin-care preparations and is extracted from the kernel of the variety *Prunus dulcis var. amara* or Bitter Almond. The Sweet Almond is grown for its nuts. Almonds are particularly nutritious: 100g provide 16.9g protein, 4.2mg iron, 250mg calcium, 20mg Vitamin E, 15mg zinc and 0.92mg Vitamin B$_2$.

Brazils *(Bertholletia excelsa)*

A native of South America. The nuts that we see in the shops actually grow inside a hard woody pod rather like a coconut shell which has to be broken open to expose the 12–24 nuts inside. Brazils are high in fat (66%) and protein (14%). 100g of brazils provide 12g protein, 2.8mg iron, 180mg calcium.

Cashews *(Anacardium occidentale)*

Native to America but now grown extensively in India and East Africa. It will withstand rather drier conditions than most other nuts. The nut we buy in the shop grows in a curious way on the tree, hanging below a fleshy, apple-like fruit. 100g of cashews provide 17.2g protein, 60 µg Vitamin A, 3.8mg iron.

Chestnuts *(Castanea sativa,* Sweet Chestnut *)*
A native of Southern Europe but planted elsewhere extensively for both nuts and timber. It was probably introduced into Britain by the Romans. Chestnuts can be used in soups, fritters, porridges, stuffings and stews, as well as being roasted or boiled whole. Preserved in syrup, they become the famous delicacy, Marron-glacé. A Chestnut-based nut roast is a delicious savoury: quite often vegetarians eat it for Christmas Dinner as it combines well with the traditional Christmas fare of sprouts, roast potatoes, cranberry sauce.

100g of chestnuts provide 2g protein (the lowest of all nuts), 46mg calcium. Although they are not as nutritious as other nuts, their taste does make them perfect for special occasions. Mix with cashews to improve nutritional content.

Coconuts *(Cocos nucifera).*
The coconut palm is common in tropical regions all over the world. All parts of the tree are useful, the trunks for timber, the leaves for thatch. The fibrous husk produces coir – for ropes and coconut matting, and the nuts are used for food. Unripe nuts contain coconut milk. The nut-meat can be eaten fresh or dried (desiccated coconut). A valuable oil is also extracted from the nut meat and used for cooking, margarines, soaps and detergents. 100g of fresh coconut gives 3.2g protein, desiccated gives 5.6g protein.

Hazelnuts *(Corylus avellana).*
Hazel, also called Cob, is a common wild tree in Europe and Asia Minor. Its nuts have been eaten by humans since earliest times; they were collected by Mesolithic peoples and there are references to them in Theophrastus and Pliny. The cultivated varieties are bigger and the filbert *(Corylus maxima)* is a similar but bigger species from S outh East Europe. 100g of hazel nuts gives 7.6g protein, and they are lower in fat than most other nuts.

Macadamia nuts *(Macadamia ternifolia,* Queensland Nuts *).*
A native of North Eastern Australia now also grown commercially in Hawaii. 100g Macadamia nuts gives 7g protein, 40mg calcium.

Peanuts *(Arachis hypogaea).*
Also known as Ground Nut or Monkey Nut, it is actually a legume. Of South American origin, it is now an important crop all over the tropics and subtropics and in the USA as far north as Virginia. It gets its name 'ground nut' because as the pods ripen, they are actually forced underground. Peanuts are highly nutritious with 30% protein and 40–50% oil and they are an important crop. The oil is used in cooking, as salad oil, in margarines, and the residue is fed to animals. Whole peanuts can be eaten raw or roasted or made into peanut butter. As they are usually inexpensive, they can be mixed with other kinds of nuts to bring down the cost of making nut roasts etc, while still maintaining flavour and good nutrition. 100g of peanuts gives 24.3g protein, 110 µg folic acid, 2mg iron, 61mg calcium.

Pecans *(Carya illinoensis).*
A native of North America where they are used extensively in ice cream, cakes, nut bread and confectionery. Nowadays you can find them in British shops but they are still not as common as almonds, brazils, walnuts and hazels. The flavour is rather like that of a mild, sweet walnut. 100g of pecans gives 9.2g protein, 130 µg Vitamin A, 2.4mg iron, 73mg calcium.

Pine nuts *(Pinus pinea).*
These are the seeds of the Stone Pine, a native of the Mediterranean region, but the seeds of various other pines are eaten in various parts of the world, including the seeds of the Chile Pine or Monkey Puzzle tree. 100g of pine nuts gives 31.1g protein.

Pistachios *(Pistacia vera).*
Native to the Near East and Central Asia but has long been cultivated in the Mediterranean region and more recently in the Southern United States. The kernels are green and prized as much for their decorative colour as for their flavour. They are more expensive than most other nuts. 100g of pistachios gives 19.3g protein, 14mg iron, 140 mg calcium.

Walnuts*(Juglans regia)* **, Black Walnut** *(Juglans nigra)*
Butternut *(Juglans cinerea)*
Juglans regia is native to Southern Europe and West & Central Asia but is now grown in the British Isles, California and China as well. It is grown for timber as well as its nuts. Walnut oil has been used for centuries in the preparation of artists' paints. *Juglans nigra* is a native of North America, introduced into Britain in the 17th century. *Juglans cinerea* is also from North America. These two have much thicker shells than European walnuts. 100g of walnuts gives 10.6g protein, 2.4mg iron, 61mg calcium.

Seeds

Pumpkin *(Cucurbita pepo and allied species).*
Can be eaten raw or cooked in both sweet and savoury dishes. Sprinkle on salads or breakfast cereal. 100g of pumpkin seeds gives 29g protein, 11.2mg iron, 51mg calcium.

Sesame *(Sesamum indicum).*
Of African origin, but now common in tropical and sub-tropical Asia. It is an annual plant growing up to six feet high and looking rather like a bellflower. An oil is extracted from the seed and used for cooking, salad oil and margarines, and the whole seeds can also be eaten and are most often seen as a decoration on cakes, confectionery etc. Sesame seed paste, tahini, is rather like peanut butter. Halva, a sweet made from sesame seeds is often found in health food shops. 100g of sesame seeds gives 26.4g protein, 12.6mg Vitamin B_3, 7.8mg iron, 131mg calcium, 10.3mg zinc.

Sunflower *(Helianthus annus).*
An annual plant belonging to the daisy family *Compositae.* It probably originated in North America or Mexico and was introduced into Europe in the 16th century. The oil extracted from its seeds is used in margarine, varnishes and soaps, but the seeds can be eaten whole, raw or cooked. They can be added to breads and cakes, made into savouries, sprinkled over salad or breakfast cereals. 100g of sunflower seeds gives 24g protein, 7.1mg iron, 120mg calcium.

Cereals

All too often, cereal products are thought of as nothing more than starchy fillers, and indeed, when you consider how some commercial products like cakes and biscuits and breakfast cereals are made from over-refined grains with nearly all the nutrients except the starch extracted, and then loaded with fat, sugar, artificial flavourings etc, you might be forgiven for thinking this is true. But go back to the original, unrefined grains and you have a wealth of nutrients in a small package.

Grains have been the staple foods of many civilisations for thousands of years – wheat, barley, oats and rye in Europe; maize in America; quinoa in South America; rice in the East; millet in Africa. Nowadays, we are not confined to the grain which grows best in our climate, we can enjoy a wide variety imported from all over the world.

The word 'corn' is sometimes applied specifically to maize, but is often used simply to designate the staple cereal grown in a particular country, so in Britain, wheat is often called corn.

Nutrition Cereals are seeds of plants, usually members of the grass family, but there are a few exceptions. They are annuals, that is they have to be planted every year, and at the end of summer, when they have produced ripe seeds, they die down. Like all seeds, cereals are very nutritious because they contain all the nutrients the embryo plant needs to start growing. Unrefined cereals are valuable sources of proteins, energy, B vitamins and also contain some fat, iron, Vitamin E and trace minerals, and are a very good source of fibre in the diet. Some cereals contain the protein gluten, which is essential for bread-making. Without sufficient gluten, the bread will not rise, so not all cereals can be used to make the familiar western-type loaf. In some parts of the world unleavened (unrisen) bread is the norm.

Cereals can be used in other ways, besides being ground into flour for bread, cakes etc. Whole cereals can be added to stews and casseroles, or boiled until soft. Flaked cereals can be added to muesli or used to make porridge, or, in many cases, added to a nut or bean roast. Meal, a coarse kind of flour can be used to make porridge, thicken soups, or mixed with wheat flour, to add interesting flavours and textures to ordinary breads, biscuits, muffins etc.

The protein in cereals is not complete in itself. Cereals are usually lacking in the amino acid lysine, so they have to be eaten with another protein source, such as pulses or dairy produce, in order to make a complete protein. They are a good source of the essential amino acid methionine and so mix very well with pulses to form complete protein dishes. They are usually cheap to buy and are a valuable source of variety in the vegetarian diet.

Barley *(Hordeum distichon)*
Barley grows in a wider variety of climatic conditions than any other cereal. It used to be a very important source of direct human food, but over the last 250 years it has given way to wheat. It is now used almost exclusively as animal feed or for making beer and whisky. It has a high gluten content and can be made into bread but is more usually found in the shops as whole or pot barley, or with the outer husks removed, as pearl barley. The whole barley is more nutritious with 100g providing 10.5g protein, 2.1g fat, 69.3g carbohydrate, 4g fibre, 50mg folic acid, 6mg iron and 50mg calcium. Vegetarians can use it cooked on its own as a pleasant alternative to rice, pasta or potatoes, or it can be added to stews.

Buckwheat
Buckwheat is not a true cereal as it is not a member of the grass family. The name is given to *Fagopyrun sagittatum* (or *esculentum*) and allied species, and they are relatives of sorrels and docks. If you look at docks closely, you

can see that the seeds, though smaller, have the same distinctive triangular shape. Buckwheat is a native of Central Asia but is now grown in Europe, North America and the USSR. It is widely used in Britain. It can be boiled and served like rice but needs sautéeing first, like millet, or you can add it to stews and casseroles. Buckwheat flour can be added to cakes, muffins and pancakes. It imparts a distinctive flavour. Look out, too, for buckwheat spaghetti. 100g of buckwheat provides 11.7g protein, 3.9mg iron and it is very high in calcium with 114mg per 100g. It is gluten-free.

Maize *(Zea mays)*

Maize is the principal food plant of America and was unknown in other parts of the world until Christopher Columbus reached America in 1492. It was grown by the Maya, Inca and Aztec civilisations, and by various North American Indian tribes, and now has spread to Canada, USSR, Italy, Spain, Egypt and South Africa. It is used for human food, animal feed and as a source of raw materials for industry.

100g maize gives 9g protein, but it is deficient in the amino acid tryptophan. This is no problem in a normal mixed diet, but people who use maize as a substitute for wheat because of its gluten-free properties should be aware of this. Whole maize, rather than the grain, is often available (as sweet corn or corn on the cob). We see maize as cornflakes or popcorn, but cornmeal or 'polenta' is also available and can be added to soup, pancakes, muffins etc. Tortillas are made from maize meal, as are many snack foods.

Millet

Millet is the name applied to a variety of grasses first cultivated in Asia or Africa, including *Pennisetum glaucum, Panicum milliaceum, Panicum ramosum*. It is a staple crop in Africa because it is drought-resistant and keeps well. If you thought it was just for budgies, think again! 100g millet provides 9.9g protein, and 6.8mg iron (higher than other cereals).

Millet makes a delicious alternative to rice but the tiny seeds need to be cracked before they will absorb water easily, so they should first be sautéed with a little vegetable oil for 2–3 minutes until some are seen to crack, then add water (care!), bring to the boil and simmer for 40–45 minutes until fluffy. 1 cup of millet requires 3 cups water. It is gluten-free. Millet flakes can be made into porridge or added to muesli, and millet flour is available.

White Oats *(Avena sativa),*
Red Oats *(Avena byzantina)*

Oats are thought to have originated in Western Europe and may originally have appeared as a weed in barley and so were spread with the barley. They are now grown in many parts of the world including North West Europe, USSR, America, Canada, Australia and China. They are mostly used as animal feed but are equally nutritious for humans. In fact, as they are usually inexpensive to buy, they can be a real boon to people trying to achieve a good diet on a low budget. 100g oats gives 13g protein, 55mg calcium (more than any other cereal except buckwheat), and 4.6mg iron. They are available as groats (whole grains with the husks removed) but more usually as oatmeal, rolled oats or flakes. All the latter can be used to make porridge, combined with ground nuts to make a roast, or added to stews. Oatmeal is low in gluten so can not be used to make a loaf, but can be mixed with wheat flour to add flavour and texture to bread, muffins and pancakes.

Quinoa

This is an ancient crop which fed the Aztecs and Incas for thousands of years, and which has recently become available here in Britain. Unlike most grains, it does not belong to the grass family, but is a relative of a garden weed called Fat Hen. It is very nutritious, containing between 13–14% protein with a good amino acid composition, but has no gluten so it cannot be used for bread-making. Instead, it is boiled and used like rice.

Rice *(Oryza sativa)*

Rice is one of the world's most important crops. It originated in Asia but is now grown throughout the humid, sub-tropical regions. It differs from most other cereals in requiring land that is submerged in water to grow, though some varieties do grow in upland areas.

Rice is a good source of carbohydrate but does not have quite as much protein as some other cereals (6.5g per 100g). Unpolished rice is a good source of B vitamins too. There are two basic kinds, long grain and short grain – the first used traditionally in Indian cooking, the second in Chinese cooking, but it is really just a matter of personal preference which you use. Rice is gluten-free and so very useful for people suffering from coeliac disease and other gluten allergies. Rice flour is available, but because of the lack of gluten, it cannot be used to make an ordinary, yeasted loaf and so has to be used for cakes, biscuits and pancakes.

Rye *(Secale cereale)*

is the least important cereal crop and is usually grown only where conditions are relatively unfavourable and other cereals don't do well. It probably originated in South West Asia, but the name occurs in Northern European languages, which suggests early cultivation in that area too. It is very hardy and so is grown in the cooler regions and at high altitudes, and it is very tolerant of poor soil fertility. It is the only cereal apart from wheat that has enough gluten to make a conventional yeasted loaf, but it has less gluten than wheat, so rye bread is denser. It is more usual to mix rye flour with wheat flour. Kibbled rye is often added to granary-type loaves. You can also add rye to stews, and rye flakes are available, which can be used in muesli. 100g of rye gives 9.4g protein.

Wheat

This is the most familiar cereal used in Britain today. It is used for bread, cakes, biscuits, pastry, breakfast cereals and pasta. All the present varieties of wheat seem to be derived from a hybrid wild wheat that grew in the Middle East 10,000 years ago. Over 30,000 varieties are said to be in cultivation, but almost all belong to two species, *Triticum aestivum*, or bread wheat, and *Triticum durum*, or macaroni wheat, which is used for making pasta. Wheat can be grown in a very wide range of climatic conditions but is most successful in temperate zones including the UK, North America, Southern Russia and South West Australia. Nutritionally, 100g of whole wheat provides 14g protein, 2.2g fat, 69.1g carbohydrate, 2.3g fibre, 3.1mg iron, 36mg calcium.

Wild rice *(Zizania aquatica)*

'Wild Rice' is not a rice at all but an American grass used as an important food by the Indians and early settlers. Difficulty in harvesting makes it expensive, but with its purplish-black colour, and its subtle nutty flavour, it is a good base for an exceptional meal.

INFORMATION

Flour Advisory Bureau,
    21 Arlington Street, London, SWIA 1RN.
Oat & Barley Association
    6 Catherine Street, London, WC2B 5JJ.
Maize Growers Association,
    Richard Weller, IGAP, Church Lane, Shinfield, Reading.

Food shopping

Food! Whether you are a vegetarian for health reasons or for ethical reasons, food is the one area in your life that you have made the decision to change. Vegetarians come from all walks of life, and all kinds of political and religious backgrounds. There is one thing that we all have in common – we don't eat meat, and we scan our food carefully to be sure that no meat products, fish or poultry, or dead animals of any kind find their way onto our plates.

The information in this section is arranged alphabetically. Within this structure, you will find information about foods to avoid (and why!), information about vegetarian alternatives to non-vegetarian foods, and information about special foods created especially for vegetarians and vegans.

In the last edition of *The Vegetarian Handbook*, we tried to list all vegetarian food products. In this edition, we have mentioned only the food products which are licensed to carry the Vegetarian Society's ϒ Symbol. These products have been checked by the Society to be sure that they meet our standards. The manufacturers all support the work of the Vegetarian Society by buying the right to use the symbol.

There are many products which are suitable for vegetarians that are not mentioned specifically in this section – the section on reading the label, which follows, plus the food additives and E Numbers lists at the back of the book should give you all the information you need to be sure of choosing the right products.

Baby food

There is a special section on feeding babies later in this book, which contains full details on infant diets and recipes. The following baby milks and foods have been authorised to use the ϒ Symbol:

Cow and Gate
- Formula S infant formula
- Olivarit garden vegetable with rice
- Olivarit garden vegetable risotto
- Olivarit vegetable & rice casserole
- Olivarit vegetable & pasta casserole

Farleys
- Ostersoy infant formula

H J Heinz Co Ltd
- Braised country vegetables
- Sweetcorn & potato hotpot
- Macaroni cheese
- Vegetable & lentil hotpot
- Bean, rice & tomato casserole
- Braised vegetables with mushrooms
- Cottage potato & vegetable dinner
- Cheesy potato pasta & tomato
- Spaghetti napolitan
- Tomato & vegetable risotto

Wyeth Nutrition
- Wysoy Infant Formula

Biscuits

Look out for animal fats (lard! If it was butter, they would SAY butter!), and also for whey and non-vegetarian colourings and food additives. Check the E Numbers against the list further on in this book.

Foodwatch International
- Banana Cookie Mix

Kroustie European Bread
- ☐ Oat bran biscuits

J Sainsbury PLC
- ☐ Carob coated ginger & orange finger biscuits

Bread

Sometimes made with non-vegetarian E Numbers, sometimes made in tins greased with animal fat, sometimes glazed with milk or egg. If in doubt, buy from your health food shop – or try making your own! It's a very therapeutic occupation! The Vegetarian Society's Cookery School runs occasional bread-making courses – phone for details.

Goswell Bakeries
- ☐ Speciality breads:
- ☐ Continental wholemeal
- ☐ Bagels
- ☐ Pretzels
- ☐ Polish rye
- ☐ Prewetts wholemeal loaf
- ☐ Doves Farm wholemeal loaf
- ☐ Doves Farm white loaf

Kroustie European Bread
- ☐ Five grain special bread
- ☐ Raisin five grain pumpernickel
- ☐ European dark rye bread

Natural Way Food Company Ltd
- ☐ Manna bread, carrot & raisin, sunseed, fruit

Clements Vegetarian Cuisine
- ☐ Cheese scones

J Sainsbury PLC
- ☐ Spiced poppadums
- ☐ Plain poppadums
- ☐ Spiced pappads
- ☐ Wholegrain rolls.

Other Sainsbury's breads are suitable for vegetarians and will shortly carry the Ⓥ symbol.

Breakfast cereals

Some brands have added vitamins and minerals which may be from dubious sources. Some brands are laden with sugar! You can easily make your own muesli. There are lots of recipes; one you might try is in *First Steps In Vegetarian Cooking* by Kathy Silk, available from the Vegetarian Society.

Burgers & bangers

Although we hate to admit it, veggie burgers are every vegetarian's stand-by! Frozen vegetarian bangers and burgers may contain battery eggs – beware.

Buss Foods
- ☐ Vegetable burger
- ☐ Nut tofu burger
- ☐ Vegetable sausage

Dietburger Co Ltd
- ☐ Frozen dietburger
- ☐ Dietburger mix
- ☐ Superveg burger

Droyt Products
- ☐ Vegetas

Clements Wholefoods Cuisine
- ☐ Chilli burgers
- ☐ Vegetable burgers

Foodwatch International
- ☐ Lentil burger mix
- ☐ Vegetable burger mix

Goodlife Wholefoods
- ☐ Vegetable & sesame cutlet
- ☐ Tandoori cutlet
- ☐ Nut cutlet
- ☐ Mexican cutlet
- ☐ Beanbangers, herb, spicey

Smits Reform BV
- ☐ Vegetable burger mix

Suma Wholefoods
- ☐ Tinned beans and vegetarian burgers
- ☐ Tinned beans and vegetarian sausages

J Sainsbury PLC
- ☐ Crispy crumbed vegetable burgers
- ☐ Vegetable burgers

Rayner Burgess
- ☐ Mortadella style sausage
- ☐ Mixed grain and vegetable sausage
- ☐ Vegetable burger with tofu
- ☐ Savoury tofu burgers

Zeras Vegetarian Foods
- ☐ Soya burger
- ☐ Millett & cheese burger

Soya Health Foods Ltd (Sunrise)
- ☐ Vegetarian burgers, spicy, tandoori, mexican chilli

Caffeine

Not strictly a vegetarian issue, but it is worth cutting down on your coffee drinking, especially if you suffer from stress or are expecting a baby. There should be several varieties of caffeine-free beverages available from your health food shop.

London Herb & Spice Company
- Natural Break vegetable snack drink

Modern Health Products Ltd
- Vecon light savoury drink

Cake

Again, check for animal fats and dubious additives. There are some egg-free cakes available, and it is possible to make a cake using purely fruit and nuts! ('Fruitarian Cake', in Eva Batt's *Vegan Cookery*, published by Thorsons, available from the Vegetarian Society.)

Clements Wholefoods Cuisine
- Date slice
- Apple cake
- Bread pudding
- Dairy free carrot cake
- Sugar free carrot cake
- Cherry almond tart
- Banana & walnut cake
- Apple sultana pie
- Apricot pie
- Iced apricot loaf
- Iced pineapple loaf
- Date scones
- Macaroon slice

Foodwatch International
- Waffle & pancake mix
- Banana cake & pudding mix

Holland & Barrett
- Blackcurrant crunch
- Chocolate flapjack
- Carob flapjack
- Apricot crunch
- Lemon cake
- Ginger crush cake
- Carrot cake
- Orange & carob chip cake
- Honey flapjack

Norfolk Punch
- Sunday pudding
- Christmas pudding

RHM Grocery
- Robertsons luxury wholefood Christmas pudding

J Sainsbury PLC
- Fruit malt loaf
- Wholemeal Christmas pudding
- Mincemeat

- Mincemeat premium brand
- Special recipe mincemeat

Matthew Walker (Derby) Ltd
- Vegetarian plum pudding

Wholebake
- Apricot & apple slice
- Date slice
- Fig slice
- Carob coated pineapple & almond slice
- Yoghurt coated apple & ginger slice
- Christmas pudding

Wilkinson's Home Bakery
- Date & walnut cakes

Zeras Vegetarian Foods
- Carrot & walnut cake
- Carrot & ginger cake
- Oatmeal date slice
- Oatmeal apricot slice

Capsules

All capsules are made from gelatine. This is not suitable for vegetarians, but most health food shops continue to sell them because no satisfactory vegetarian alternative has yet been found. Look for tablets instead. See section on vitamins and supplements for details of herbal remedy and health supplement tablets which have been authorised to use the Υ symbol.

Carob

Caffeine-free alternative to chocolate which crops up in drinks, biscuits and confectionery. Often carob products are sugar-free because carob is naturally far sweeter than cocoa. Frequently carob products are dairy-free, but don't take it for granted. Some carob products contain whey which is not considered suitable for vegetarians.

Cheese

Most of the cheeses you will find on sale in supermarkets and High Street shops are not completely vegetarian. One of the first steps in the process of making cheese is to coagulate the liquid milk by adding a substance called rennet. This is the common name for an enzyme, rennin, found in the stomachs of baby animals, including humans. It helps the baby to digest milk, but as the baby grows and starts to eat solid foods, its production of rennin declines. When adult humans drink milk, it is clotted in the stomach, not by rennin but by the hydrochloric acid present there. As is usual with enzymic reactions, only a small amount of rennin is needed to clot a large volume of milk. According to the *Dairy Handbook*, one part of rennin can coagulate 10–15,000 parts of milk in about 40 minutes at 30°C. The usual source of rennin for commercial cheese-making is the stomach of slaughtered calves. The fourth stomach or abomasum is used, from a newly-slaughtered two-week-old calf. The lining of this stomach is washed, dried, cut into small pieces and macerated in water containing about 4% boric acid at 30°C. for about five days. Another method of extraction is to use a brine solution instead of boric acid. Pepsin can also be used to coagulate milk but this is mixed with rennin. A 50:50 rennet is half pepsin, half rennin.

Incidentally, the liquid that is left after the clotted fraction of the milk has been removed is called whey. This turns up in a lot of products, for example margarine, but unless a vegetarian enzyme was used, whey cannot be considered a vegetarian ingredient.

A soft cheese can be made through the natural souring process. Bacteria normally present in milk produce lactic acid which acts as a clotting agent. This is sold as lactic cheese, but we suspect that all so-called lactic cheeses are not completely vegetarian, some may have had rennet added. Other strains of bacteria, eg *Bacillus subtilis*, *Bacillus prodigiosum*, produce a true rennin. It is from this bacterial enzyme that 'vegetarian' cheeses are produced.

There are now lots of vegetarian cheeses on the market. The Vegetarian Society has a list of vegetarian cheeses, and can also give information to caterers on buying vegetarian cheese in bulk.

The following is a list of vegetarian cheeses which have been given authority to use the ℣ symbol:

Abergavenny Fine Foods Ltd
- Goats milk cheese

Avonmore Foods (Ireland)
- Vegetarian Cheddar cheese

Bailey Milk Products Ltd
- Organic Edam cheese

Bongrain UK Ltd
- Vegetarian tartare cheese

Capitol Foods
- Cottage cheese

Caterers Choice (for caterers)
- Vegetarian cheese

Caws Cenearth
- Welsh cheese

Central Midlands Co-operative Society
- Vegetarian Cheddar, mild, medium, mature

Express Foods
- Vegetarian cheese
- Eden Vale cottage cheese:
  natural
  fruity pineapple
  savoury onion and chive
  crunchy peanut, carrot and celery
- Eden Vale vegetarian Cheddar

Fromageries Triballat
- Le Roule, Herb, Spiced, Strawberry, Mint & Choc

Galbani Ltd
- Mascarpone
- Ricotta
- Gorgonzolla
- Dolcelatte
- Mozzarella

Holland & Barrett
- French brie

Ingle Smokehouse
- Smoked cheese

M D Foods AMBA
- Danish mozzarella

Oldenburger UK Ltd
- Oldenburger German white rindless Cheddar cheese
- Oldenburger German white rindless Tilsit cheese
- Oldenburger German white rindless Edam cheese
- Oldenburger German white rindless Gouda cheese
- Goldrauch Natural smoked cheese

Perratt & Sons
- Full fat soft cheese

Rosary
- Goats Cheese

J Sainsbury PLC
- Low fat soft cheese
- Welsh goats cheese
- Welsh goats cheese with sweet peppers
- Bavarian soft cheese
- Bavarian soft cheese with horseradish
- Creamy full fat cheese

- Half fat creamery cheese
- Cottage cheese with chives
- Cottage cheese with pineapple
- Cottage cheese with sweetcorn, mixed beans & peppers
- Cottage cheese with onions and peppers
- Natural cottage cheese
- Cream cheese
- Cream cheese with pineapple
- Cream cheese with chives
- Curd cheese
- Skimmed cheese
- Half fat cottage cheese
- Half fat cottage cheese with pineapple
- Half fat cottage cheese with chives
- Continental style cottage cheese
- Vegetarian cheddar
- Danish blue cheese
- Cardigan cheese
- Acorn cheese
- Soft cheese with garlic and parsley
- Mozzarella cheese.
- Fromage frais

Sarah's Kitchen
- Low fat creamery cheese

Sodaerasens
- Sunflower cheese

H T Webb & Co
- Exquisa sport low fat cheese

Westland Kaasspecialiteiten BV
- Ball Edam (Dutch)

Wyke
- Farmhouse cheese

Chips

May be fried in animal fat, or in the same container as pieces of meat, fish and chicken.

Convenience foods

Vegetarianism has never been so convenient! Chilled and frozen ready-meals, and dried packet mixes, are available in sizes suitable for home cooking and for caterers.

Addler (West Germany)
- Cheesey
- Kaese Pastete

Brooke Bond Foods
- Beanfeast, 4 flavours

Butcher & Baker
- Vegetable pasties

Clements Wholefoods Cuisine
- Pizzas
- Mushroom & pepper pizzas
- Quizzas
- Hazelnut roast
- Peanut roast
- Nut roast
- Curried rice quiche
- Nut & cauliflower quiche
- Cheese & potato pie
- Picnic loaf
- Vegan pie
- Bean & vegetable pie
- Curried triangles
- Scotch eggs
- Cheese & vegetable pasties
- Cheese & lentil loaf
- Spinach & lentil lattice

Cook Inns Ltd (for caterers)
- Butterbean & vegetable curry
- Lentil & pepper casserole
- Spaghetti with lentil & tomato
- Blackeys bake
- Bean goulash
- Bean & vegetable stew hotpot
- Curried chickpeas
- Spicy bean rissotto
- Oriental black bean casserole
- Mushroom saute rissotto
- Tuscan beans with pasta
- Vegetarian paella
- Bean & mushroom casserole
- Curried chickpeas with tomato & pineapple
- Lentil bake
- Nut roast & mediterranean sauce
- Broccoli & cauliflower crumble
- Curried bean bake
- Curried wonder crumble

Country Cooks
- Mixed vegetable crumble
- Nut lasagne
- Vegetable curry
- Mushroom & cashew nut pilaf
- Blackeyed bean bake

Emile Tissot Foods Ltd
- Vegetable lasagne
- Vegetable au gratin
- Wheat & walnut casserole
- Vegetable biryani
- Vegetable chilli
- Vegetable moussaka
- Vegetable stroganoff
- Broccoli & cream cheese pie
- Shredded vegetable pie
- Macaroni cheese
- Potato dauphinoise

- Cauliflower cheese
- Tagiatelle nicoise

Farmer Giles Foods
- Mushroom & broccoli flan

Foodwatch International
- Versaloaf

Ginsters Cornish Pasties
- Pasti Italiano
- Ploughman's pasty
- Country vegetable savoury slices

Golden Wonder
- Chilli con carne pot rice
- Chicken supreme pot rice
- Spicy beef curry pot noodle
- Beef & tomato pot noodle
- Chicken curry pot noodle

Goodlife Wholefoods
- Vegetable biriani
- Peas and rice
- Fruit and nut rice
- Organic smoked tofu satay

Granose Foods Ltd
- Brazil nut roast mix
- Cashew nut roast mix
- Nut roast mix
- Lentil roast mix
- Sunflower & sesame roast mix
- Mexican corn roast mix

Holland & Barrett
- Wholemeal spicy pasty
- Nutty jacket egg
- Wholemeal vegetable pakora
- Wholemeal spicy country pie
- Wholemeal ratatouille pie
- Wholemeal breakfast pie
- Asparagus quiche
- Mushroom quiche
- Cheese & onion quiche
- Provençal quiche
- Fruit salad

Impulse Foods (Bean Cuisine)
- Lentil shepherds pie
- Lentil lasagne
- Three bean goulash
- Haricot hot pot
- Bean and vegetable curry
- Bean ratatouille
- Chilli con lentil
- Lentil bolognese
- Green bean moussaka

Jus-rol (for caterers)
- Pullman vegetable & cheese pasty

Mearns Food Company Ltd (for caterers)
- Vegetarian moussaka
- Chilli beans
- Chickpeas and tomato
- Ratatouille
- Mushroom curry
- Vegetarian lasagne

Molly's Kitchen (for caterers)
- Vegetarian savoury crepe
- English vegetable mornay
- Cheesy leek & potato casserole
- Mushroom stroganoff
- Cauliflower & chickpea korma curry
- Mexican chilli
- Pasta italienne
- Courgette & mushroom lasagne
- Spicy broccoli au gratin
- Nut roast provençal

The Nestlé Company Ltd
- Vegetable hot pot
- Vegetable chilli
- Vegetable curry
- Vegetable lasagne

Rani Frozen Foods
- Chickpea curry
- Corn & mushroom curry

Rayner Burgess
- Crispy tandoori grills, tandoori, farmhouse, Italian
- Shanghai sweet & sour vegetables with tofu
- Cantonese stir fry vegetables with tofu in black bean sauce
- Indonesian vegetables and tofu in spicy satay sauce
- Punjabi vegetable biriani with tofu
- Spicy tofuloni
- Country tofuloni

Response Foods
- Red dragon pie
- Leek & pecan pancakes
- Vegetable curry
- Mixed bean ratatouille
- Spicy garbanzo beans
- Chilli vegetariani

J Sainsbury PLC
- Garlic mushroom jacket potato
- Baked bean jacket potato
- Neeps & tatties
- Potato & leek flan
- Vegetable chilli flan
- Vegetable dhansak
- Spicy vegetables
- Vegetable samosa
- Spring rolls

- Vegetable tikka masala
- Mushroom & courgette lasagne
- Mixed beans & peppers
- Deep & crispy vegetable pizza
- Mixed beans in mild curry sauce
- Mixed beans in spicy pepper sauce
- Mixed beans in sweet & sour sauce
- Vegetable enchilladas
- Cauliflower au gratin flan
- Vegetable bake
- Vegetable grills
- Potato latkes
- Vegetable canneloni
- Vegetable moussaka
- Vegetable pakoras
- Tagliatelle vegetali
- Leek & potato crumble
- Nut roast
- Deep filled pizza with cheese
- Bombay potato pasty
- Vegetable ragout
- Gobi aloo sag
- Vegetable curry & spiced basmati rice
- Vegetable slice
- Ploughman's pasty
- Potato cheese & onion pasty
- Vegetable samosas
- Crispy crumbed cauliflower florets & onion dip
- Crispy crumbed mushrooms with garlic dip
- Pizza flans
- Party size vegetable rolls
- Vegetable casserole
- Vegetable curry with rice
- Vegetable chilli
- Lasagne vegetali
- Potato bake
- Mushroom flan with cream sauce filling
- Cheese & onion flan
- Courgette provençal
- Ratatouille
- Vegetable pasty
- Vegetable pies
- Chunky vegetable pies
- Fruit pies
- Broccoli in white sauce
- Broccoli provençal
- Broccoli & cheese flans
- Vegetable slices
- Onion bhajias
- Vegetable pizzas
- Celery quiche
- French bread pizza
- Authentic Indian chickpea dhal
- Lobia masala & palak paneer

Sarah's Kitchen
- Tagliatelle bake
- Vegetable & hazelnut roast

- Cashewnut & apple roast
- Soyabean crumble
- Lentil lasagne
- Spicy blackeyed beans
- Authentic Indian lentil dhal

Simpson Ready Foods Ltd
- Vegetable curry, mild, hot
- Lentil dhal
- Mexican beans
- Bean range
- Vegetable chilli
- Sweet & sour vegetables

Soya Health Foods Ltd (Sunrise)
- Tofu pies

Suma Wholefoods
- Baked beans
- Tinned hummus
- Aubergine hotpot
- Brazilian bake
- Zuchinni lasagne
- Aduki nitzuki
- New Delhi choley
- Calcutta alu domm
- Bombay vegetable jhal phirezi
- Madras vegetable sambar

Westler Foods (for caterers)
- Spicy vegetable chilli

Vandemoortele
- Provamel soya dessert, vanilla, carob

Wholebake
- Vegetable pie
- Vegetable pasty
- Potato with seitan pie
- Seitan and mushroom pie
- Cheese & onion pie
- Curry pasty
- Picnic pie
- Picnic pie with mushroom
- Picnic roll
- Picnic roll with mushroom
- Savoury potato pasty
- Chilli beans
- Shepherds pie
- Lasagne
- Seitan grills
- 12" quiche
- Individual quiche
- Pizza

Zeras Vegetarian Foods
- Aduki bean rissole
- Vegetable hot pot
- Falafel
- Baked peanut loaf
- Cashew & lentil loaf

- Onion bhajias
- Cheese & onion pasty
- Ratatouille vegetable pasty
- Nut loaf

Cooking aids

Clements Vegetarian Cuisine
- Pastry case

Foodwatch International
- Pastry mix
- Baking powder
- Whipped topping mix
- Custard powder

Granose Foods Ltd
- Mincemeat

Master Foods
- Yeoman mashed potato

Nelsons of Aintree
- Simply Good mincemeat

Norfolk Punch
- Fruit Mix

RHM Grocery
- Robertsons luxury mincemeat

J Sainsbury PLC
- Onion bhajia mix
- Naan bread mix
- Wholemeal pizza base mix
- Vol au vent cases, medium and cocktail size

Tilda Rice
- Basmati
- Brown basmati
- Easy cook basmati
- American long grain
- American easy cook
- Brown easy cook
- Surinam brown
- Pudding rice
- Natural wholegrain
- American brown easy cook
- American natural wholegrain
- Italian pudding rice

Crisps

Frequently contain lactose, a milk sugar unsuitable for vegans, or whey, which acts as a carrier for flavourings. Beef flavouring is usually made from yeast extract, but chicken flavouring is generally from an animal source.

Imagefarm Ltd
- Vegetable potato chips

Kelp Farm
- Kelp Crunchies

Walkers Crisps
- Beef & onion crisps

Drinks

Fruit and vegetable juices can be an excellent way to top up your vitamin intake.

John Powell Wines
- Apple juice
- Tomato juice
- Pineapple juice
- Beetroot juice
- Golden grape juice
- Carrot juice
- Mixed vegetable juice
- Rosy cheeks red
- Rosy cheeks gold
- Red grape juice
- 11 + 11 multivitamin juice
- Blackcurrant & pear juice
- Mixed berry juice
- Grape, pear & lemon juice
- Grape, passionfruit & cherry juice
- Summertime nectar
- Grapefruit nectar
- Pear nectar
- Peach nectar
- Orange & buckthorn nectar
- Apricot nectar
- Prune nectar
- Cherry nectar
- Blackcurrant nectar
- Cranberry nectar
- Eisenblut (tonic with iron & vitamins)

Norfolk Punch
- Norfolk punch

Dripping

Animal fat.

Eggs

Buy free range, not battery eggs (see section on FACTORY FARMING). Most if not all mass produced food items which contain eggs are made with battery eggs. Unless the manufacturer clearly states on the packaging that he is using free range, it is safe to assume that he is not.

Fish

**VEGETARIANS DON'T EAT FISH!
...OR PRAWNS ... OR ANY KIND OF
SHELLFISH ... OR JELLIED EELS ... OR
ANY THING THAT HAS TO BE KILLED
BEFORE YOU CAN EAT IT!**

Gelatine

Made from the boiled-down bones and connective tissue of slaughtered animals. Found in confectionery, desserts, sweet and savoury jellies. Vegetarians can use alternatives such as Gelozone, which is based on carrageen moss, or agar agar which is based on a sea vegetable.

Gravy

Make it without adding animal fats or meat stocks. Beware of it in restaurants as it is likely to be meaty.

Foodwatch International
- Gravy mix

G F Dietary
- Gravy mix

Jessup Marketing
- Naturally Good gravy powder

McCormick/Schwartz Foods
- Onion & mushroom gravy

J Sainsbury PLC
- Vegetarian gravy granules

Haggis

NOT a small furry animal that lives in the Scottish Highlands, but a sheep's stomach stuffed with offal! There is a vegetarian haggis on the market, made by MacSweens of Edinburgh.

Honey

Often avoided by vegans because of possible cruelty to bees.

Ice cream

Could contain non-milk fats whose source is not given. May contain gelatine, non-vegetarian additives and battery eggs. There are more healthy alternatives in health food shops and some supermarkets, including soya ice-cream and frozen yoghurt. If you have a freezer you can make your own!

Allied Frozen Foods
- Vive ice-Cream

Berrydales
- Tofu ice-cream: Berry, Maple & walnut, Ginger & honey, Bitter chocolate, Honey vanilla

Gaia Jerseys
- Rookbeare farm Jersey ice-cream

Granose
- Sweet sensation vegan ice-cream

Soya Health Foods Ltd (Sunrise)
- Sunrise carob ice
- Soya dream dessert
- Ice dream

Unisoy
- Marinelli's ice-cream: Raspberry ripple, Chocolate, Vanilla

Jam

The jam in biscuits might be made more sticky with gelatine. In general, jam should be suitable for vegetarians. If in doubt, try making your own. It's extremely messy but great fun and very rewarding! Some ' Pick Your Own ' farms now grow organic fruit.

Jelly

Usually made with gelatine, although there are now some vegetarian jellies and jelly crystals available.

Just Wholefoods
- Jelly crystals: lemon, strawberry, tropical fruit

Junket

Made with gelatine.

Margarines

Usually contain vitamins added in the form of fish oils. Look for the Ⴤ symbol.

Lakes Foods
- Clarified butter (ghee)

Proctor & Gamble (for caterers)
- Whirl oil/margarine
- Prep frying oil

Rakusens Foods
- Tomor
- Sunflower spread

J Sainsbury PLC
- Sunflower margarine
- Solid sunflower oil
- Soya margarine

Silebury Marketing
- Soya margarine

Suma
- Margarine

Vandemoortele (UK) Ltd
- Vitelma margarine

Meat

Obvious? Not always. Beware of meat stock and scraps of bacon and ham in soups, quiches, pasties and stews. It is easy to be caught out, and this can be very distressing.

Milk

Cows, goats and sheep are all used for their milk. Many people find that they are allergic to cows' milk or unable to digest it properly. As awareness of the cruelties involved in the dairy industry grows, more people are seeking alternatives. Soya milks are readily available and most are suitable for vegans.

J Sainsbury PLC
- Non-dairy cream.
- Soya milk

Soya Health Products Limited
- Sunrise soya milk

Unisoy
- Gold soya milk

Vandemoortele UK Ltd
- Provamel soya milk, sugar free, carob, honey & malt

Mousse

A pudding usually made with gelatine and eggs.

Muesli

Look out for unnecessary sugar, and whey.

Nougat

Usually contains gelatine.

Oxtail

Literally the tail of an ox, used in soups.

Pasta

Sometimes contains battery eggs. There is a black variety of pasta which is coloured with 'ink' from squid.

Pastry

Animal fats are used in most ready-baked pies, pasties and so on. Check the ingredients in ready-made pastry dishes and also in frozen pastry.

J Sainsbury PLC
- Wholemeal shortcrust pastry
- Fresh puff pastry
- Fresh shortcrust pastry.

Pâte

Some vegetable pâtes contain gelatine or are coated with a jelly of some kind. Others contain battery eggs. Pâte is one of the easiest things to make if you have a food processor.

Linden Lea Fine Foods Ltd
- Vegetable pâte

Rayner Burgess
- Vegetarian pâte, 4 flavours
- Smoked tofu pâte

J Sainsbury PLC
- Felafel pâte
- Vegetable pâte
- Mushroom pâte
- Peanut butter, wholenut, crunchy, smooth

Pepperoni

Sliced sausage, sometimes found hiding under the cheese on your pizza. Much prized by Teenage Mutant Hero Turtles.

Pork scratchings

Pig skin treated and sold as a snack.

Salad dressings

Often contain battery eggs. There are vegan alternatives which have become more popular since the salmonella outbreak brought to public attention the possible health risks involved in eating uncooked eggs.

Clements Wholefoods Cuisine
- French dressing

Rayner Burgess
- Soyannaise tofu dressing

Soya Health Foods Ltd (Sunrise)
- Sunrise eggless mayonnaise with garlic

Salads

Make sure the ready-made salads you purchase have been properly refrigerated, keep them at the correct temperature, and do not use them after the 'sell-by' date.

Clements Wholefoods Cuisine
- Brown rice salad
- Sweetcorn salad
- Mixed bean salad
- Coleslaw
- Tabbouleh
- Celery salad
- Carrot, sultana & nut salad
- Hummus

J Sainsbury PLC
- Hummus
- Tzatziki
- Onion & garlic dip
- Yoghurt & mustard seed dip
- Thousand Island dip
- Blue cheese dip
- Bombay potato
- Red cabbage salad

Soya Health Foods Ltd (Sunrise)
- Tofu salad, Japanese, Chinese, Brazilian, Hungarian

Suma Wholefoods
- Bean salad in tomato sauce
- Bean salad in vinaigrette

Sandwiches

Even the humble sandwich is a potential stumbling block for vegetarians. If you are lucky enough to find a cheese salad roll, is it made with vegetarian cheese? Is it made with vegetarian margarine?

Holland & Barrett
- Vegetarian Cheddar cheese & salad sandwich
- Vegetarian Cheddar cheese & tomato sandwich
- Vegetarian Cheddar cheese & pickle sandwich
- Vegetarian Cheddar cheese & apple sandwich
- Mixed salad sandwich
- Mushroom, onion & tomato sandwich
- Cream cheese & pineapple sandwich
- Peanut butter & peach sandwich
- Avocado salad sandwich
- Vegetable tikka sandwich

Smits Reform BV
- Vegetable sandwich cream

Travellers Fare (British Rail)
- Egg & cress sandwich
- Egg salad sandwich
- Soft cheese & cucumber sandwich

Sauces

Watch out for meat stock.

Brooke Bond Foods
- Ragu pasta Sauces

D'Silva Foods
- Rechard marinating pastes

Goodlife Wholefoods
- Organic peanut satay sauce

Grammas
- Grammas concentrated pepper sauce

Master Foods
- Dolmio sauces: Vegetable, Napoletana (jars or chilled)

J Sainsbury PLC
- Fungaiola pasta sauce
- Vegetarian bolognese sauce
- Napoletana sauce
- Onion sauce mix
- Parsley sauce mix
- White sauce mix
- Special choice creamy garlic & chive sauce mix
- Bread sauce mix

Sea food/fruits

VEGETARIANS DO NOT EAT SEA FOOD! 'Sea fruits' is another way of saying 'sea animals'.

Sea vegetables

Seaweed, vegetarians do eat this! There are varieties called Arame and Hiziki, and you can find them dried in health food shops. Try them crumbled into savoury dishes. The Vegetarian Society's Merchandise Department sells books on cooking with sea vegetables.

Soup

Even 'vegetable' soup in a restaurant may contain meat or fish stocks, or even little pieces of meat. Check first. There may also be a risk of contamination in tinned soups if the manufacturer uses the same equipment to make meaty soups.

Baxters of Speyside Ltd
- Chinese-style vegetable soup
- Tomato & orange soup
- Cream of courgette soup
- Spiced parsnip soup
- Spicy yellow pea soup
- Country garden soup
- Bean & mixed pepper soup
- Carrot & butter bean soup
- Scotch vegetable soup
- Vegetable korma soup
- Minestrone soup
- Potato & leek soup
- Italian bean & pasta soup
- Mediterranean tomato soup
- Cream of tomato soup
- Gazpacho
- Mushroom soup

Brooke Bond Foods - Batchelors
- Dutch cauliflower & broccoli 'cup a soup'
- French leek & potato 'cup a soup'
- Spicy vegetable 'snack a soup'
- Mushroom 'cup a soup'
- Golden vegetable 'cup a soup'
- Tomato 'cup a soup'
- Cream of onion 'cup a soup special' with croutons
- Cream of mushroom 'cup a soup special'
- Cream of vegetable 'cup a soup special' with croutons
- Cream of asparagus 'cup a soup special' with croutons
- Cream of tomato packet soup
- Cream of vegetable packet soup
- Cream of asparagus packet soup
- Cream of mushroom packet soup
- Farmhouse vegetable packet soup
- Lincoln pea packet soup
- Golden vegetable packet soup
- Golden vegetable 'slim a soup'
- Asparagus 'slim a soup'
- Golden vegetable 'slim a soup special'
- Tomato & vegetable 'slim a soup special'
- Spicy tomato 'slim a soup special'
- Leek & potato 'slim a soup special'

Brooke Bond Foods (Foodservice, for caterers)
- Farmhouse lentil & barley soup
- Farmhouse french onion soup
- Farmhouse clear vegetable soup
- Farmhouse thick vegetable soup

CPC (UK) Ltd
- German harvest soup

New Convent Garden Soup Co Ltd
- Mushroom soup
- Spicy tomato soup with chilli peppers
- Summer tomato soup

- Green pea & mint soup
- Borscht
- Parsnip soup with cumin
- Spinach & nutmeg soup

J Sainsbury
- Bean & pepper soup
- Winter vegetable soup
- Fresh watercress soup
- Extra thick vegetable soup
- Spinach & lentil soup
- Spicy tomato & chickpea soup
- Fresh vichyssoise soup
- Fresh gazpacho
- Reduced calorie vegetable soup
- Minestrone soup
- Mushroom soup
- Vegetable soup
- Cream of tomato soup
- Tomato soup
- Celery soup
- Carrot & orange soup
- Vichyssoise
- Fresh vegetables for leek & mushroom soup

Suma Wholefoods
- Organic leek & potato soup
- Organic parsnip & celery soup
- Organic mushroom soup

Stock

Very often in restaurant kitchens there is a stock pot, into which all the peelings and scraps are put to produce a basic stock for sauces and soups. In a vegetarian restaurant the stock will be suitable for vegetarians but in restaurants which serve meat this might not be the case. There are lots of vegetarian stocks available in shops; some may contain lactose which makes them unsuitable for vegans.

Brooke Bond Foods Ltd
- Oxo vegetable cubes

CPC (UK) Ltd
- Knorr vegetable bouillon
- Knorr vegetable stock cubes
- Marmite

Darenth Health Foods Ltd
- Darenth valley vegetable stock

Just Wholefoods
- Vegetarian stock powder

Kallo Foods
- Friggs vegetable cubes:
- vegetable
- tomato & herb

- sweet pepper
- low salt vegetable
- french onion

Modern Health Products
- Vecon
- Vecon stock powder

The Nestlé Co Ltd
- Fonds de legumes (for caterers)
- Maggi vegetable boullion (for caterers)

RHM Ingredients Ltd
- Vegetable bouillon
- Vegetarian "chicken" bouillon
- Vegetarian "beef" bouillon

J Sainsbury PLC
- Vegetable stock tablets
- Yeast extract
- Garlic & herb stock tablets
- Spicy vegetable stock tablets
- Onion stock tablets

Smits Reform BV
- Vegetable broth granules
- Vegetable broth cubes

Stuffing

Most stuffing mixes contain beef suet. There are alternatives available in health food shops. Sometimes scarce around Christmas time, so get yours early! You don't have to stuff it into a dead bird – use a separate bowl.

J Sainsbury PLC
- Country herb stuffing mix

Suet

Solid animal fat. There are vegetarian alternatives, and these are available in many supermarkets.

RHM Grocery
- Atora vegetable suet

Sweets

Watch out for gelatine in chewy sweets and also in mints. Animal fat may be used in biscuit style confectionery. Non-vegetarian colourings may crop up, check the E Numbers. So-called 'healthy' snack bars are often full of sugar.

Food For Thought
- Niki bar

Itona Products Ltd
- Orange & lemon bar
- Decaffeinated chocolate bar

Smits Reform BV
- Natural liquorice
- Fruit muesli bar

Taramasalata

Pink paste with the consistency of hummus, made out of fish.

Tempeh

Fermented soya beans pressed into a block. Suitable for vegetarians.

Impulse Foods
- Tempeh

Tempeh Foods
- Tempeh

Tequila

A fashionable cocktail drink, sometimes has a worm at the bottom of the bottle. Non-vegetarian macho types derive hours of mindless entertainment from this gimmick.

Tofu

Vegan product made from soya beans.

Rayner Burgess
- Original, natural smoked, and marinated tofu

Tofu cheese

Not necessarily suitable for vegans, check for dairy products.

TVP

Textured vegetable protein. You can buy dehydrated packs of mince or chunks for bulking out casseroles. TVP seems to have a bad name, and is sometimes seen as a poor man's substitute for meat. Sometimes it appears in non-vegetarian dishes, flavoured with meat stock.

GMB Proteins
- Bontrae beef flavour brown mince
- Bontrae beef flavour brown pieces

Granose
- Soya supreme, mild, rich

Vitamins

Sources can be dubious. See information on medicines and supplements later in this book.

Worcester sauce

Usually (but not always) made with anchovies. Look out for it as a flavouring in pies.

Yoghurts

Often contain gelatine.

Fromageries Laiterie
- Sojasun soya yoghurt

Holland & Barrett
- Live low fat yoghurt:
  natural
  strawberry
  raspberry
  apple & damson

black cherry
lemon, orange, hazelnut & raisin
apricot, guava & banana
strawberry & red cherry
- AB live yoghurt:
  natural
  peach & guava
  apricot & mango
  strawberry & vanilla
  honey & almond
- Greek style yoghurt

Perratt & Sons
- La creme fraiche
- Greek style yoghurt

J Sainsbury PLC
- Fromage frais

This information has been compiled with the help of Lesley Wilkinson, the Vegetarian Society's Υ symbol Liaison Officer.

Alcohol by Chris Olivant (Information Officer, VSUK)

The use of animal derived products in the production of alcoholic beverages is fairly widespread – not because no alternatives exist, but because they always have been used and there is little demand from the consumer for an alternative.

The main obstacle when trying to judge the acceptability to vegetarians of any given product is a clause in the 1984 Food Labelling Regulations which excludes from the 1984 Food Act all drinks with an alcohol content exceeding 1.2% by volume (ABV), leaving only very low or non-alcoholic beers, wines and ciders being required to list all ingredients.

The main use of animal derived products is in the fining or clearing process, though others may be used as colourants or anti-foaming agents. It must also be pointed out that alcohol is routinely tested on thousands of animals each year (though this is not usually done directly by any individual company).

Beer

Cask-conditioned ales need fining to clear the material (especially the yeast) held in suspension in the liquid. This is invariably done by adding isinglass – derived from the swim bladders of certain tropical fish, especially the Chinese sturgeon – which acts as a falling suspension. If you were to hold a pint of real ale up to the light and see cloudy lumps swirling around that would suggest that the cask had been recently disturbed and the isinglass shaken up from the bottom.

Bottled Naturally Conditioned beers do not have to go through a similar fining process.

Keg Beers are pasteurised and passed through Chill Filters, as are canned beers and some bottled beers. The only animal derived ingredient involved in the production of Keg Beers is E471 glyceryl monostearate, which is occasionally used in place of 900 dimethylpolysiloxane as a foam-control agent.

Wines (and fortified wines)

With wine it is again in the fining process that animal derived ingredients make an appearance. Finings can be isinglass, gelatin, egg albumen, modified casein (from milk), chitin, (derived from the shells of crabs or lobsters) or ox blood (rarely used today). But alternatives do exist in the form of bentonite, kieselguhr, kaolin and silica gel or solution. You may like to note that the Wine Development Board claims that the fining agents are 'removed at the end of the process with the possible exception of very minute quantities'.

Spirits

All spirits appear to be acceptable to vegetarians, with the possible exception of Malt Whisky, some Blended Whiskies and Spanish Brandies which may all have been conditioned in casks which had previously held sherry. (Brandy itself is not produced from wine which has undergone any fining processes).

Colourants: E120 cochineal produced by extracting the red body material from pregnant scale insects of the species *Dactilopius coccus* is used as a colourant in some red wines, soft drinks and Campari.

SUPPLIERS

Disos
104 Remer Street, Crewe, Cheshire, CW1 4LT. Tel: (0270) 584183. or 50 Springfield Road, Gatley, Cheadle, Cheshire. Tel: (061) 428 7666.

Haughton Fine Wines
Chorley (near Cholmondeley,) Nantwich, Cheshire CW5 8JR. Tel: (0270) 74 537 or (0836) 597 961.

HDRA Sales Ltd
National Centre for Organic Gardening, Ryton-on-Dunsmore, Coventry CV8 3LG. Tel: (0203) 303517.

Brian Morris Wines
34 Borden Lane, Sittingbourne, Kent ME10 1DB

John Powell Wines
Harding Way, St Ives, Huntingdon, Cambs. PE17 4WR.

Mark Richardson Trading
290 Fulham Palace Road, London SW6 6HP. Tel: (071) 381 9924.

Seddlescombe Vineyards
Robertsbridge, E. Sussex TN32 5SA

Vinature Wines
16 Cotton Lane, Moseley, Birmingham B13 9SA. Tel: (021) 449 1781.

Vincermos
Unit 10, Asley Industrial Estate, Wakefield Road, Ossett, West Yorkshire WF5 9JD. Tel: (0924) 276393

Vintage Roots
25 Manchester Road, Reading, Berkshire RG1 3QE. Tel: (0734) 662569.

West Heath Wines
West Heath, Pirbright, Surrey GU24 0QE. Tel: (04867) 6464.

Reading the label

Not every product on the shelf carries the ϒ symbol. Sadly, some products such as alcoholic drinks are not yet required by law to be fully labelled, and buying from delicatessen counters can be a problem when food items are not labelled.

You made the decision to go vegetarian, and it is up to you and nobody else to see that the decision is enforced. Of course, avoiding meat and fish should not be too difficult. But vegetarianism goes deeper than that. An ethical vegetarian will refuse any product that contains any slaughterhouse ingredients. There may be only the tiniest amount of an animal derived ingredient in the dish that you are contemplating buying, but the manufacturer of that product is buying from the slaughterhouse on a grand scale in order to meet his manufacturing requirements.

Reading the label can be seen as a chore or as an exercise for the inquisitive mind, but it is an essential habit for vegetarians. Unless the product displays the ϒ symbol, in which case the ingredients have already been checked by The Vegetarian Society, it is up to you to find out whether that product meets your requirements. The labels are there for your information – but sometimes the information can be difficult to understand.

This chapter supplies a list of names to watch out for – names which do not initially ring any warning bells because they may not be automatically associated with meat. You may find that a favourite product contains an ingredient which is not considered to be suitable for vegetarians. Of course, whether you continue to use the product is a matter for your own personal choice – but do bear in mind that the position taken by ethical vegetarians can sometimes be undermined by the actions of less scrupulous vegetarians who are seen to be accepting slightly dubious ingredients. If a dubious product finds a vegetarian market, then the manufacturer will have no incentive to change his product for the better. Why not write to manufacturers to ask why they feel it necessary to include a tiny amount of an ingredient which makes their whole product unsuitable for vegetarians? What is the ingredient used for? Is there a vegetarian or vegan alternative, and if so, has the manufacturer considered changing the formulation in order to reach a new vegetarian market?

One final word of warning – once you have discovered a vegetarian product that you enjoy, it may be a mistake to assume that the ingredients will never change. Formulations change all the time, and this can even be a selling point. Watch out for signs on the packaging that indicate that a change has taken place, and scrutinise the label again. If you don't like what you see – write to the manufacturers.

Additives

The chapter which follows this one deals in greater depth with chemical additives which crop up in foods under vague names like 'preservatives', 'improving agents' and so on, and also goes into greater detail about the sources of specific chemicals which are often used in the food industry.

Things to avoid

Albumen

… from egg. It is safe to assume that all eggs and egg products that are used in mass-produced food products are from battery eggs. Part of the reason for this is that free-range producers find it difficult to meet the huge levels of demand from large-scale manufacturers. Manufacturers often buy their eggs in bulk in powdered form, and powdered free-range eggs are hard to find. This is not to say that a few manufacturers may not have been able to convert to using free-range eggs – but you can be sure that if the manufacturer is going to the trouble and extra expense of using free-range eggs he will make sure that the consumer knows about it – he will list free-range eggs on the label.

Anchovies

… don't forget, anchovies are fish! They can turn up unexpectedly on pizzas and are usually an ingredient in Worcester Sauce.

Aspic

… savoury jelly derived from meat and fish.

Battery eggs

The vegetarian creed does not mention eggs, and does not state that vegetarians should not eat eggs (apart from some Indian vegetarians who do not eat eggs). However, when the guidelines for vegetarianism were first drawn up, the battery system for factory farming of hens had not been devised. Perhaps battery eggs would not have been included in the definition of vegetarian if battery eggs had existed. Battery hen farming remains one of the most cruel, and also one of the most insanitary forms of farming in Britain today, and most vegetarians avoid eating battery eggs either on ethical or on health grounds.

Brawn

… animal brains, still sometimes crop up in butchers' shops and are used in stews and casseroles. The BSE scandal makes the consumption of the nervous system of animals a highly questionable practice in terms of the health risk involved – to say nothing of the ethical concerns.

Roe

… fish eggs, obtained by killing the female fish and extracting the eggs from her abdomen. Caviare is basically fish eggs, which means that caviare is not suitable for vegetarians, but I can't say I miss it.

Cochineal

… a red colouring made from beetles, found in all kinds of red foods.

Collagen

… the connective tissue from meat, which once unfortunately found its way into being used as the skin for 'vegetarian' sausages!

Edible fats

… may mean animal fats. If it were anything that could be used as a selling point, like butter, then the manufacturer would be sure to use it to his advantage on the label!

Fatty acids

… may be animal or vegetable.

Fish oils

… also known as marine oils. Often added to margarine to give extra vitamins. There are alternative vegetarian margarines.

'Fortified'

… some cereals, drinks and margarines are 'fortified' with extra vitamins, but the source of the added vitamins, especially Vitamin D_3 may be dubious.

'Fried'

… when you buy vegetable spring rolls, samosas, bhajias and so on, from the delicatessen counter, ask the assistant whether they were fried in animal fat.

Gelatine

… also 'gelatin'. Thickener obtained by boiling animal skins, tendons, ligaments, bones etc with water. Used in confectionery, ice cream, sweet and savoury jellies.

Glycerine

… also glycerol. Can be manufactured from petroleum, from the fermentation of sugars (rarely), or as a by-product of the soap industry, in which case it is usually an animal product.

Gravy

… often contains animal fats or meat stock.

Hydrolysed protein

… may be animal, vegetarian or vegan, depending on the source of the protein.

Isinglass

Clearing agent used in beer and wine manufacture. Derived from swim bladders of fish. Japanese isinglass is made from seaweed.

Kosher

… the Jewish dietary system bans the consumption of animals with cloven hooves, and shell fish. It states that milk (and dairy products) and meat should not be eaten at the same meal. The 'kosher' label is no guarantee that a food is suitable for vegetarians.

Lactose

… a milk sugar, not suitable for vegans. Often used as a carrier in homoeopathic tablets.

Lard

… solid animal fat. Used in pastry, biscuits, 'lardy cake'; also used in some ointments.

Lecithin

… can be from soya or from (battery) eggs.

Oils

… can be fish oils, liquid animal fats, vegetable oils, or mineral oils. Refined 'edible oils' may have been chemically treated.

Quinoline

… a yellow dye, not always vegetarian.

Rennet

… an enzyme taken from the stomach of freshly-slaughtered calves and used in the cheese industry. Look for vegetarian cheese, which is made with a vegetarian alternative to animal rennet.

'Shortening'

… can be animal fats; used in pastry and biscuits.

Suet

… solid animal fat, usually appears at Christmas as little white lumps in mincemeat and Christmas puddings. There are vegetarian mincemeats and mince pies available, and vegetarian Christmas puddings too.

Whey

… is not considered to be suitable for vegetarians. It is derived from milk, but is usually made using animal rennet as a by-product of the cheese industry.

'E Numbers' and all that…

At the back of the book you will find a full listing of 'E Numbered' and other additives. It is not what you might call a thrilling read, but if you want to look up exactly what you find on the label… err, that's where it is.

Special diets...
special people

Vegetarians are different, not just from the meat-eating many but from one another. They come in all varieties... some chose to be vegans, others are obliged by allergy or illness to follow a specialised diet. Others are at a stage or an age of life that itself dictates what they eat. So here it is... for the young, the old, the pregnant, the podgy, the poorly and worried-well... and if you cannot find yourself in here, get back to the planet Zaarg!

Veganism

Vegans endeavour to live lives which do not cause any suffering at all to animals, or exploit animals in any way. This normally involves ceasing to eat any eggs or dairy produce, or honey, and ceasing to wear or use leather, silk, wool and similar animal products.

Cutting out dairy produce.

Many people find that after they have been vegetarian for a while, they want to take things a stage further and cut out eggs and dairy produce as well, so that their diet is not dependent on animals in any way. If you do this, there are some aspects of your diet that you have to plan a little more carefully.

Protein

Getting enough protein isn't really a big problem; even without eggs and milk, you still have all the other main vegetarian sources of protein at your disposal: pulses, cereals, nuts and seeds and soya products. There is more information on protein in our section on nutrition.

Vitamin B_{12}

Vitamin B_{12} isn't produced at all by plants, with the possible exception of some seaweeds. It is produced by micro-organisms. Non-vegetarians get it from meat because animals like cows and sheep have the necessary micro-organisms living in their guts. The B_{12} also passes into the milk, so lacto-vegetarians are not usually short of this vitamin. If you decide to cut out milk and cheese you must make sure you have an alternative source of B_{12} in your diet. Many vegetarian foods have been fortified with B_{12} – including some yeast extracts, some TVPs, some soya milks and some breakfast cereals; but do check the label to see that the brands you are buying contain B_{12}!

115

Vitamin D

Vitamin D is not found in plant foods. It is present in dairy produce in variable amounts (depending on how the cows were fed and how much sunshine they received), and it is added to vegetable margarines. So if you cut out dairy foods, your only dietary source of Vitamin D will be that in fortified foods. Normally, this isn't much of problem, humans can make Vitamin D for themselves when the skin is exposed to sunlight. You don't have to bare all and grill yourself in the hot sun, normally bright daylight is sufficient and only hands and face need to be exposed for between 20 minutes and one hour a day. The body can store Vitamin D so people who go out of doors regularly can build up enough stores to tide them through winter and cloudy periods so taking advantage of a summer holiday to spend more time out of doors is worthwhile. People who are confined indoors however, especially the elderly and invalids, also very young children, should take a Vitamin D supplement as a precaution. Vitamin D_2 is never of animal origin – D_3 may be animal-derived. Follow the instructions on the label very carefully as it is possible to overdose on Vitamin D with adverse results, including excessive calcium being absorbed from the diet. Levels as low as ten times the recommended amount have caused toxic effects in infants; adults are less susceptible, but should still take care.

Calcium

Milk tends to be the main source of calcium in British diets, whether vegetarian or omnivorous. Meat is, in fact, a poor source of calcium, so vegetarians are not at a disadvantage in this respect. If you cut out milk, there are still plenty of good calcium sources such as: tofu, watercress, parsley, dried figs, nuts (especially almonds), soya flour, dried apricots, cabbage, oatmeal, bread and sesame seeds.

So, you must take a little trouble to see that such foods are consumed regularly. White bread is actually better than brown in this respect, as it has had calcium added. If there is some doubt as to whether you are getting enough calcium, you might consider using half-and-half white and wholemeal bread. If you are using soya milk to replace cows' milk, you should be aware of the fact that the nutritional content of soya milks varies from one brand to another, and some are far less nutritious, especially in terms of calcium, than cows' milk. Some soya milks however, have been fortified to bring their nutritional content close to that of cows milk – again, you should check the label carefully before buying.

INFORMATION

FOR FURTHER INFORMATION ABOUT THE VEGAN DIET AND LIFESTYLE CONTACT

The Vegan Society
    7, Battle Road, St Leonards On Sea, East Sussex, TN37 7AA Tel: (0424) 427 393
The Movement for Compassionate Living
    9, Moyle Terrace, Hobson, Europerfield, Co. Durham

THE VEGETARIAN SOCIETY'S MERCHANDISING DEPARTMENT SELLS A WIDE RANGE OF VEGAN RECIPE BOOKS

Macrobiotic diets

The term 'Macrobiotic' was coined by George Oshawa to mean the study of a healthy and creative diet. Foods are classified according to the ancient Chinese principles of Yin and Yang, the idea being to achieve a Yin – Yang balance in the diet. The following are just a few of the differences between foods classified as Yin and foods classified as Yang.

Yin – female, passive	Yang – male, active
Sweet, hot foods	Salty, bitter foods
Fruits and leaves	Roots and seeds
Purple, blue or green foods	Red, yellow or orange foods
Acidic foods	Alkaline foods

To become expert at assessing the relative Yin and Yang qualities of a food, it is really necessary to study macrobiotics. Foods that are avoided include all processed foods, meat and dairy products, and refined flours and sugars. Fish, nuts and fruits are regarded as optional. Vegetarians should note that macrobiotic food is not necessarily vegetarian food.

INFORMATION

FOR FURTHER INFORMATION ON MACROBIOTICS, INCLUDING COOKERY COURSES, AND RELATED ISSUES SUCH AS SHIATSU MASSAGE, YOGA AND MEDITATION, AND T'AI CHI, CONTACT:

The Community Health Foundation
188, Old Street, London, EC1V 9BP. Tel: 071 251 4076

Raw food diets

Some people believe that a diet of raw food is the most healthy for humans, and they only consume raw fruit and vegetables, nuts and seeds (sometimes) and raw sprouted seeds and grains. Where possible these should be organically grown. Raw food diets are used in the holistic treatment of cancer and AIDS. Some people combine raw food with a fasting régime to cleanse the system.

Fruitarian

Some vegetarians believe that it is wrong to kill plants for food. To obtain vegetables, which are from plant roots, it is necessary to dig up the plant and kill it. Fruitarians live on nuts and fruits which can be harvested without causing damage to the plant.

INFORMATION

FOR FURTHER INFORMATION SEND SAE FOR FREE LITERATURE TO:
Wilfred Crone
14 Walkford Way, Christchurch, Dorset, BH23 5LR

Organic diet

Because of the high levels of residues from chemical fertilisers, pesticides and fungicides found in fruit and vegetables, many people are turning towards organically-grown foods. There is a section on organic/veganic gardening and organic foods later in this book.

INFORMATION

The Soil Association
86 Colston Street, Bristol, BS1 5BB

Diets for allergies

When people say that they are 'allergic' to a certain food, they usually simply mean "It makes me feel ill"! What is really happening *might* be a genuine allergy. It might equally be something called 'food aversion' – a strong dislike of the food combined with a sincere *belief* that it makes one ill. Possibly it is a more tangible physical problem: some people cannot tolerate milk because they don't produce enough of the enzyme, lactase, which is needed to digest it. Whatever and whichever, the obvious remedy is to avoid the food that makes you feel ill!

Some people become vegetarians because they find, or suspect, that something in meat makes them feel ill. Some people – not necessarilly the same ones! – find that having become vegetarian they are reacting badly to a food that they are now eating much more often.

The most common allergens are the things we eat frequently, and may crave if we occasionally miss them. Top of the league are wheat, milk, eggs, chocolate, coffee, tea, 'additives' and citrus fruits.

People are sometimes allergic to several foods, and just cutting out one food for a few days will not make them any better, even if it *is* one of the culprits. Any foods 'excluded' must be religiously avoided (read food labels!) for a week or so before any conclusions can be drawn. If you plan to exclude quite a few things from your diet you should check with your doctor first.

'Allergies' get blamed, rightly or wrongly, for a diverse range of problems – arthritis, asthma, eczema, mood changes, digestive disorders, runny noses, ringing ears, and behaviour problems. Your suspicion that you have an allergy is always worth investigating, but bear in mind that it is possible that your nose is running because you have a cold and that you are depressed because your life has been just plain depressing lately!

INFORMATION

Food Watch
Butts Pond Industrial Estate, Sturminster Newton, Dorset, DT10 1AZ
Food Watch publish an excellent recipe book excluding all the common 'baddies', with recipes for biscuits, bread, cakes, savoury meals and other problem areas (and it's vegetarian!). They also have a mail order service supplying alternative foods which can be difficult to obtain.

Action Against Allergy
43 The Downs, London, SW20 Tel: (081) 947 5082
Action against Allergy are very helpful with queries, and can provide names of local clinical ecologists.

Dietary Therapy Society
33 Priory Gardens, London, N6 5QU

The Asthma Society
300 Upper Street, London, N1 2XX

The Coeliac Society of the UK
Box 220, High Wycombe, Bucks, HP11 2HY
Produce a magazine called *The Cross Grain*. SAE with enquiries appreciated.

The British Diabetic Association
10 Queen Anne Street, London, W1M 0BD

General Designs Ltd
PO Box 38E, Worcester Park, Surrey, KT4 7LX
Make artificial egg-powder

Barbara Berman Ltd
20 Roundway, Grimsby, S Humberside, DN34 5AS
Make specialist diabetic foods

G F Dietary Supplies
494 Honeypot Lane, Stanmore, Middlesex, HA7 1JH
Make low-protein gluten-free ready meals

Diets for illnesses

There is no doubt that the quality of our diet can affect our health, and it is now thought that dietary therapy can not only help prevent the onset of disease, but also help once disease has appeared. Perhaps the most well known example of this is at the Cancer Help Centre in Bristol where cancer sufferers are taught to use a diet which is almost vegan, and relies heavily on raw and organic foods, to help give their bodies the best chance for healing. They have published a cook book explaining the diet. The Centre can also give advice on many other aspects of dealing with cancer.

INFORMATION

The Cancer Help Centre (Bristol)
　　Grove House, Cornwallis Grove, Clifton, Bristol, BS8 4PG
Nature Cure
　　Kingston Clinic, Edinburgh, EH15 5UQ

Arthritis and rheumatism

Many practitioners are recommending a vegetarian diet to help relieve some forms of arthritis and rheumatism. Below is a brief outline of recommendations generally given and some references for further reading. We must stress that we are not medical experts; the following is a digest of advice provided by several practitioners. How appropriate any particular diet might be for you and your condition is very much a matter to be discussed with your own physician.

A person suffering from arthritis is often recommended to try a low-fat, wholefood vegetarian diet, with a large, raw salad or lightly steamed vegetables every day. There is considerable emphasis on eating raw foods, and some books suggest that one or two days a week should be 'raw-food only' days. It is said that an allergic reaction is a factor in some kinds of arthritis.

To make sure your vegetarian diet does not contain a high level of fat, you must ensure that you do not simply replace meat with cheese and eggs. Explore the other alternative protein foods. Try not to fry food at all, but if you must, use a minimum of sunflower, safflower, or soya cooking oils – these are low in saturated fats. If you use milk, choose skimmed milk rather than full-cream milk. You are advised to avoid some things altogether. These include:

All meat, Salt, Sugar, White-flour products, Cows' milk and its products (some say milk should be avoided altogether, others say use goat's milk instead), Acid fruits like citrus fruits and strawberries, rhubarb, and Alcohol.

Some practitioners recommend that you also cut out tea, coffee, and chocolate, and you should keep any kind of processed food to a minimum or cut it out altogether if possible.

Some people find certain foods trigger an attack. The main suspects are:

Dairy products, Tomatoes, Potatoes, Aubergines, Peppers, and Wheat, and, though not a food, Tobacco in any form.

Keeping a diary of what you eat and what symptoms you suffer can help you identify any foods that might trigger off an attack for you.

The following supplements are also sometimes recommended:

Zinc (15mg daily), Vitamin C (1000mg three times daily), Pantothenic Acid (100mg twice daily), Pyridoxine (50mg twice daily).

Other things you can do to help

When the pain subsides, take some gentle exercise to help keep the joints supple, yoga is often beneficial. Osteopathy has been found to be helpful, particularly if the therapy is started at an early stage of the disease. You may also experience good results from massage, hydrotheraphy and acupuncture. The knowledge that you are taking responsibility for your health by controlling your diet can help you to maintain a positive outlook.

INFORMATION

Why Endure Rheumatism and Arthiritis
    by Clifford Quick, Unwin (this author is a vegetarian naturopath)
Arthritis: self help
    by Leon Chaitow, Thorsons
Relief from Arthritis the Natural Way
    by John E Croft, Thorsons

In later life...

The information that follows is for people who are still responsible for their own intake of food. For those who care for the elderly, a different type of advice is applicable.

Sound nutritional principles apply to all age groups, but for older people it is not appropriate to be over-zealous with healthy eating guidelines, as this may impose irksome dietary restrictions. Good nutrition leads to a healthy immune system – helps to ward off those diseases and infections to which older people are more prone.

Potential nutritional problems Research has shown that some older people tend to have a lower intake of some nutrients than is desirable. These nutrients are Vitamin C, the B vitamins (particularly Folate, Riboflavin and Vitamin B_{12}), Vitamin D, Iron, Potassium, other trace elements and fibre. This does not mean that you should reach for a multi-vitamin supplement, unless you choose to, but simply that you should be aware.

Recommended daily amounts (RDA) There are no special requirements for specific nutrients for older people. As with younger vegetarians, supplements should not be needed if a healthy, varied and balanced diet is consumed.

Although your intake may be smaller than the RDAs, unless it is a lot lower you should not worry unduly if you are otherwise in good health. Some adaptation to a lower intake does occur.

Energy Unless you are very active, you need less protein and 'energy food' than you once did. Your need for vitamins and minerals, however, is *not* reduced. So try not to 'fill up' on foods you do not really need, such sugar and other confectionery.

It may seem obvious, but it is worth saying that if you are gaining weight you are eating more (sweet or fatty) 'energy food' than you need!

Vitamin C Too little of this and you may feel depressed and tired, also cuts may take a long time to heal. Fresh fruit and vegetables are the best sources, particularly citrus fruits. If you find fresh fruit too hard or difficult to eat, include fresh fruit juice or raw vegetable juice in your diet.

B vitamins These vitamins are very important for energy utilisation and the functioning of the nervous system. Folate is often lacking in the diets of older people. The best source of this vitamin is green leafy vegetables, so make sure you include some spinach, broccoli or greens regularly in your diet.

If you have been vegetarian for many years and have avoided dairy products, it is possible that you have exhausted your body stores of Vitamin B_{12}, (unless you have included a good supply in your diet). Many people adapt to a low intake of this vitamin, but if you are concerned about your Vitamin B_{12} levels you could ask your doctor to do a test for you.

Vitamin D Vitamin D is found only in animal-derived foods, including dairy produce and eggs. Vitamin D is also produced by the action of sunlight on the skin, and most vegetarians get quite enough in this way. So... get out in the sunshine when you can, and bear in mind that Vitamin D can be stored in the body. A case of "stocking-up for winter"! Vegetarian margarines are supplemented with Vitamin D.

Potassium and sodium Most foods, particularly unrefined cereals and vegetables, contain moderate amounts of potassium – a balanced vegetarian diet should supply all you need.

You are unlikely to get short of sodium, quite the reverse, because we get it in ordinary table salt. There is no need to *restrict* salt in your diet, unless you have a tendency to high blood-pressure or your doctor recommends it.

Calcium If you are trying to get away from animal products altogether do make sure you include a good vegetable source of calcium in the diet, such as sesame seeds (tahini). Other sources of calcium include dairy products, green vegetables, and almonds.

Zinc and iron A balanced diet with plenty of fresh vegetables will contain all the minerals you need. The problem is that your ability to *absorb* them may be impaired. Remember that drinking tea with meals can reduce the absorption of minerals. If you do have a drink with meals it is better to have fruit juice.

Fibre Most vegetarians consume healthy amounts of fibre, and for this reason should be less prone to diverticular disease, constipation and varicose veins in later life. If you do feel that you need to increase the amount of fibre in your diet, remember to do this gradually, as your body will need time to adapt. Do not take bran on its own (unless medically advised), as this can create unpleasant digestive problems. More fluid is also required with a diet high in fibre.

Fluid It is very important to include sufficient fluid in the diet. Take regular drinks, even if you do not feel thirsty. Have a variety of drinks, such as fruit juice, milk, vegetable juice, herb teas as well as moderate amount of ordinary tea and coffee. If you have a poor appetite have your drinks between meals rather than with meals.

Exercise Some form of gentle exercise is especially important in later life. Exercise prevents bone loss and protects against osteoporosis. Some form of activity will keep your muscles healthy and create a healthy appetite.

Special nutritional problems

Diabetes Older people are more likely to suffer from diabetes, particularly if there is a history of it in the family. although it is far less common in vegetarians. A vegetarian diet is healthy for diabetics, as it tends to be high in fibre, low in fat and low in sugar. The diet should be tailored to your individual needs by your dietitian or doctor.

Osteoporosis Osteoporosis is a thinning of the bones which can eventually lead to fractures and breakages in later life, and is particularly a problem for women. A good intake of calcium and Vitamin D, combined with exercise is recommended. Vegetarians seem to have an advantage in that, over a lifetime, they store-up more calcium than meat-eaters.

Summary
A good vegetarian diet is a recipe for good health in old age. You should not need any special foods (unless they are advised for a particular medical condition), but a good variety of the foods you have consumed all your life. Remember variety is the spice of life!

Finally, if you have any problems that the Vegetarian Society may be able to help with – like obtaining vegetarian 'Meals on Wheels' – please contact us and we will do our best.

Advice for slimmers
If you find you are putting on weight after changing to a vegetarian diet, check that you are not making one or both of the following mistakes:

Eating too much fat This is easy to do if you use a lot of cheese or eggs to replace meat. Dairy products are mostly high in fat, so do try to make full use of the alternative sources of protein: nuts, pulses, seeds, soya products and cereals. Try to limit eggs to a maximum of three a week. If you wish to use cheese occasionally, look for low-fat varieties. Avoid fried foods. Use skimmed milk or soya milk instead of full-fat milk. Some items like avocados, brazil nuts, soya pâté, soya sausages and burgers, commercial cakes and biscuits are also high in fat, so use with discretion.

Eating too much carbohydrate A traditional meal has three kinds of food on a plate: meat for protein, potatoes for carbohydrate, vegetables for vitamins and minerals. A vegetarian savoury (nut roast, for example) contains quite a lot of carbohydrate as well as protein, yet people still think of it as just the protein component and are tempted to add a serving of potatoes, rice or pasta etc to provide the carbohydrate. This may not be necessary unless you are a very active person, or engaged in heavy manual work, pregnant or breast-feeding, or you are a growing child. Try a very small serving of extra carbohydrate, or none at all. If your plate looks as though it has a gap on it, fill it with salad or green vegetables instead.

The unrefined carbohydrates, including sugar, sweets, cakes, biscuits and alcohol should be avoided as much as possible by slimmers.

Additional advice
• Avoid processed and refined foods as much as possible. It is physically harder to eat too much when you are on a wholefood diet. Highly processed foods make it easy to consume too many calories without feeling full.
• Don't weigh yourself too often, once a month is sufficient.
• Regularly take some brisk exercise – walking, cycling or swimming.
• Crash diets don't work. It took you a long time to put on weight. Don't expect to be able to take it off in a day or two. It is better to work out for yourself a healthy way of eating that you feel you can stick with for the rest of your life.

Diet plans 'Weight Watchers' and *Slimming Magazine*'s Slimming Clubs both offer a diet plan for vegetarians – you have to join to get it.

The Good Health Company manufactures a rotation diet package which is available from health food stores and is suitable for vegetarians.

The Libra One Diet Plan is a vegetarian diet sheet. Write to Delta Publishing Ltd, 39-41 Wilson Street, Largs, KA30 9AQ.

Cures for flatulence

We get some letters from people complaining of indigestion or excessive flatulence after changing to a vegetarian diet. Here are some pointers that might help.

Make the change to a vegetarian diet gradually. Vegetarians have quite different intestinal flora (bacteria that aid digestion) from meat-eaters, so give your body time to adapt, particularly if you have not been used to a high-fibre diet previously.

Try to avoid stress. The digestive system is very sensitive to stress, and ignoring early warning symptoms may lead to ulcers or other severe problems. Flatulence can be a warning that your digestive system is finding your lifestyle hard to take! Don't eat when you are in a hurry, or if you are experiencing any kind of violent emotion like anger or fear. Try to arrange things so you have time for a calm, unhurried meal. Chew your food well, digestion in the stomach starts in the mouth with an enzyme produced in the saliva. If you eat hurriedly and don't chew properly, this enzyme doesn't have time to start working and it is rendered ineffective by the acid conditions in the stomach.

Take a look at how much fibre you are eating. A high fibre diet is good for health, but remember we are all individuals and react differently to what we eat. You need to find a balance where you are eating enough fibre to avoid constipation but not enough to give you flatulence. If you think this is the cause of your problem, try going half-and-half with refined and unrefined foods, eg half wholemeal pasta/half white pasta, half wholemeal bread/half white, or vary the proportions until you find a mixture that suits.

Some people are sensitive to particular kinds of foods. It might be worth keeping a diet diary for a few days, noting when symptoms appear so you can pinpoint the culprits! Beans are often the cause.

It is very important to make sure that all beans are thoroughly boiled; they must be at boiling point for at least 10 minutes and then simmered until soft.

If using dried pulses, never cook them in the soaking water. Always discard the soaking water, rinse thoroughly and cook in fresh water. Adding a little dill or caraway seed during cooking might also help (this applies to any food that causes flatulence, not just beans. Cabbage is another common culprit that benefits from a sprinkle of dill seeds). Some people cannot digest beans easily because they are short of an enzyme that breaks down the polysaccharides they contain, so if all the above measures fail, you may have to avoid beans altogether. The hard beans like soya and red kidney are worst; Soft beans – lentils, split peas – don't usually cause trouble.

Some people are sensitive to certain mixtures of foods, for example, mixing starches and proteins. Also, mixing high fibre foods with high sugar foods can cause problems. Again, you may have to identify the culprits and avoid them.

Many people find the Hay Diet helpful. Basically, this avoids mixing starches and proteins at a meal. In this system, you should have one protein meal, one starch meal and one alkaline meal a day. The alkaline meal could be fresh or dried fruit, salad or lightly-steamed vegetables; jacket potato (without cheese!), avocado or vegetable soup. Examples of starch meals are sandwiches with salad filling, rice and pasta with salad or vegetables. Protein meals can be eggs, cheese, nuts. Pulses count as 'starch'. Fresh vegetables other than potato, nuts (except peanuts), butter, vegetable oils, egg yolk and cream can be eaten with either protein or starch meals. Most fruits – except 'starches' such as bananas, dates and figs – can be eaten with protein meals. Dry wine complements a protein meal, and beer a starch meal. Allow at least four hours between eating foods in different classes.

Herbal remedies All the following have been suggested as possible cures for flatulence in one Herbal or another:

• Dill or caraway: add to food while cooking or chew a few seeds after a meal.
• Nutmeg: take a pinch of ground nutmeg in hot water before a meal.
• Thyme: as tea or raw with the food.
• Angelica: chew a small piece of the root.
• Ginger: take one teaspoon of ground ginger in half a cup of hot water.
• Charcoal biscuits.
• Herbal teas: made by adding 1 teaspoon of the dried herb to half a pint of boiling water and leave to infuse for five minutes. As with medicines, it is important not to exceed the recommended dose. Try peppermint or sage.

Tiredness

Many people complain of feeling tired much of the time. Sometimes this may be related to poor diet, but not always. A change to a vegetarian diet should not cause tiredness in itself. Some of the main causes of tiredness are given below. It is up to the individual to decide which relates to his/her own lifestyle, and to take the appropriate action.

Lack of Iron: Tiredness is a symptom of iron-deficiency anaemia. If you suspect this is the case, you should go to your own doctor for accurate diagnosis. Vegetarian sources of iron include: dried fruits, leafy green vegetables, pulses, oats, wholemeal bread, brown rice, nuts, molasses, and curry powder. As vegetable sources of iron aren't as easily absorbed as animal sources, it is important that you have a diet rich in Vitamin C, which aids absorption of iron. (Vitamin C in fruits, green vegetables, potatoes, salads etc). It is a good idea not to drink tea with meals as this inhibits iron absorption. Wait for at least an hour before having a cuppa.

Lack of Calories: If you are not eating enough food overall to satisfy your energy requirements you may well feel tired. This usually only occurs on a very strict slimmimg diet – in which case try relaxing your diet and allow yourself an extra 500 calories – or if illness is upsetting your digestion or appetite, in which case you need to consult a doctor.

Hypoglycaemia: This refers to low levels of blood sugar. Severe cases need medical treatment, but you can help yourself by eating several small meals spaced out at about 3-hourly intervals through the day. Avoid large concentrated sources of sugar (sucrose, glucose, dextrose) but try to include some unrefined carbohydrate in every mini-meal, e.g. wholemeal bread, crispbread, potato, pasta, brown rice.

PMS Women who feel very tired just before and during their periods are suffering from a form of PMS. You can help yourself by taking as much rest and relaxation as you can at this time; avoid alcohol; eat small meals at three-hourly intervals as prescribed for hypoglycaemia. Further advice can be obtained from: The National Association for Pre-Menstrual Syndrome, 2nd Floor, 25 Market Street, Guildford, Surrey, GU1 4LB. Helpline (0483) 572806.

Lack of exercise This makes you feel sluggish and tired. Try walking, cycling, swimming two or three times a week. Exercise also encourages deep breathing and gets more oxygen into the blood stream.

Overweight If you are very overweight, you will feel tired. Try cutting out sweets, biscuits, cakes etc, all fried foods, and increase the amount of exercise you take.

Lack of Sleep and Relaxation: Don't overlook the fact that you might simply be physically tired. The maxim about burning the candle at both ends is true. Try getting half an hour's extra sleep a night. Try to make some time for holidays and relaxing hobbies.

Boredom: If there is not much happening in your life, it can make you feel sleepy! Switch off the TV and look out for new interests.

Stress: Stress and anxiety can also make you feel tired. It may seem blindingly obvious but do try to sort out the problems in your life, don't just worry about them. Taking the first simple step – talking to the Citizen's Advice Bureau, your doctor or a friend – can shed the energy-draining burden of stress almost instantly! Rest, relaxation and a good diet can help combat the *effects* of stress, so can meditation or yoga, or a relaxation cassette, but the thing is to deal with the cause.

Depression and grief: People suffering from severe depression and grief from a bereavement or similar loss may sleep a lot and feel listless. In this case, expert medical help is needed.

Diet for sports

Carbohydrates If you are a sports person you should increase your intake of complex carbohydrates i.e. bread, pasta, cereals, peas and beans, in order to maintain the body's energy requirements. Remember the best time to eat for re-fueling is straight after training. Carbohydrates are as important to the 'explosive' type events as they are to the endurance events.

Fluid Make certain you drink plenty of water or electrolyte drinks before and during training. If you are training for any length of time your fluid level will go down through sweating. You can take in fluid during training by: (a) Breaking up the training and having rest periods or, (b) by sipping small amounts of fluid. There are many good 'sweat' replacement drinks on the market and none of them should contain animal ingredients.

Protein There have been more arguments about the benefits of animal protein as opposed to vegetable protein for sports people than any other nutritional subject. *You do not need red meat to build muscle!* – in fact most sports nutritionists recommend a reduction of red meat for a 'sports diet'. You can get the required amount and quality of protein from vegetable sources by mixing them together e.g. beans, grains and peas etc. Alternatively, if you do need large amounts of protein – for weight lifting, for example – then use a protein supplement. Most of the brands on the market are from vegetable sources. Some do have fish or egg ingredients – check the label first.

Other points

Alcohol – It is best not to drink during the 24 hours before a competition or major sporting event. Alcohol depresses the central nervous system and also causes dehydration.

You need food for energy – don't skip meals. Take more but smaller meals throughout the day.

Don't try any new diet on competition day – try it in training first.

Eat about 3 to 4 hours before competition and make it a light carbohydrate meal. The myth that meat before a competition is essential is rubbish.

Bodybuilding

A special note about bodybuilding on a vegetarian diet is included here, because we do get calls from bodybuilders and endurance athletes who are concerned about whether their diet is sufficient for their needs, and whether they should take non-vegetarian supplements.

A recent article in the American magazine *Vegetarian Times* (April 1990) by Victoria Moran looks into the subject and interviews several vegetarian body builders.

Bill Pearl was Mr Universe four times. He is a lacto-ovo vegetarian and has been for some 20 years. He claims that his vegetarian diet has eased his blood pressure, high cholesterol and high uric acid levels, and reduced the pain in his elbows and knees.

Andreas Cahling is a vegetarian who eats egg whites but no other dairy or egg products. He was winner of the 1980 'Mr International' contest. He says: "If I included more animal foods in my diet, I would be getting a lot more toxins and be in trouble in the long run. Since I stopped using dairy products, my joints are better, enabling me to continue bodybuilding for life".

Cahling also says that some professional bodybuilders who do eat meat find it more difficult to obtain a chiselled shape because of water retention, and a build-up of protein waste products between the muscle and the skin.

Barbara Brehm, Assistant Professor of Exercise and Sports Physiology at Smith College in Northampton, Massachusetts, draws attention to the fact that you do not need to eat muscle to make muscle, any more than you need to eat liver to make liver. She suggests that bodybuilders and endurance athletes should aim for a protein intake around 10% higher than less active people.

Ron Weston is a Canadian athletic trainer who eats a raw food diet. He thinks that such a diet may make it difficult to get enough calories to go into professional competitive bodybuilding, but says that non-professional weight lifters may find a raw food diet beneficial, as it helps the body to build strong cell tissue.

Spice Williams is an American actress and stunt-woman, whose latest role is a female Klingon in *Star Trek V*. She is a vegan who supplements her diet with dairy-free vitamins and supplements.

This is a very specialised area of nutrition and the Vegetarian Society does not claim expertise in this field. It would seem that eating meat is not necessary for athletes and bodybuilders, and that a vegetarian or vegan diet can be beneficial.

The experts are available to help you out if you can afford a long distance phone call. Andreas Cahling offers bodybuilding consultations by phone on a limited basis – you can make an appointment by phoning USA 818 360 7122. Ron Weston lectures and works as a personal trainer in Canada – phone him on Canada 416 964 1575. Bill Pearl has written a book called *Getting Stronger – Weight Training for Men and Women*. It was published in 1988 by Shelter Publications.

Pregnancy and babies

The Vegetarian Diet During Pregnancy

A pregnant vegetarian has the same needs as a pregnant non-vegetarian. Both require well-balanced meals, both have to watch their weight carefully, and both have to get far more calories, vitamins and minerals and in particular, more protein than before.

The nine months of pregnancy is a period of readjustment as well as growth. There are three divisions of three months called 'trimesters' during which the mother's mood, activity, diet and appetite vary.

0 – 3 months: A mother may feel 'different', and possibly sickly and tired. It is advisable to avoid rich and eggy foods. Each meal or snack should start with fresh fruit or juice. Avoid salt at the table, and cut down on sugar – use honey instead. If you intend to breastfeed, give up tea and coffee – the caffeine can affect your baby.

3 – 6 months: A mother usually feels more like herself and is often hungry, while the child visibly grows bigger and begins to develop bones and a mobile body. Weight control is an important factor at this time. It should be brought about by eating more fruit, salads and protein foods, and less starchy and sweet foods. Cheese, eggs and nutmeat are probably less fattening and provide adequate protein, while white bread, biscuits, cakes and puddings are more fattening. If you are hungry between meals, nibble on raw fruit or vegetables.

6 – 9 months: The baby matures while the mother eases up on her activities and prepares for the birth. By this time the space occupied by the child in its bag of 'liquor' can reduce the capacity of the mother's stomach, so she may have to eat smaller portions, more frequently. As long as a well-balanced diet is followed there should be no problems. However, some complications in the last months of pregnancy are associated with an increase in weight, high blood pressure, and signs of strain on the kidneys. These are likely to be reduced or even avoided by a good diet, sufficient relaxation, fresh air, lack of stress and anxiety, and a real enjoyment of the pregnancy. Make sure you drink plenty of fluid.

Breast Feeding

Whether you are a vegetarian or not, you may need to add one or more extra servings from both milk and cereal groups. Vegans should substitute soya milk and soya products.

General Advice:

• If you do not already eat a wholefood diet, try to increase your intake of unrefined and unprocessed foods, for example by using wholemeal bread and wholegrain cereals.

• During the first 4 months, all tablets and medicines should be avoided unless prescribed by a doctor. Because the action of vitamins and minerals is closely interrelated, it is best not to take any vitamin or mineral tablets or tonics without consulting your doctor first. However, if you should want to add supplements to your foods, kelp (a powdered seaweed), wheatgerm, and brewers yeast will do no harm as long as the manufacturers' instructions are followed.

• Where possible, avoid all foods containing artificial additives and pre-servatives. Eat fresh foods or frozen foods, in preference to tinned ones.

• Avoid sweets, cakes, sugar and soft drinks as much as you can. They often contain few or no vitamins and minerals. The odd cake, chocolate or biscuit will do no harm, but fresh fruit or vegetables, unsalted nuts and raisins are better for you.

• Eat plenty of iron and zinc-rich foods – for example eggs, unless you are a vegan, and dried fruit. Vitamin C aids absorption of iron from plant foods. Serve vegetables and fruits that are rich in Vitamin C with food that contain iron – for example, orange with breakfast cereals, salads and vegetables with main pulse or seed meals.

• Try not to drink more than 5 cups of tea or coffee during one day, and especially not with a meal, as iron absorption can be inhibited, and protein availability may be affected. Ideally, drink water, milk (animal or soya), mild herbal teas and pure unsweetened fruit juices – fresh or in cartons. Avoid fruit drinks because they contain little or no fresh fruit.

• Vegans may need a Vitamin B_{12} supplement from their doctor, because Vitamin B_{12} is found almost entirely in animal foods. It is also added to many yeast extracts and seaweed products which are widely available.

A free information sheet is available from the Vegetarian Society.

Vegetarian diet for infants

Weaning infants

Up to the age of six months, a full-term infant can get adequate nutrition from breast milk or formula, although an iron supplement is needed after the sixth month if breast-milk continues to be the sole food. During the period of weaning, a baby's nutritional requirements are extremely high. A baby requires more protein and calcium, and more of most other nutrients, than at any other time in life.

By six to eight months, most babies are able to eat solids, but milk should still play a large part in their diets. When you begin introducing solids to your baby, introduce one food at a time, and leave three or four days between each new food. This way, you will be able to tell if your baby is allergic or sensitive to any particular food.

Bringing up your child as a vegetarian, you will want to accustom him to the five basic food groups: cereals, beans and nuts, dairy produce, fruit, vegetables. You can introduce your child to virtually all adult foods from these groups by the end of his second year. Your baby may reject strong-tasting foods, such as as broccoli, cauliflower and cabbage, at six months, but may take them enthusiastically several months later.

When purchasing ready-prepared baby foods, it is advisable to choose those which have no additives, including sugar or salt. This will be better for your child in the long run by avoiding the development of a sweet tooth or taste for strong, salty flavours in later life. Carried to extremes, these may lead to health problems.

Iron is probably the most important nutrient when you start introducing your baby to solid food. Iron-rich foods include: figs, prunes and prune-juice, apricots and other dried fruits, molasses, brewers yeast and cocoa. Although wheatgerm, lentils and spinach contain good quantities of iron, its availability is limited by the other substances present. Vegetables such as potatoes, beetroot, broccoli, tomatoes, cauliflower and cabbage may be better sources of iron because they contain less of the inhibitory substances, and more Vitamin C which aids iron absorption. Serve combinations of iron and Vitamin C – for example, orange juice with the breakfast cereal, salads and vegetables with main pulse or seed meals.

It is also a good idea to cook in iron pans to add traces of iron to your food, except for foods rich in Vitamin C, because iron can destroy Vitamin C during cooking.

Calcium is another example of food that is absorbed to varying extents depending upon where it comes from. The calcium in milk, especially in mothers' milk, is absorbed better than calcium from other sources.

If you continue to breastfeed into your child's first year of life – your concern should be as much for your own nutrtion as for the child's. If *you* are eating well, so is your child. Remember, you are *still* eating for two!

Baby food

As children's teeth come through, they can eat a greater variety of foods. By the age of two or so, they can be eating much the same foods as adults, which makes it easier for the mother to buy food and cook meals. However, babies and young children have different dietary requirements from older children and adults. During the first year, the child's weight normally triples, but there is a marked slowdown in growth from the age of one until puberty. This explains why some one-year-olds seem to loose their appetites, at least for a while. They may eat far less, or far more, than the officially recommended allowances, but generally they require food which will provide them with plenty of calories (energy) as well as nutrients. However, because babies do not have the capacity to eat large quantities of food, they do not require a diet which is bulky and high in fibre.

Fibre: Although all wholefoods should not be avoided, high-fibre diets fill up a child before his nutritional needs have been met, and they may also interfere with absorption of minerals, such as zinc, iron and calcium. Bran should not be added to a young child's diet because of this. If you think that the baby is constipated, give it extra water or fruit juices. A constipated older child should be encouraged to eat extra fruit and to drink more fluid.

Milk: Do not give skimmed milk to a child under the age of five, unless your doctor advises it. It does not provide the high concentration of calories a baby or young child needs – nor does skimmed milk have the Vitamin A and D content of whole milk.

Salt and sugar: These should be avoided in the diet of babies and young children. A baby's kidneys are not mature enough to cope with too much salt; and sugary foods and drinks are a prime cause of tooth decay. In addition, a baby who is encouraged to develop a sweet tooth may have problems with obesity in later life. Having said this, there is nothing wrong with allowing a small child the occasional packet of crisps or sweets, as treats. Depriving a child of certain foods creates emotional stress and possibly greater difficulties in feeding habits.

Feeding Problems: Most children, not just those brought up as vegetarians, go through phases of not wanting to eat what their parents want them to eat; or they prefer one or two foods to anything else. Unfortunately, the more you nag or scold about what a child eats, the less likely the child is to co-operate. In fact, your anxiety may provoke a worse reaction.

If your child looks well, is about the right size and weight for age, and is lively during waking hours, there is no need for concern. Experiments have shown that children have an inborn ability to meet their nutritional needs after weaning without any detailed direction from their parents, provided that ample fresh and wholesome foods are offered, and highly processed foods and drinks (cakes, biscuits, soft drinks etc) are not easily available.

Hints

• Establish and reinforce good habits by providing the right atmosphere and setting a good example. Eat breakfast with your children.

• Make sure there are plenty of nutritious foods and snacks readily available, but do remember that a few treats will not do any real harm.

• Do not prepare elaborate meals to try to tempt your child. This will only add to your frustration when they are rejected!

• Whichever 'unhealthy' food your child may insist on eating, try combining it with nutritious food, for example chips and beans, sandwiches with white (rather than wholemeal) bread and yeast extract or peanut butter.

• Try to involve your child in the preparation of meals – most children love to eat anything they have cooked or concocted themselves.

You have complete control of the foods your child eats during infancy, but you will gradually lose out to other influences: TV, other children, school meals and birthday parties.

Your children will encounter meat when they are away from home. This can be a problem, because children do not like to be different from their friends. Explain simply to your child why you are a vegetarian, but do not try to force your view. This may well cause resentment and rebellion. Face the challenge squarely by providing tastier scrummier (but veggie) food at home!

A free information sheet giving details of how to prepare nutritious and appetising vegetarian meals for babies and young children is available from the Vegetarian Society.

Aluminium in soya milk

Aluminium levels in soya milk caused a scare last year when it was suggested that babies were being fed soya milk with a dangerously high aluminium content.

There is no cause for alarm over this issue. Aluminium occurs naturally as a trace element in soya beans, but also in many other foods and in vegetables.

Soya milk actually contains substantially less aluminium than cows milk.

Babies should not be given soya milk liquids as these are quite rich, and are not designed to feed babies. Proprietary brands of soya milk baby feeds are suitable as long as they are not used for babies who were premature or suffer from kidney problems.

INFORMATION

MANUFACTURERS OF VEGETARIAN BABY FOODS

BEECH-NUT (Eliko Food Distributors)
Vegetable and fruit foods, cereals and juices. No added sugar
or salt, gluten-free. Available in chemists and health

BIKKIPEGS
Very hard baby biscuits, made from wheat flour, wheat-germ
and water. No added salt or sugar.

BOOTS
Baby meals in jars. Instant baby foods

COW & GATE
Formula 'S' Soya Food. Olivarit baby foods (see 'Food Shopping' page 97)

FAMILIA (G. Costa and Co. Ltd)
Swiss Baby food, available in raw sugar and sugar-free varieties

FARLEY'S
Ostersoy Formula.

GRANOSE
All the range is vegan, eight varieties, organically grown,
no lactose or dairy products, artificial flavouring or colourings.

HEINZ baby foods
(see 'Food Shopping' page 97)

THURSDAY'S CHILD
Organic wholemeal dry foods, sugar- and salt-free.

WYETH NUTRITION
Wysoy Baby Milk. Progress Junior Milk.

THIS LIST HAS BEEN COMPILED FROM VARIOUS SOURCES. IT IS PRODUCED AS A GUIDE ONLY AND DOES NOT
SIGNIFY ANY SPECIAL APPROVAL OF THE PRODUCTS LISTED. YOU ARE ADVISED TO READ LABELS.

BOOKS ON PREGNANCY BABIES AND CHILDREN

First Foods
VSUK

Vegetarian Baby
Sharon Yntema.

Pregnancy, Children and the Vegan Diet
Michael Klapper MD.

New Recipes for Young Vegetarians
Sammy Green.

Vegetarian Children
Sharon Yntema.

The Vegetarian Lunchbox
Janet Hunt.

Children's Food – The Good, The Bad and The Useless
Tim Lobstein

Good Children's Food
Christine Smith.

KIDS OWN BOOKS

The A-Z of Vegetarianism
VSUK

Some People Don't Eat Meat
Jan Inglis.

Full of Beans
Evelyn Findlater.

The Kitchen Crew
Stephanie Lashford

Let's Cook It Together
Peggy Brusseau

TO ORDER BOOKS, PHONE THE MERCHANDISE DEPARTMENT OF THE VSUK FOR DETAILS.

The real world

Vegetarianism is a growing movement but we are still a minority – most of areas of life are geared up to the meat-eating majority. This section deals with how veggies fare (sometimes literally!) in a rather oddly assorted range of circumstances.

Eating out

Happily, finding vegetarian food in restaurants is not as difficult as it used to be. Many restaurant proprietors are offering at least one vegetarian dish so that they will not lose any trade from parties with vegetarian members. However, at worst the so-called 'vegetarian choice' might be a cheese omelette made with battery eggs and non-vegetarian cheese. Some caterers are still labouring under the misapprehension that vegetarians eat fish! It may be worthwhile making your requirements crystal clear, or even taking the precaution of booking in advance. Personally, I always feel unhappy about having to book a vegetarian meal in advance – why should vegetarians be made to feel different?

The Vegetarian Society produces a leaflet called *Catering for Vegetarians*. Aimed at caterers, it explains fully the requirements of vegetarians. You can use these leaflets to explain your requirements to restaurants. If you enjoy your meal, do thank the proprietor for his consideration and perhaps contact the Editor, who will investigate whether the establishment is suitable for a listing in the *The Vegetarian Travel Guide*. You could contact your local branch to see if they are aware of the good service available, and also contact Bronwen Humphreys at The Vegetarian Society. She will write a letter to the establishment asking them to consider offering a discount to card-carrying members of the VSUK.

On the other hand, if you are given a meal which does not meet your expectations, make your feelings known to the proprietor. Try to be constructive. Perhaps you might give him a *Catering For Vegetarians* leaflet so that he knows what he should be aiming at. If you are presented with a meal which you know contains meat or fish, do not under any circumstances accept it – the proprietor will make a mental note that vegetarians will accept little pieces of meat, or that vegetarians eat fish, and this will make things very awkward for the next vegetarian to visit the establishment.

Always make sure that you book vegetarian meals well in advance if you are staying at a hotel or guesthouse. Again, sending a *Catering for Vegetarians* leaflet with your booking form may help.

The Vegetarian Society publishes *The Vegetarian Travel Guide*. This lists hundreds of restaurants, hotels, guesthouses, pubs and cafés which have been investigated by the Society, and which are able to provide meals which meet Vegetarian Society standards. Every establishment which is listed has signed a declaration to this effect – if it is not living up to this declaration, the Editor would like to know! The *Guide* covers the whole of the British Isles. All establishments are listed alphabetically in county order within regions – there are useful maps too. *The Vegetarian Travel Guide* is the sister volume to this book. If you have not already bought the set, why not treat yourself? Phone the Vegetarian Society to place your order.

Fast food

I recommend a book called *Fast Food Facts* published by The Food Commission – fascinating stuff! Wimpy offer a 'Beanburger', but it is fried in the same vessels as pieces of fish and chicken. The oil used by Wimpy is vegetable oil. Kentucky use hardened soya fat, but both McDonalds and Burger King fry in beef fat.

Outside caterers

There is a growing army of vegetarians who have set up catering businesses, plus a number of caterers who offer vegetarian options. Vegetarian caterers may be able to make the arrangements for a vegetarian or vegan wedding buffet, or cater for a vegetarian business conference lunch. When you need to cater for a party, and you want to impress, booking a vegetarian caterer might be the answer. The VSUK can provide a free list of vegetarian caterers.

Travel

The Vegetarian movement knows no boundaries! Vegetarianism is everywhere. Unfortunately, it is still easier to find food suitable for vegetarians in some countries than it is in others, partly due to cultural differences. If you are not an expert linguist, you may have difficulty in explaining your exact requirements to a waiter or chef. Sometimes your problems can begin almost as soon as you leave Britain, when the airline meal fails to live up to expectations, or even to materialise at all!

Do not despair – you need your own personal copy of the *Vegetarian Travel Guide!* Produced by The Vegetarian Society, it includes all the information you need when travelling either in this country or abroad. All the British entries have signed a declaration that they can provide meals which meet strict Vegetarian Society standards; all the foreign addresses have been verified by international vegetarian organisations. Wherever you go, you will be able to find good food, meet up with fellow vegetarians, explain your requirements using our translations, and enjoy your trip!

The book also contains addresses of tour operators who can cater for vegetarians; and ideas for activity holidays of all kinds. It really is a *must* for the glove box or rucksack! Available in good bookshops and from the Vegetarian Society – phone for mail order details.

Places you don't want to go to!

Hospitals

In theory, all hospitals are obliged by the Department of Health to cater for all patients. In practice, hospital food is at best, varied and wholesome, and at worst, poisonous. There are no specific guidelines. It is up to the area health authority to set its own catering standards. Some authorities take the need for special diets very seriously, providing a range of healthy, balanced meals for all diets, be they religious, medical or ethical.

A survey carried out by Surrey University concluded that only 22% of vegetarians have to spend time in hospital. Perhaps this is why hospitals are not used to providing vegetarian meals! Another survey found that the average vegetarian costs the NHS £12,340 in a lifetime, as compared with the average cost to the NHS of a meat-eater, £58,062! It must be in the best interests of the NHS to campaign for everybody to go vegetarian!

Obviously, if your arrival in hospital is sudden, you will not have time to make any enquiries or arrangements. If you do have time, check with a catering officer, a hospital dietitian, and the ward sister, that you will be able to eat properly during your stay. If necessary, bring in some ideas or your favourite recipes. If you are in for a long stay, ask your visitors to bring in some fresh fruit!

Prison Catering

Vegetarians are catered for in all of HM Prisons. Vegetarian cheese is used, but unfortunately not free-range eggs. The meals are all nutritionally balanced and are in fact sometimes exceed the NACNE recommendations.

There is usually a choice of dairy or non-dairy (vegan) in most long term prisons. Of a total of 146,000 meals served daily to prison inmates in England and Wales, 15,000 are for vegetarians and 1,200 for vegans. (*The Independent* 7.12.89).

Careers for vegetarians

Employment

There is no specific legislation to ensure that, where appropriate, employers provide vegetarian alternatives to meals. If you have a problem in this respect, your trades union representative may well be the person to help.

Increasingly, young vegetarians are coming to realise that many jobs involve cruelty to animals, either directly or indirectly, and naturally they wish to plan their careers to avoid this.

Careers which may involve cruelty, and require investigation

Beauty therapist, research technician, horticulturist, caterer, soap manufacturing, all medical fields, vet (you may be asked to administer to farm animals treatments that are mainly for improving profits rather than the animals' welfare), sales assistant (you may have to handle meat, furs etc), fashion designer, cosmetics manufacturer, pet trades, science teaching, home economics teaching, shoe manufacturing and retailing, jockey.

Careers with animals

There are a number of ways in which you can work directly with animals without causing suffering, although some careers (such as veterinary surgery or even working for the RSPCA) may require some conscience-testing personal compromises.

RSPCA The Society's Inspectorate employs approximately 250 uniformed Field Officers in stations throughout England and Wales. Candidates must be aged 22 – 35, possess a good general education, hold a full, clean, current UK driving licence, be physically fit, and be prepared to serve anywhere in England and Wales. There is a 7 month training course, after which the successful applicant becomes a 'probationary inspector' for 12 months before finally achieving the rank of inspector. Previous experience of working with animals, including voluntary work, is likely to be of benefit to applicants; as is experience of working with the public. You should be aware that the RSPCA still destroys animals for which it cannot find homes.

RSPCA, Causeway, Horsham, West Sussex, RH12 1HG.

RSPB The Royal Society for the Protection of Birds stress that "while the number of people seeking jobs in nature conservation increases every year, the number of posts that arise remains small." However, a number of temporary and permanent positions do arise each year, on the Society's 121 reserves throughout the UK. The temporary category includes work as a 'Summer Warden' from April to August. Applicants must be competent and reliable ornithologists, and be prepared to undertake physical work for long hours if necessary. The most outstanding Summer Wardens may then be offered permanent employment as 'Assistant Wardens' or full 'Wardens' when vacancies arise. Like the RSPCA, the RSPB also has occasional vacancies in administrative, educational and research posts at its headquarters and regional offices. These positions are advertised in the national press and other relevant publications.

RSPB, The Lodge, Sandy, Bedfordshire, SG19 2DL.

Royal College of Veterinary Surgeons for details of a career as a veterinary surgeon. 32 Belgrave Square, London, SW1X 8QP.

British Veterinary Nursing Association for details of a career as a veterinary nurse.15 Manderville Road, Northolt, Middlesex, UB5 5HD.

Please note, in either of the above two careers it is highly probable that you will be required to do some dissection during training!

Guide Dogs for the Blind Association for details of work as a Guide Dog instructor. Applicants should, be aged 20 – 24, possess 4 GCSE passes or equivalent including English, be able to drive, have physical stamina and be willing to undergo a three year training period.

Alexandra House, 9 Park St, Windsor, Berks, SL4 1JR. Tel: (0753) 855711.

The British Horse Society for details of work as a riding instructor. Applicants must be at least 18 years of age and possess 4 GCSE passes or equivalent.

British Equestrian Centre, Kenilworth, Warwickshire, CV8 2LR.

Nature Conservancy Council for details of work with the NCC.

Recruitment Section, PO Box 6, Goodwin House, Huntingdon, Cambs. (You might also contact your local wildlife sanctuary or animal refuge to see if they have vacancies.)

Science careers without vivisection

FRAME Although the Fund for the Replacement of Animals in Medical Experiments "does not have many employment opportunities per se... it is in a position to advise science graduates on how to pursue a career in alternative research." Such research might include the development and production of computer programmes, the establishment of databanks or studies in the application of tissue techniques. FRAME states that they are happy to recommend suitable research posts in their own laboratories and in other academic or industrial establishments to interested students. Clearly, graduate or even postgraduate qualifications are needed for work of this nature.

FRAME, Eastgate House, 34 Stoney Street, Nottingham, NG1 1NB.

Miscellaneous

There are lots of charities and other organisations that work for the welfare of animals and the environment – VSUK, CIWF, BUAV, League Against Cruel Sports, Animal Aid, etc. They don't usually employ many staff, but occasionally a vacancy will arise, so it is probably worth sending your CV to them if this is the sort of job you really want; or subscribe to their magazines as this is where positions are most frequently advertised. *The Vegetarian* has a good 'Situations Vacant' column and Friday's issue of *The Guardian, Environment Guardian,* is where jobs in conservation are often advertised.

Don't forget that even if you can't find a job that's totally acceptable, many careers will offer opportunities to 'spread the message' in a subtle way. For example, a nutritionist or dietitian may have to handle meat during training, but once qualified, he or she will be in a position to give people authoritative advice about vegetarianism.

Before you accept a job, even if at first sight it doesn't appear to involve anything objectionable, do check your contract of employment, and do investigate what other jobs inside the same organisation entail. For example, we know of a girl who had accepted a job as a window dresser in a department store. At first, she was working with innocuous materials, but later she was transferred to the fur department. To avoid a similar experience, you must insist on its being written into your contract of employment that you will not be required to handle certain materials, or work in certain departments. Asking a few questions at the beginning can save a lot of distress later.

INFORMATION

Careers in the Environment
£1.25 inc. p&p, from Council for Environmental Education, School of Education, University of Reading, 24 London Road, Reading, RG1 5AQ.

Working in Nature Conservation
£1.95 from Careers and Occupational Information Centre, Sales Department, Freepost, Sheffield, S1 4BR.

Working Out: Work and the Environment
from World Wide Fund for Nature, Panda House, Godalming, Surrey.

Careers with Animals
from the Universities Federation for Animal Welfare, 8 Hamilton Close, South Mimms, Potters Bar, Herts, EN6 3QD. This might be useful for the addresses it contains, but watch out – the UFAW considers farming, animal experimentation and zoo-keeping to be acceptable careers!

Careers in Conservation
by John McCormick, published by Kogan Page, £3.25.

Job Search

During the past year our Cookery School Co-ordinator, Rosemary Billings, has noticed that a number of people who come to 'Parkdale' for a cookery course are either looking for work or looking for staff. They may be young people, hoping to set up their own vegetarian restaurant or guest house in the long term, who need experience. Or they may be hoteliers who need suitable help. We do also get letters and telephone calls from people who are looking for vegetarian staff or for employment. It seemed sensible to keep a note of jobs available and to try to match them with workers available.

This service has become very popular. Employers can now register an interest in finding people to work as cooks, caterers, chefs, waiters and waitresses, or in other positions including office work, child-minding, parents' help, cleaning and domestic work, and animal welfare work. If Rosemary is able to find the right person for the job she will ask for a donation of at least £20 paid by the employer to the Cookery School.

If you are an employer looking for somebody with an interest in vegetarianism, cookery, or animal welfare, you could find the person you need through the Vegetarian Society's Register. If you are looking for a job in one of these areas, why not contact Rosemary to discuss your qualifications and requirements.

The Vegetarian Society cannot take responsibility for the character or work of any person on the Register. We simply provide a service, without recommendation. It is the responsibility of the employer to contact and interview potential employees.

Pets and domestic animals

Some vegetarians may choose not to keep birds in cages, (budgerigars are flock birds), rabbits in hutches (they are family animals), fish in tanks (artificial environment) and so on. There is some debate over the ethics involved in keeping any pets or domestic animals. Some people feel that keeping animals as our pets is unnatural and demeaning to the animals, and that humans have no right to interfere with the natural lifestyle of animals. Others feel that the human race benefits by living in close harmony with pet animals; that developing a close relationship to a pet can encourage compassion towards less fortunate animals (including those that are killed for meat); and that anyway, some animals are ill-equipped genetically to live in a world which is no longer suitable for their free way of life. The argument rages on!

One of the most difficult problems for vegetarian and vegan pet owners is how to feed pets which would normally be fed meat. Many vegetarians find it difficult to handle meat. Of course, pet food is made from the slaughterhouse products that are not considered fit for human consumption… and, bearing in mind what is considered suitable for human consumption these days, the contents must be dreadful! Vegetarians feel unhappy that they are feeding this waste to their pets, and also feel angry that by buying pet food they are contributing to the profits of the meat industry.

There are also arguments over whether it is ethical to feed an animal such as a dog on a vegetarian diet, when dogs are naturally carnivorous. I do not propose to wade into the fray! Suffice it to say that it *is* possible to feed a dog, and to keep it happy and healthy, on a vegetarian or vegan diet. Cats are more difficult – they require an amino acid called Taurine if they are to stay healthy. The richest source of Taurine is meat. Sadly, although cats will happily eat fruit and vegetables, they will suffer a serious deterioration in their sight if their diet is low in Taurine, and in time they may go blind. The only way to feed a cat a vegetarian diet without risk to its health is to provide a special food supplement. Katz Go Vegan supply a supplement called 'Vegecat' – they can be contacted through the Vegan Society.

The Vegetarian Society can supply very detailed information about feeding vegetarian dogs and cats; if you are resolved to do this, it is something that really must be done properly!

INFORMATION

Katz Go Vegan
c/o The Vegan Society, 7 Battle Rd., St Leonards-on-Sea, East Sussex, TN37 7AA .
Supply Vegecat supplement which can make up any deficiencies in a vegetarian diet for cats.

Wafcol
Vegetarian dog food. The Nutrition Bakery, Haigh Av, Stockport, Cheshire SK4 1NU. Tel: (061) 480 2781.

Happidog
Vegetarian dog food. Bridgend, Brownhill Lane, Longton, Preston, Lancs PR4 4SJ
Tel: Preston (0772) 614952.

Green Ark
Cereal mix. Ullston Cumbria Tel: (0434) 381766

Vegetarian dogfood
Made fresh at home by: Leda Schoen, 64 Crouch Hill, London, N8 9EE.

Christopher Day
British Association of Veterinary Surgeons, Chinham House, Stanford-in-the-Vale,
Faringdon, Oxon, SN7 8NQ. Send for a list of homoeopathic vets.

Ganymede
Make the Assisi range of cruelty-free pet care products. Heesom Green Farm,
Middlewich Road, Toft, nr Knutsford, Cheshire, WA16 9PQ.

Pampurred Pets
Aromatherapy products for pets. 7-9 Bank Street, Wakefield, W.Yorks. Tel: (0924) 372372.

Homoeopathic Development Foundation
Publishes a book called *Homoeopathy for Pets*. Harcourt House, 19a Cavendish Square,
London, W1M 9AD. Tel: (071) 629 3205.

National Petwatch
Campaigns against pet stealing, offers advice on how to protect your pet and help
if your pet is missing. PO Box 16, Brighouse, W Yorks, HD6 1DS. Tel: (0484) 72411.

National Canine Defence
League Maintains rescue centres throughout the country for lost, abandoned and
unwanted dogs. No healthy dog is ever destroyed. Conducts a dog sponsorship scheme
whereby dog lovers can adopt a dog which is resident at one of the kennels.
1-2 Pratt Mews, London, NW1 0AD Tel: (071) 388 0137 or 10 Seymour St, London W1H 5WB.

Dogs and Cats Go Vegetarian
by Barbara Lynn Peden. (Available from Katz Go Vegan)

The Celebrity Vegetarian Cookbook
Contains a recipe for home-made vegetarian dog biscuits supplied by Carla Lane.
You can order the book from the Vegetarian Society.

Denes Veterinary Herbal Products Ltd
Write for help with illnesses etc. 14 Goldstone Street, Hove, East Sussex,
BN3 3RL. Tel: 0273 25364.

Cats Protection League
20 North Street, Horsham, W. Sussex RH12 1BN

RSPCA
Causeway, Horsham, W. Sussex RH12 1MG

Universities Federation for Animal Welfare
8 Hamilton Close, South Mimms, Potters Bar, Herts EN6 3QD
SAE for leaflet *How to choose a cage for your pet mouse, gerbil or hamster.*

Food and Gardening

Compiled by Bronwen Humphreys with information supplied by N. I. Cooper (craftsman gardener).

Organic food

Organically-grown food is becoming increasingly easy to find in shops and supermarkets, and presents vegetarians with something of a dilemma.

On one hand, there are cogent arguments for growing crops organically, as this method of production is better for the environment, and better for human health. Organic growing uses no herbicides, only a very limited number of pesticides, (those with a proven safety record and good bio-degradability), and no artificial fertilisers.

On the other hand, some of the fertilisers used are *not* vegetarian – things like fishmeal, bonemeal, dried blood. Inorganic fertilisers are usually simple chemicals obtained by mining or as by-products of the steel industry with no animal content.

There is a 'veganic' method of growing which uses no animal products, but this is only as yet practised on a very small-scale. On the other side of the argument, pesticides and herbicides, besides polluting the environment and presenting a danger to health if used unwisely, have probably been tested on animals. In the UK, there is little or no animal testing of fertilisers. On balance, organic growing probably does less harm, but you should be aware that not all products used conform to vegetarian standards.

Gardening for vegetarians

Fertilisers

Try not to use peat if you can help it. Britain's peat bogs are rapidly disappearing with the consequent destruction of wildlife. Two million tonnes of peat are sold to gardeners every year! Use home-made compost if you can, or buy composted forest bark – a renewable resource from managed plantations. A brand new product will be appearing in garden centres during 1990 – composted coconut fibre. This consists of the outer husks of coconuts so it is an ecologically acceptable, renewable resource. Trials have shown that it performs as well as peat-based compost.

Spent mushroom compost, spent hops (as a top dressing) and composted stable manure are alternative fertilisers.

Dried blood and fishmeal are often used to add nitrogen to the soil. These are definitely not vegetarian products. You should also look out for various kinds of 'composted manures' that are on sale these days – some even labelled 'organic', as many of them contain manure from factory-farmed animals, or droppings from battery-kept chickens. Seaweed fertilisers are a good and acceptable substitute. Bonemeal is a slaughterhouse by-product, in addition to being non-vegetarian. We hear that now organic growing is on the increase, bonemeal is being imported from South American countries, where cattle ranching is helping to destroy the rainforests! Don't use a product called 'worm compost' without investigating its source. Some methods of making it are acceptable, but others may cause injury to the worms, or even kill them.

If you make your own compost, you know what has gone into it, so you can be sure that it is acceptable! Invest in a compost bin, or make your own;

or, if you are really short of space, use a heavy-duty polythene sack. Put a shovelful of soil at the bottom to provide the organisms that start off the fermenting process, then add layers of kitchen waste, fallen leaves, grass cuttings and any other organic waste matter. Even shredded paper will compost. Tough things like cabbage stalks and banana skins should be cut into smaller pieces. Annual weeds can be put in whole, but perennial weeds should have their roots cut off and discarded. Never put any part of the plant Bindweed into your compost – even small pieces will root, and your garden will have a wonderful crop of Bindweed when you spread the compost!

Make sure you don't add quantities of extra soil when you add weeds. It can slow down the fermentation process. If you are using the polythene sack method, tie the sack off when it is nearly full, and pierce two or three holes in the sides and leave to rot down until about a third of the original bulk is left. Then turn out and spread on your soil. Most compost bins have provision for you to remove compost from the bottom without emptying the entire bin, so the process can be continuous.

Pest Control

Perhaps the best way to control insect pests is to invite natural predators into your garden. If you have room, dig a pond to encourage frogs. This needs to be an irregularly-shaped pond, with varying depths, and at least one side sloping up gradually, so the frogs have easy access. Toads, too, are good friends. They don't spend as much time in water as frogs, but they need some undisturbed, dampish nooks and crannies to hide in. Always have a bird bath and make sure it is kept topped up with clean water and that it doesn't freeze over in winter. Encourage the birds to stay near your garden in winter when there are few insects, by putting out bird food. Plant some leafy bushes or small trees so that the birds have places to hide in and feel secure. Shrubs with berries on in winter are even better, as they provide more winter food. Encourage hedgehogs by not being too tidy – leave some scrub and leaf litter under sheltered hedges and in dark corners for them. If you have a large garden, consider nesting boxes for birds (advice from the RSPB) and little kennels for hedgehogs to hibernate in. Leave some corners of the garden deliberately undisturbed for wildlife.

Natural insect predators can be encouraged into the garden by having a variety of plants. Don't plant up large beds of the same crop; have small patches interspersed with bright flowering plants like Marigolds. This not only attracts insect predators, but makes it harder for the pests to spread rapidly should one patch of the crop become infected.

Ladybirds are your friends! Avoid disturbance of hedge-bottoms, where they lie up in winter. Common predatory insects are ladybirds, blue bottles and green bottles, and lacewings. Natural predators for various pests can be purchased if you don't have them in the garden already. Look for 'Biological Controls' in gardening magazine small ads.

Try physical barriers against pests, for example, a 'fence' of polythene sheeting around carrot plants stops carrot flies from getting in. Tight-fitting discs of felt or old carpet, around Brassicas, discourage cabbage root fly. Plastic plant pots, lined with newspaper and balanced upside down on the top of garden canes, will trap earwigs and vine weevils, which can then be carried away from the garden. Large pests like caterpillars can also be picked off by hand, and carried away. Pests like greenfly can be washed off plants with a medium to high pressure hose.

Plant resistant varieties; plants that are in good health have a better resistance to pests, so always make sure that you provide the optimum growing conditions for any particular variety – take care with things like soil pH, light, drainage, and exposure to winds. The use of home-made compost strengthens plants and increases resistance to pests. Liming discourages Brassica 'club root.'

You should be aware that Derris and Pyrethrum, the pesticides allowed in organic horticulture, are not particularly selective, and may kill beneficial insects like ladybirds, bees and butterflies. They are also poisonous to fish if they get into a pond or stream. Chemical pesticides, on the contrary, may be highly selective. Of course, you have to remember they may have been tested on animals. So please think very carefully before you spray anything. Ask yourself "is it really necessary?" Try other methods of pest control first, and if you feel that spraying *is* absolutely imperative, make sure you are using the right one for the job.

Don't be in too much of a hurry to spray. Pests initially increase at a faster rate than their natural predators – often, if you wait, the predators will catch up and do the job for you!

Slugs are a nuisance, but most commercial slug-killers contain the very poisonous Metaldehyde. This kills off beneficial soil organisms as well as slugs. It is dangerous to pets, hedgehogs and other animals, and the poisoned bodies of the slugs may be eaten by birds, which are poisoned in turn. If you don't want to kill slugs, you can protect susceptible plants with a physical barrier like soot, sharp gravel or sand – slugs don't like irritants on their delicate under-surfaces!). You can trap slugs alive by putting out half orange skins, or sinking pots into the soil with some bait inside, then take them away from your garden. *Gardening Which*, in one of its trials, found that the 'beer-trap', so beloved of organic gardeners, actually killed more beneficial creatures than it killed slugs! They advised drinking all your beer, and then cutting 4 inch deep rings from the plastic bottles to make slug barriers for individual plants. These need to be buried at least 1cm deep in the soil. These proved very effective at keeping slugs out until the plants had grown enough to be able to withstand a little slug damage. By the way, it is the little grey and white slugs that damage plants, the big black and brown ones are useful scavengers! There is a compound called 'Nobble' which acts as a kind of slug birth control by destroying the eggs in the soil.

If garden ants are getting into your kitchen, find the point of entry, and place a line of red chilli pepper, paprika or dried peppermint there to deter them. Washing kitchens with equal parts of vinegar and water may also work.

Mammals can sometimes cause damage to gardens. Cats can be deterred by placing stems of pruned roses around the base of plants. Old lemonade bottles or jam jars, half full of water and left in strategic points around the garden, can also help persuade cats to go elsewhere!

Moles are said to dislike vibrations. Sticking children's plastic windmills in their runs may persuade them to go next door! The same effect can also be produced by sinking bottles into their runs, so that the wind blowing over the open top makes a noise. It is said that mice can be deterred by 'companion-planting' with Spurge *(Euphorbia lactea, Euphorbia lathyrus* or Caper Spurge). It should be sown around the garden, one plant every six metres. I've also heard that mice don't like getting their feet dirty and a ring of soot around seedlings will keep them away!

Endangered Species

Do be careful when buying bulbs. Often these are gathered from the wild in vast quantities; so much so that they are becoming endangered species.

Don't encourage this trade. Always check that your bulbs come from a reputable supplier and are nursery-propagated. If in doubt buy a named variety, not the species, because you can be sure it has been nursery-bred.

Grown in Britain

If we decided to depend solely on crops that could be grown only in Britain, we could still manage as vegetarians but we would have a rather different diet from the one we enjoy now. We have come to take for granted the vast variety of products that is displayed on the supermarket shelves, and tend to think that we could not survive without them. Yet this excess is a comparatively new trend (except in the case of the very rich, who have always been able to import luxuries). Two hundred years ago, the average family in Britain would have lived on home-grown produce. Here is a list that could be grown in this country:

Cereals *Wheat, Barley, Oats, Rye.* No problems here, oats are probably the original cereal of our islands. The others have been in cultivation for centuries.

Nuts *Hazels, Walnuts.* Hazels used to be grown extensively in this country, but the acreage has declined in recent years. For example, in the South East the acreage has dwindled from 7,325 in 1913, to 732 in 1951, to about 150 in 1990. Nuts need a low input of pesticides. A tree has a useful cropping life of over 100 years and provides a refuge for native wildlife. If we are seriously 'green' we should be demanding more home-grown hazels, cobnuts and filberts (all the same family).

Pulses *Garden peas, broad beans, runner beans, yellow split peas, field peas.* Beans and peas are a traditional British crop so again, there is no problem, although our choice would be slightly more limited than at present.

Vegetables and salads *All the common Brassicas – cabbage, broccoli, sprouts, cauliflower, kale, calabrese. Potatoes, turnips, swedes, carrots, parsnips, beetroot, radish, onions, lettuce, watercress, land cress, celery, chives, Jerusalem artichoke, parsley, fennel, spinach, asparagus, chard, leeks, sweetcorn, many herbs like mint, thyme, marjoram, chervil, borage, sage, rhubarb* and, although not a table vegetable, *sugar beet.* Most of the vegetables commonly eaten in Britain can be grown here. Glasshouses would extend our choice even more.

Fruits *Apples, pears, cherries, plums, damsons, quinces, raspberries, greengages, strawberries, gooseberries, red and blackcurrants, rosehips, bilberries, elderberries, tayberries, loganberries.* We would miss citrus fruits, though rosehips and blackcurrants are very rich in Vitamin C. One problem is that our orchards have been run down in recent years.

Oil bearing seeds *Rape, flax.*

Seaweeds *Laver, dulse, carragheen.*

Crops that will grow in Britain given some protection   *Cucumbers, tomato, peppers, mushrooms, aubergines, marrows, peaches, apricots. Vines will grow in sheltered places, as will sweet chestnuts.*

Experimental crops Growers are currently experimenting with new crops which, if they prove successful, will considerably extend the range of crops available to British farmers and horticulturists. Many are oil-bearing seed crops with specialist applications, like Borage which yields an oil rich in gamma linolenic acid for medical use.

Of particular interest to vegetarians are:

Amaranth: Better known to the gardener as Love-lies-bleeding. The seeds of this plant are rich in carbohydrates and balanced proteins, yet contain no gluten. It has a protein content of 16% (compared to 14% for wheat) and unlike wheat, is rich in the essential amino acid lysine.

Quinoa: A distant cousin of our weed Fat Hen, it has been grown in the Andes for thousands of years. The first commercial British crops were harvested in 1989, and it can be found in some health food shops. It contains about 15% protein with a good balance of amino acids.

Other crops on trial are *sunflowers, chickpeas, lentils and buckwheat.*

Wild plants that are edible but not commonly eaten *Nettles, sloes, mushrooms, sorrel, Fat Hen (or Good King Henry), dandelion.*

Leaf Curd We could also expand our range of options by using leaf curd as a primary food. Leaf curd, produced by mechanically removing most of the fibre, is a way of concentrating nutrients. It is a good source of protein, beta carotene, iron, calcium, folic acid and Vitamin E and makes use of leaf crops not normally grown for human consumption in this country – nettles, swede and carrot tops, lupins, lucerne and clover.

Leaf curd production fits very nicely into a stockless system of farming. The plants used enhance a rotation of organically-grown crops – the juice left over can be used as a fertiliser, and the fibre residue can be composted. It is thought that leaf curd could replace imported soya to a large extent.

'Plants for a Future'

This is a vegan alternative plant project being carried out on 20 acres of land in Cornwall. It shows the very wide variety of plants that can be grown in this country – all with a contribution to make to human needs.

Emphasis is on perennial plants because they cause minimal soil disturbance, minimal environmental impact and minimal work. At present over 12,000 species are being grown. There is a register of useful plants, and a growing collection of plants for sale. Information from the register is freely available for all who wish to consult it. The aim is to show that a balanced and healthy diet is perfectly possible without recourse to either animal products or imported foods, because all we need can be grown in this climate. Visitors are welcome by prior arrangement.

Contact: A Morais & K Hennesey, The Field, Higher Penpoll, St Veep, near Lostwithiel, Cornwall, PL22 0NG. Tel: Bodmin (0208) 873554.

Grown in Europe

If we include food grown in European countries, we can extend our list to encompass: *Maize, Buckwheat, Almonds, Sweet Chestnuts, Pine Nuts, Pistachios, Sunflower, Flageolet Beans, Lentils, Olives, Citrus Fruits, Sweet Potatoes.*

Similarly, we could get soya beans, peanuts, dates, red kidney beans, navy beans, pinto beans, black-eyed beans, rice, wild rice, buckwheat, maize, pecan nuts, and many citrus fruits from the USA.

Virtually all edible plants have been carried by human agency to countries far from their original home. Unless foods are clearly labelled, giving the country in which the main ingredients were grown, not just where they were packed or processed, it is going to be very difficult to stick to any 'Britain-only,' or 'Europe-only' or 'developed-country-only' rule!

There are good arguments for encouraging the production of as much home-grown food as possible.

- The greater variety of crops is good for the environment and wildlife.
- The food is fresher when it arrives in the shop.
- It saves fuel used in transport, refrigeration and, possibly, avoids any need for irradiation.
- It provides jobs and is good for our balance of payments.

Britain could be much more self-reliant than it is now, as the war years proved. A vital corollary to this issue is the argument that modern methods of agriculture, with their emphasis on very large acreages of just a few crops are depleting fertility, causing soil erosion, loss of forests, and other environmental problems. The Permaculture Movement tries to redress this by designing integrated systems of housing and food production based on the concept that trees are very important, and so is diversity of species. Permaculture encourages the creation of a stable and self-reliant system of food production where materials and nutrients are recycled.

INFORMATION

Biodynamic Agriculture Association
Woodman Lane, Clent, Stourbridge, West Midlands, DY9 9PX. (0562) 884933. Promotes non-chemical agriculture, based on the indications of Rudolf Steiner, which includes the use of homoeopathic biodynamic preparations to enhance the forces of nature.

Country College
5 Roseberry Terrace, Frieze Hill, Taunton, Somerset, TA1 1EZ. Tel: (0823) 88232. Country College (founded 1977) is now offering a correspondence course in 'Health and Wholefood Diet' in addition to 'Organic Crop Production', and local classes. Contact Anthony Wigens.

Good Gardeners' Association
Arkley Manor Farm, Rowley Lane, Arkley, Barnet, Herts, EN5 3HS. (081) 449 7944. To foster and encourage the keen amateur gardener in organic growing without the use of poisonous chemicals. Supplying a variety of products grown under the Soil Association Symbol. Contact C R G Shewell-Cooper.

Henry Doubleday Research Association
Ryton Gardens, Ryton-on-Dunsmore, Coventry, CV8 3LG. Tel: (0203) 303517 National Centre for Organic Gardening, research and advice, the preservation of rare vegetables, biological pest control etc. Gardens open all year. Publishes the *Organic Food Guide*.

Organic Living Association
St Mary's Villa, Hanley Swan, Worcester, WR8 0EA. Promotes the production and consumption of organic foods; aims to improve awareness of nutrition and alternative medicine; encourages the establishment of ecological, self-sufficient villages.

Organic Farm Foods
Unit C, Hanworth Trading Estate, Hampton Road West, Hanworth, Feltham, Middlesex. Tel: (081) 755 2401 Distribution centre for organically-grown produce, including free-range eggs. SAE for list of stockists. Also cash and carry for private customers. Soil Association standards where possible.

The Soil Association
86 Colston Street, Bristol, BS1 5BB. Tel: (0272) 290661
Promotes the knowledge and practice of organic husbandry for health, nutrition, and a balanced environment, within a holistic philosophy.

Working Weekends on Organic Farms (WWOOF)
19 Bradford Road, Lewes, Sussex, BN7 1RB. Tel: (027347) 6286
If you want to try working on an organic farms, send SAE to this address. Mention that you are a vegetarian, as they have vegetarian farmers on their lists.

Farm Hands
Croes Philip, St David's, Pembrokeshire, Dyfed, SA62 6PU. Tel: (0437) 720768
Farm Hands (Smallholders' Holiday Exchange) provides a nationwide holiday relief service for smallholders.Alternatively, the Smallholders' Holiday Exchange Scheme exists for those preferring to try a 'busman's holiday'.

The Organic Food Manufacturers Federation
20 Princes Rd, Bromham, Bedford MK43 3QD

The Good Gardeners Association
Two Mile Lane, Gloucester, GL2 8DW

Farm Verified Organic Info Centre
86 Easton St, High Wycombe, Bucks HP11 1LT

Natural Pest Control
Yapton Road, Barnham, Bognor Regis, W Sussex (this is a commercial company!)

National Centre for Alternative Technology
Llwyngwern Quarry, Machynlleth, Powys. Tel: (0654) 2400.

Organic Farmers and Growers
Abacus House, Station Yard, Needham Market, Ipswich, Suffolk, IP6 8AT. Tel: (0449) 720838.

Parents for Safe Food
Britannia House, 1-11 Glenthorne Road, Hammersmith, London, W6 OLS.

UKROFS (organic produce standard)
c/o Food from Britain, 301-344 Market Towers, New Convent Garden Market, London, SW8 5NQ.

Farmers Third World Network
The Arthur Rank Centre, National Agriculture Centre, Stoneleigh, Warwickshire, CV8 2LZ.

The Permaculture Association (UK)
8 Hunters Moon, Dartington, Totnes, Devon, TQ9 6JT. Tel: (0803) 867546.

Movement for Compassionate Living (vegan)
47 Highlands Road, Leatherhead, Surrey, KT22 8NQ.
They publish a booklet *Sustaining and Sustainable* at 60p.

Find your Feet
Information about leaf curd. 318 St Paul's Road, London, N1 2LF.

Veganic Garden Suppliers
AE Barwick, Weavers Way, Heath Farm Rd, Worstead, Norfolk NR28 9AH

Springhill Farm Foods Ltd
PO Box 463, Portslade, BN4 1AJ

Peatlands Campaign
RSNC, 22 The Green, Nettleham, Lincoln

Chase Organics
Coombelands, Addlestone, Surrey KT15 1HY

Veganic Gardening
> by Kenneth Dalziel O'Brien, Thorsons
> Veganic gardening depends entirely on products of vegetable and natural mineral origin,
> combined with a special no-digging technique and natural weed control without poisons.

Organic Gardening Magazine
> PO Box 4, Wiveliscombe, Taunton, Somerset TA4 2QY.

Planning the Organic Vegetable Garden
> Dick Kitto

Planning the Organic Herb Garden
> Sue Stickland

Planning the Organic Flower Garden
> Sue Stickland

Green Gardeners Handbook
> Elphinstone & Langley

Forest Garden
> book available from the Institute for Social Inventions, 24 Abercorn Place, London, NW8 9PX.

An A to Z of Fresh Fruit & Veg
> The Ethical Consumer, no 7, £2. 00. ECRA Publishing, 100 Gretney Walk, Manchester, M15 5ND.

Medicines and alternative therapies

Many people turn to vegetarianism for health reasons, and there is no doubt that a vegetarian diet is both healthy and humane. It has even been suggested that vegetarians have greater peace of mind because they are convinced that their diet is free from unnecessary cruelty. This peace of mind can have a marked effect on health, as many illnesses can be brought on or exacerbated by a pessimistic outlook.

To live a full and fullfilling life, it is essential that we all take responsibility for our own health. We know that smoking, eating red meat and animal fats, and taking too little exercise can damage our quality of life. To a very great extent, our health and happiness are in our own hands.

Many vegetarians become interested in alternative medicine and therapies because they are determined to find natural solutions to their own health problems; they wish to make use of a treatment which seems to be more personal to them. Many 'alternative' therapies involve treating the patient's state of mind, as well as his or her physical symptoms. Some say that one of the reasons behind the success of 'alternative' medicines is that they can induce a more positive outlook from the patient.

Another reason for considering 'alternative' medicines is that the vast majority of medical drugs has been repeatedly tested on animals. Although it may be very unwise to dismiss conventional medical treatments out of hand, there are often cases where very minor illnesses or discomfort can be successfully treated without recourse to strong drugs. Alternative treatments have gained credibility over hundreds of years. Often they originate from countries whose cultures are more open to the concept of the link between body, mind and spirit than the modern West.

There are hundreds of books on the market on all kinds of alternative therapies – from simple personal treatments like stress management and meditation, to complicated treatments such as acupuncture, which must only be administered by trained professionals. Although there *are* practitioners who can achieve good results without being qualified, contacting the regulating body for the type of therapy which you find particularly interesting can save difficulties in the long run. The regulating organisations (of which there is a list at the back of this book) may also be able to give advice if you are interested in learning more about becoming an alternative practitioner yourself. It can be a wonderfully fulfilling way of helping other people.

For names and addresses of alternative health clinics, see the Classified Advertisement pages of your favourite health magazine. Good sources of information include *The Vegetarian Magazine, Here's Health, Homoeopathy Today, Yoga and Health* and the *Journal of Complementary Medicine*. Not every health clinic views vegetarianism as a priority – it is not necessarily a foregone conclusion that they will be exclusively vegetarian. Make sure that they can cater for your needs.

Medicines and supplements – things to look out for

Amino Acids May have been derived from animals. Crop up in bodybuilding supplements, slimming formulae.

B$_{12}$ See nutrition section. B$_{12}$ is generally obtained from meat such as desiccated liver, although vegetarians can find alternative sources.

Calcium Check source. May be derived from animal bones, but in general is from a mineral source such as chalk.

Capsules Oddly enough, this is about the only area that most health food shops fall down on. All capsules, hard and soft, are currently made from gelatine. Research continues to seek an alternative, but until a vegetarian capsule can be found, health food stores seem to make an exception for this non-vegetarian item. Look for alternatives – tablets, liquids, drops.

DNA Sometimes crops up in supplements, may be animal-derived.

Insulin A very difficult dilemma for vegetarians who are diabetic, as insulin is generally from an animal source. There is also a synthetic source – check with the British Diabetic Association.

Oestrogen A female hormone which can be used in hormone replacement therapy, cosmetics and body building supplements.

Prescriptions Medicines on prescription have usually been tested on animals repeatedly, and may contain animal ingredients. This is very difficult to check.

Progesterone A female hormone, sometimes obtained from the urine of a pregnant mare, used in hormone creams.

Royal Jelly A food produced by worker bees for the queen bee, recently 'discovered' as an 'anti-ageing' supplement, sometimes crops up in cosmetics but generally in capsules as a supplement. Not considered to be suitable for vegetarians by some, because of the cruelty involved.

Stearates Meat industry by-product used in bodybuilding supplements.

Steroids Possibly animal-based. Used in bodybuilding and for the treatment of certain chronic illnesses.

Testosterone The male hormone – used in bodybuilding supplements and hormone therapy. May be animal-derived.

Homoeopathic Most homoeopathic medicines readily available from health food stores come in the form of little white pills that melt on your tongue. These pills are unfortunately not suitable for vegans because they are made with lactose, a milk sugar. Practising homoeopathic doctors may be able to offer an alternative. Some homoeopathic remedies contain animal products, such as snake venom. Apis Mel is the remedy which is made with stings taken from bees, although apparently the bees are already dead.

Immunisation Another tricky area. Animal testing will almost certainly have been involved. Some countries insist that foreign visitors are vaccinated against certain illnesses before they arrive in the country.

The Pill The development of the contraceptive pill will have involved animal experimentation, and the source of the hormones used is not clear. There is some concern over the health risks involved in using the Pill over a long period. In the past there have been some doubts expressed over the effectiveness of the pill for vegetarian users. The Vegetarian Society understands that the vegetarian diet can alter the ability to digest and absorb foods through the stomach wall. However, the efficacy of the pill is very unlikely to be affected and this should not be a cause for alarm. If you are a vegetarian on a low-dose pill and suffer unexpected bleeding, you should contact your doctor who will probably prescribe a different pill with a higher dose.

A balanced vegetarian diet should provide all the essential vitamins and minerals that you need. Many supplement pills contain minute quantities of animal-derived ingredients such as Vitamin D_3, and fillers such as stearic acid. Gelatine capsules are not considered to be suitable for vegetarians. There are many of special supplements formulated for vegetarians on the market now – check the label, and also to see if the label indicates that the product has been tested on animals.

There is a list of medicines and remedies authorised to use the Vegetarian Society's ⋎ symbol at the back of the book.

Related issues

> *The individual path to vegetarianism often starts from some other issue... concern about experiments on animals, for example. Similarly, people who become vegetarians for reasons of their own personal health and welfare usually become actively concerned about the well-being of animals and of the environment.*

The Vegetarian Society often receives letters asking for information about Animal Rights – what to do to stop hunting taking place, how to avoid dissecting animals at school, where to find a local homoeopathic doctor. Although we are not specialists in any of these fields, we work closely with related organisations and have a very wide range of contacts. The best solution to any query is to go straight to the experts – and if The Vegetarian Society cannot help directly, we usually know somebody who can!

This section is intended both to answer queries and to stimulate an interest in issues which are often quite closely related to the vegetarian lifestyle. Very often interest in one field can lead to involvement in another. Look back at the reasons that caused Vegetarian Society staff to become vegetarians. You will notice that Christine Tilbury, our Cookery School Tutor, first became interested in the subject when she read a leaflet from Beauty Without Cruelty about the unnecessary suffering caused to animals by tests on cosmetics. Bronwen Humphries our Branch Liaison Officer was a student of agriculture with a keen interest in the causes of and solutions to famine in the Third World when she first made the connection with vegetarianism.

The connection seems to work both ways. New vegetarians move on to considering avoiding products that have been tested on animals, or considering alternatives to conventional medicines. People who are involved in campaigning to protect the environment or prevent cruelty to animals may go on to become vegetarians.

Animal rights

There are all kinds of Animal Rights groups operating in the UK. Some protest actively while others work to change laws and educate the public about animal abuse. Some publish magazines. The following addresses may be of use to vegetarians who wish to take their involvement with Animal Rights further.

Animal Aid
7 Castle St
Tonbridge
Kent, TN9 1BH
(0732) 364546

As well as alerting the public to the horrors of animal abuse in factory farms, slaughterhouses and vivisection laboratories, Animal Aid highlights the many alternatives to animal suffering, encouraging a cruelty-free lifestyle.

Animaline
P. O. Box 10
Ryde, Isle of Wight
PO33 1JX
(0983) 616980 (Office)
(0898) 444033 (Inf.)

The aims of Animaline are: to promote a positive relationship between man and animals, and to educate the public into an awareness that the suffering caused to animals is a) unneccessary, b) something which we all have the power to influence. Individuals are encouraged to adopt a humane lifestyle, a vegetarian diet etc.

Animal Rights Movement (N. I.)
3 Donegal Street
Belfast, BT1 2FF
(0232) 240671

Campaigns peacefully but forcefully against all forms of animal abuse through education, protests, political lobbying and the compiling of information on all aspects of animal exploitation.

Animals Vigilantes
James Mason House
24 Salisbury Street
Fordingbridge, Hants
(0425) 53663

Their work involves the education of young people in the care and welfare of animals and the teaching of respect for all life.

Artists For Animals
P O Box 18
South PDO, Manchester
M14 5NB

"Through the use of exciting and innovative music and art we raise public awareness to all forms of animal abuse. For lists of AFA records, merchandise and events, send SAE."

The Athene Trust
3a Charles Street
Petersfield, Hants
GU32 3EH
(0730) 68070

An educational charity promoting harmony between humanity, animals and the environment. Educational resources list available, with details of videos/books etc. for all age groups.

Beauty Without Cruelty (Charity)
11 Limehill Road
Tunbridge Wells
Kent, TN1 1LJ
(0892) 25587

Beauty Without Cruelty campaigns against the exploitation of animals for vanity e.g. the fur trade; and the testing of cosmetics on animals.

Captive Animals' Protection Society
36 Braemore Court
Kingsway
Hove, East Sussex
BN3 4FG.

Campaigns against the inclusion of performing animals in circuses. Non-stop press panel circulates local councils asking them to refuse sites to circuses.

Care for the Wild
26 North Street
Horsham
West Sussex, RH12 1BN
(0403) 50557/56641

Opposed to bloodsports. Works to stop suffering of wildlife and to protect its habitat. Educates the public, particularly young people, in the care of wildlife and environment.

Crusade Against All Cruelty to Animals
Avenue Lodge
Bounds Green Road
London, N22 4EU
(081) 889 1595

Founded in 1955 to promote humane and ethical standards of behaviour towards the animal kingdom.

Pagan Animal Rights
23 Highfield South
Rock Ferry, Wirrall
L42 4NA
(051) 645 0485

Works to promote respect and love for Mother Earth and all her creatures, and uses meditative and magical techniques to this end.

Quaker Concern for Animal Welfare
Webb's Cottage, Saling
Braintree, Essex
CM7 5DZ

Quaker Concern exists to encourage members of the Society of Friends (Quakers) to witness against the cruel exploitation of animals.

RSPCA
The Manor House
Causeway, Horhsam
West Sussex, RH12 1HG
(0403) 64181

The Society deals with many animal welfare issues, including animal experimentation, farm animals, and wildlife.

Student Campaign For Animal Rights
Mandela Building
99 Oxford Road
Manchester

Our aim is to promote, amongst the student population, an awareness of animal abuse and to encourage students to campaign against such abuse, particularly that relevant to them in their colleges.

Teachers for Animal Rights
29 Lynwood Road
London, SW17 8SB

Committed to sharing young people's attitudes towards animals through the educational system. Information pack dealing with dissection, meals, literature, classroom animals, available.

Universities Federation for Animal Welfare
8 Hamilton Close
South Mimms
Herts,EN6 3QD
(0707) 58202

UFAW, an educational charity concerned with the welfare of animals symposia/workshops and publishes books on the care of animals. SAE for list.

World Society for the Protection of Animals
106 Jermyn Street
London,SW1Y 6EE
(071) 839 3026/66

WSPA works to protect all animal life and is the world's widest ranging animal protection society, having over 300 member humane organisations around the world.

Zoo Check Trust
Cherry Tree Cottage
Coldharbour, Dorking,
Surrey, RH5 6HA
(0306) 712091

Dedicated to conservation, education and anti-cruelty to animals. Seeks to find alternatives to the zoological collection in order to educate people and keep wildlife in the wild.

Wildlife

Animals in the wild need our support and protection. They are subjected to bloodsports and unlawful killing; can often be trapped or poisoned by rubbish and pollution; and sometimes lose their home environments when land is cleared for building.

Most of the general Animal Rights organisations mentioned earlier can supply more information. The following is a list of more specialised groups.

Elefriends, 162 Boundaries Road, London, SW12 8HG

Swan Rescue Service Europe, Shotesham St Mary, Norwich, Norfolk, NR15 1XX

Care for the Wild, 26 North Street, Horsham, W Sussex, RH12 1BN

Wirral & Cheshire Badger Group, P O Box 19, Warrington, WA2 8TG

Nature Conservancy Council, Northminster House, Peterborough PE1 1UA

Whale & Dolphin Conservation Society, 20 West Lea Rd, Bath BA1 3RL

British Hedgehog Preservation Society, St Tiggywinkles, 1 Pemberton Close, Aylesbury, Bucks MP21 7NY

Dartmoor Badgers Protection League
Riverside Cottage, Poundsgate, Newton Abbott, Devon, TQ13 7NU

The DBPL is Britain's only national badger group. It campaigns against badger slaughter by the MInistry of Agriculture, diggers and the destruction of badger habitat.

Sea Shepherd
UK Marine Conservation Soc., P. O. Box 5, Ashford, Middlesex, TW15 2PR

Direct action marine mammal protection and conservation group.

Peoples Trust for Endangered Species, Hamble House, Meadrow, Godalming, Surrey GU7 3JX

Hunting & bloodsports

'Sport' is a strange word to choose for activities which involve the purposeless killing of defenceless animals. Everybody should be joining the campaign to ban bloodsports, without reservation. Examples of these so-called sports which still go on in this country are fox hunting, dog fighting, cock fighting, badger baiting, stag hunting and hare coursing.

Although most people would not immediately think of it, angling is another occupation which involves pointless animal suffering. The ethics involved in many other sports in which we use animals for human enjoyment or for gambling, such as horse racing (particularly over fences), show that jumping and dog racing are also dubious.

World Society for the Protection of Animals
106 Jermyn St, London SW1Y 6EE

Korean dog campaign
Bullfighting
Chimps for photos

Campaign For The Abolition Of Angling
P. O. Box 14
Sevenoaks
Kent TN14 5NR

The CAA is a campaigning organisation dedicated solely to bringing about the demise of the bloodsport of angling. It produces a range of information sheets, merchandise and a quarterly newsletter – *Pisces*

Hunt Saboteurs Association
P. O. Box 1, Carlton
Nottingham, NG4 2JY

Aims to save the lives of animals pursued in the name of sport (angling, shooting, hunting) through the use of non-violent direct action.

International Council against Bullfighting 106 Jermyn Street London SW1Y 6EE (071) 839 3066	Merged with the World Society for the Protection of Animals in 1984.
Irish Council Against Blood Sports 31 Endsleigh, Douglas Cork, Ireland (021) 292197	Aims to secure the imposition of a ban on all bloodsports, especially hare-coursing and fox-hunting, through political lobbying, letter writing, and lively protest pickets.
League Against Cruel Sports Ltd 83-87 Union Street London, SE1 1SG (071) 407 0979	The League's primary aim is to persuade Parliament to enact legislation to protect wild animals from cruelty – particularly that involved in the hunting of foxes, deer, hares etc. with dogs. The League also purchases land (to date 36 sanctuaries totalling 2,500 acres) where wildlife can find refuge from the hunt. (*Outfoxed* Mike Huskisson £4. 50)

Fur and leather

Lynx is the best known organisation campaigning against the wearing of fur. Its campaigns are widely known and very successful – I doubt if there are many intelligent people in Britain today who would buy a fur coat. Killing animals by trapping or factory-farming them for fur is an utterly pointless pursuit, kept afloat purely by people with more money than sense. It is estimated that about 400 million animals are killed for the fur trade every year – the vast majority taken from factory farms. Animals which are caged for their fur include foxes, mink and rabbits. Although it is estimated that 38 million animals are trapped in the wild for fur every year, this figure does not take into account millions more 'trash' animals, such as domestic pets, owls, hedgehogs, ducks and swans which are killed by indiscriminate traps. Lynx can tell you everything you need to know about fur.

Lynx, P. O. Box 300, Nottingham, NG1 5HN

They have a shop in Convent Garden (79 Long Acre), and regularly run hard-hitting advertising campaigns and a 'fur amnesty' in which people are encouraged to give up their fur coats.

Many people make the decision to stop using and wearing leather, which they see as being similar to fur. Leather is a by-product of the meat industry. To some extent sales of leather support the meat trade. Many people feel uncomfortable wearing the skins of animals when they have made the decision to stop eating them. Vegans do their best to live a cruelty-free lifestyle by refusing to use any animal products whatsoever, and this includes wearing leather, silk and wool.

The Vegan Society can advise on alternatives to leather products. When looking for alternatives, it is important to bear in mind that some synthetic leathers and plastics are not biodegradable. The manufacturing process involves heavy consumption of fossil fuels and can contribute to pollution. Try to find canvas and cotton alternatives. The Vegetarian Society produces a list of non-leather shoes including sports shoes – however, a good browse around the shops should turn up some reasonable choices.

A campaign to highlight the similarity between fur and leather has been launched by CALF – the Campaign Against Leather and Fur.

CALF, Box 17, 198 Blackstock Road, London N5

Duck and goose down is also usually a by-product of the slaughterhouse. The only major exception is true Eider down. The female Eider duck plucks down from her own body to make a soft lining for her nest. After the nests have been used, they are collected and the down is sold as Eider down. The process is expensive and Eider down is not easy to find in High Street shops.

Once you become interested in trying to avoid buying slaughterhouse products such as fur, leather and feathers, there are all kinds of stumbling blocks to look out for.

Leather – manufacturers sometimes use the real leather symbol to make it easy for us to see leather at a glance. However, look out for things like chamois car cleaning cloths, crocodile skin belts, bags and jewellery, lizard and snakeskin, parchment and vellum which are made from animal skin. Books, sports equipment and some musical instruments are made with leather.

Fur – look out for it on children's toys and as 'lucky rabbit's foot' charms.

Wool – Angora, cashmere, felt, Persian lamb, mohair. Also look out for hair, in the form of shaving brushes, camel-hair coats, and furniture stuffing.

Feathers – crop up in bedding, and sometimes on hats. Quills are sometimes used in calligraphy, but these can usually be picked up from the ground.

Ivory – is almost universally condemned but it still appears in the decorative inlay of wooden boxes and furniture, and sometimes chessmen are made from ivory. Old cutlery handles and the keys on old pianos are likely to be made from ivory or bone. Bone china is actually made using animal bones, this helps to give it a translucent quality.

Silk – for clothing cannot usually be obtained unless cocoons can be unravelled unbroken. The silk worm, which makes the cocoon so that it can change into a silk moth, is killed by boiling or gas before it can escape from the cocoon. Silk is also used in some cosmetics and skin/hair care products.

Shells – are not always found on the beach – they can be taken by killing the sea creatures that live inside them. Some people may prefer not to buy ornamental shells, mother of pearl or capiz lampshades. Pearls are obtained by killing the oyster which produces them. Natural sponges are obtained from sea animals.

It is surprising how animal products are collected in the home. Some people have lucky charms made from sharks teeth, collections of dead butterflies or empty eggs, even whole stuffed animals and birds.

Beeswax – is used in furniture and floor polishes, and sometimes used to make candles. Candles can also be made from tallow, an animal fat obtained from the slaughterhouse. Many soaps are also made from this kind of animal fat.

Photography cannot be done without using gelatine, a slaughterhouse by-product, during the film processing. There may be alternatives in the future involving putting photographs onto a compact disc. Gelatine is also commonly used to coat paper to create a smooth writing surface and some DIY papermaking kits are sold with a packet of gelatine crystals.

Animal experiments / Vivisection

Every year more than 3 million animals suffer and die in British laboratories. They are burnt, blinded, poisoned, starved, given electric shocks and infected with disease. Most experiments are carried out by commercial concerns, and products tested include: household products, drugs, pesticides, food additives and industrial chemicals. But now, more than ever before, people are challenging the scientists' traditional 'right' to use animals as the disposable tools of research, calling instead for a more civilised and compassionate approach. The medieval idea that lives can be saved only by sacrificing others must be rejected.

Ethical objections are strongly reinforced by scientific arguments because people and animals are different in the way their bodies work and in their response to drugs. The finding that chimpanzees do not develop AIDS when inoculated with HIV illustrates the problem. In fact reliance on misleading animal tests can have devastating consequences for human health: the failure to induce lung cancer in animals by forcing them to inhale cigarette smoke cast doubt on human clinical findings and delayed health warnings for years, costing thousands of lives.

More could be achieved by switching resources to methods of direct relevance to people – such as human population studies, clinical investigation of patients actually suffering from the disease, and test tube experiments with human tissues derived from biopsy and post mortem samples. But with powerful vested interests at stake, public pressure will be essential to ensure that medical research concentrates on the study of people, and that alternative tests no longer remain underdeveloped. (Dr Robert Sharpe).

TESTED – Did you know?

These are a few of the products that we use every day that are commonly tested on animals. Review your purchasing habits and look for alternative products: cigarettes, hair colour and perming lotions, detergents, fabric conditioner, toothpaste, washing powder, pesticides and gardening chemicals, glues, household cleaning products, cosmetics and toiletries, food additives, aerosol sprays, weapons.

The words 'NEW', 'IMPROVED' and 'ADVANCED', and the phrases 'SCIENTIFICALLY TESTED', 'DERMATICOLOGICALLY TESTED' AND 'LABORATORY TESTED' can all mean that the product has been tested on animals.

The BUAV (British Union Against Vivisection) produces a booklet which lists cosmetics, toiletries and household cleaning products that have not been tested on animals. Vegetarians and vegans should also question the actual ingredients of such products, as they may come from animal sources. The BUAV leaflet lists vegetarian and vegan products separately.

The following products are licensed to carry the Vegetarian Society's ϒ Symbol: **Weleda UK Ltd.**, Plant gel toothpaste, salt toothpaste, calendula toothpaste, herbal toothpaste. **Maxim Pharmaceuticals**, Amber Toothpaste. **Homecare Products**, microwave plus, hob brite cream cleanser, shiny sinks cream cleanser, copper glow powder cleanser, bar keeper's friend powder cleaner. **Astley Dye & Chemical Co Ltd.**, ACDO soap powders.

Vivisection books

Against all Odds – £1. 95
What is Vivisection/BUAV – £2. 50
Victims of Science/Richard Ryder – £3. 75
The Cruel Deception/Dr Robert Sharpe – £7. 99
The Military Abuse of Animals/BUAV, Bruce Kent – £1. 20
The Animal Liberation Movement/Peter Singer – £1. 10
Up Against the Law – £1. 50
Men and Beasts/Maureen Duffy – £1. 95
Slaughter of the Innocent/hans Reusch – £3. 50
The Use and Abuse of Animals/Zoe Watson – £6. 50
Assault and Battery/Mark Gold – £4. 25

British Union for the Abolition of Vivisection
16a Crane Grove
Islington N7 8LB
(071) 700 4888

BUAV actively campaigns for an end to all animal experiments. All members receive a bi-monthly magazine *Liberator*. Network of local contacts around Britain which organises events in support of national campaigns.

The Dr. Hadwen Trust for Humane Research
6c Brand Street, Hitchin
Herts, SG5 1HX
(0462) 36819

For the promotion of the development of humane alternatives to animal experiments in medical and scientific research. No animals are made to suffer in our research programmes.

FRAME (Fund for the Replacement of Animals in Medical Experiments)
Eastgate House
34 Stoney Street
Nottingham, NG1 1NB
(0602) 584740

FRAME seeks to eliminate the requirement for laboratory animals currently used in biomedical research and toxicity testing by developing, evaluating and promoting alternative techniques.

The Humane Research Trust
Brook House
29 Bramhall Lane South
Bramhall, Cheshire, SK7 2DN
(061)439 8041

Promotes research into alternatives to animal experiments.

DAARE – Disabled Against Animal Research & Exploitation
P. O. Box 8, Daventry
Northants, NN11 4QR

National Anti-Vivisection Society Ltd
51 Harley Street
London, W1N 1DD
(071) 580 4034/631 0612

Works to bring about the abolition of vivisection within the law by educational and active means, and to support measures leading to eventual abolition.

Nurses Against Vivisection
2 Hillcrest, Bonsall
Derbyshire, DE4 2AW
(062982) 4664

Nurses Against Vivisection opposes without compromise all animal experiments. Membership is open to qualified nurses with associate membership for student nurses.

Scottish Anti-Vivisection Society
121 West Regent Street
Glasgow, G2 2SD
(041) 221 2300

Committed to the total abolition of vivisection and the promotion and recognition of Animal Rights.

Scottish Society for the Prevention of Vivisection
10 Queensferry Street
Edinburgh, EH2 4PG
(031) 225 6039

For the protection of animals from cruelty, the prevention of the infliction of suffering and the abolition of vivisection.

Cosmetics

In previous years the *Vegetarian Handbook* has attempted to list cosmetics and toiletries which are suitable for vegetarians. By this we mean that the products have not been tested on animals, and do not contain any slaughterhouse ingredients. There has been much welcome publicity recently over the issue of animal testing and cosmetics – many people feel that although they are unable to say for sure that animals should not be used for the testing of medical drugs, it is a pointless waste of life to test cosmetics on animals. Many manufacturers are ceasing to test on animals. One wonders whether this is because of a genuine concern for animals or merely a marketing ploy.

Some of the ingredients used in modern cosmetics can be dangerous. It is for this reason that the manufacturer tests them on animals. It makes you wonder why, if these ingredients are so dangerous, should anybody really want to smear them on their face?

The British Union Against Vivisection (see section of vivisection) is the expert on products which are not tested on animals, and hold comprehensive records on the subject. For this reason, I recommend their booklet on cosmetics and toiletries which are not tested on animals. The listing divides into three sections – vegan products, vegetarian products, and products which contain slaughter-house ingredients but are not tested on animals. Phone BUAV on 071 700 4888 and ask for their free *Approved Product Guide*.

Animal ingredients found in cosmetics

Dr Gill Langley has supplied information on alternatives to animal testing for cosmetics through her work with the Dr. Hadwen Trust for Humane Research.

Dr Langley also looked into the slaughterhouse ingredients which you may not be aware find their way into 'Beauty' products. How could you know, when there is no law concerning the labelling these products?

One book about cosmetics that makes interesting reading, but is not particularly aimed at vegetarian readers is *Cover Up* by Penny Chorlton (Thorsons).

Collagen – a slaughterhouse product made from animal connective tissue. Used in moisturising creams to help the skin to retain moisture, in hair conditioners to add 'body', and in some bath products.
Fatty Acids – another slaughterhouse ingredient, although these are sometimes derived from a vegetable source.
Glycerine/Glycerol and glycerol compounds – can be from the slaughterhouse or from vegetable sources. Used as an emollient (skin softner) in creams and lotions. Vegetable emollients include avocado oil and jojoba oil.

Keratin – animal protein which can be from wool or from the slaughter-house. Used in hair conditioner and nail conditioner.

Lanolin – 'Wool Wax', an emollient and emulsifier made from the natural grease found on sheep wool. Often found in lipsticks.

Reticulin – animal protein from the slaughterhouse, used in moisturisers.

Shellac – a kind of glue secreted by insects, used in lip sealer and hair spray.

Silk – It is uncertain whether gathering of silk from the cocoons of silk worms involves killing the worms before they hatch out as silk moths. Silk is used in products for moisturising and conditioning the skin and hair, in styling mousses for hair, and in some face powders and eye shadows.

Squalene/squalane – squalene is obtained either from olive oil or from shark liver oil, and hydrogenated to become 'squalane', which is used all over the place – in rouge, creams, moisturisers and sun tan preparations.

Stearic acid/stearates – Usually from the slaughterhouse although there is a vegetable source. Used as emollients (skin softeners) in creams and lotions, also in lipsticks, pressed powders, cream shampoos. Some stea-rates are used as emulsifiers and solubilisers for fragrances.

Tallow compounds – always from the slaughterhouse, for example tallow ammonium ethosulphate, an emulsifier, and sodium carboxymethyl tallow, a surfactant (has a detergent effect).

Chitin – from shrimp and crab shells, chemically treated to form chitosan, which is used as a thickener in shampoos, conditioners and skin care products. As it binds to our skin and hair, it has a moisturising effect.

Elastin – animal protein from the slaughterhouse. Has film-forming prop-erties and can be used as a moisturiser.

Milk protein and beeswax are also used in cosmetics. These would not be acceptable to vegans.

Environment

All the television programmes and magazine articles about our environment seem to have turned into stories of gloom and doom. There is no getting away from the fact that we have to act now – the planet has serious problems which could drastically affect the lives of all of us. Vegetarianism can help.

Here are a few simple things you could be doing: Recycle glass, paper, and aluminium. Don't use aerosol cans, even if they are CFC-free they are energy-intensive to produce and non-biodegradable. Buy recycled products where possible. Install a water filtration system.

British Trust for Conservation Volunteers
36 St Marys Street
Wallingford,
Oxon, OX10 0EU
(0491) 39766

The BTCV is the country's leading organisation involved in practical conservation in both urban and rural areas. Each year over 55,000 volunteers are equipped and trained to tackle hundreds of environmental projects.

Council for Environmental Education
School of Education
University of Reading
London Road, Reading, RG1 5AQ
(0734) 875234 Ext 218

Promotes environmental education and encourages communi-cation between member organisations and others interested in environmental education. Provides an advice and informa-tion service. Send S.A.E. for further information.

Council for the Protection Of Rural England
25 Buckingham Palace Rd
London SW1W 0PP
Voluntary body, with 44 county branches and 30,000 members, seeking to protect the rural landscape and the amenities of the countryside. Annual Report and members magazine *Countryside Campaigner.*

Environmental Investigation Agency Ltd
40 Bowling Green Lane
London, EC1
(071) 833 1493
Undertakes campaigns to protect wildlife such as pilot whales in the Faroes, investigating the trade in live wild animals, especially primates and birds, and investigates the illegal ivory trade to protect Africa's elephants.

Friends of the Earth
26-28 Underwood Street
London N1 7JQ
A campaigning pressure group and major force behind today's Green Movement. It is now running 10 major campaigns including Countryside, Agriculture and Pesticides.

Greenpeace
30 -31 Islington Green
London, N1 8XE
(01) 354 5100
Greenpeace is an independent and international environmental pressure group which actively campaigns against issues of abuse to the natural world including toxic pollution, release of radioactivity and the endangering of wildlife

Common Ground, 45 Shelton St, Covent Garden, London, WC2H 9HJ

Women's Environmental Network, 287 City Road, London EC1V 1LA

Men of the Trees, Turners Hill Rd, Crawley Down, Crawley, W Sussex RH10 4HL

The Ark Trust, 498-500 Harrow Road, London W9 3QA

Green Living

What is 'Green Living'? It is a blanket term to cover all those ethical 'green' concerns faced by the concerned vegetarian. Vegetarians are often attracted by alternative lifestyles and by 'green' ideas. Green living has got to be one of the biggest movements of the decade, and this is not the place to go into depth about the issues and ethics. There are many books about 'going green' available now, one of the most useful being John Button's *Green Pages* which is about the same size as a telephone book and makes fascinating reading!

Anthroposophical Society in Great Britain
Rudolf Steiner House
35 Park Road
London, NW1 6XT
(071) 723 4400
Centre for the work of Rudolf Steiner. Publishes *Anthroposophy Today* and *The Golden Blade.* Lectures, study groups, artistic activities, library, bookshop.

Green Party
10 Station Parade
Balham High Road
London, SW12 9AZ
(071) 673 0045
A political party aiming to create a sustainable life style. Campaigns on all issues – from environment and nuclear industries, to social, economic and Human Rights matters. Contests elections at all levels.

One World Week
P. O. Box 1
London, SW9 8BH
(071) 733 5500
Annual (October) focus for study and action on issues of justice, peace and world development. Organised and run locally with materials and support from national office.

Traidcraft
Kingsway
Gateshead, NE11 ONE
(091) 4873191

As an Alternative Trading Company, they sell a range of foods and other products from developing countries, from sources benefitting ordinary working people.

Women's Environmental Network, 287 City Road, London EC1V ILA

SustainAbility, 49 Princes Place, London W11 4QA

Human Rights

Animal welfare and human welfare are inextricably linked. While humans cope with grinding poverty, filthy living conditions and famine, it is not surprising that animals will suffer. Until a reasonable standard of living is available to everybody, animal rights are inevitably a secondary consideration.

Vegetarians are sometimes criticised for caring more about animals than they do about their fellow human beings. This should never be allowed to happen. The Hindu concept of 'Ahimsa' may be summed up as an ideal of non-violence which applies equally to treatment of humans and of animals. Many people believe that vegetarianism is an essential prerequisite of a non-violent lifestyle. How can we renounce violence towards mankind if we continue to perpetrate violence of all kinds against animals?

What do we mean by Human Rights? You may be surprised when you realise how basic are the freedoms and rights which have to be fought for in less fortunate countries than our own. Reading a copy of the *Universal Declaration of Human Rights* can be very enlightening. For your copy send a S.A.E. and a donation to Amnesty International.

Amnesty International
99-101 Roseberry Ave.
London EC1R 4RE

Amnesty works very hard to end imprisonment without trial all over the world.

CND
22-24 Underwood St.
London N1 7JG

If you are concerned about violence towards animals, you might be interested in helping to stop violence against mankind through the use of nuclear weapons.

There is information about how vegetarianism can help solve the world food problem in the first section of this book. There are several relief projects which try to send vegetarian or vegan food to famine struck countries, and to encourage starving people to aim at developing their agriculture towards a vegetarian or vegan output.

Enough, London House, Queens Road, Freshwater, Isle Of Wight, PO40 9EP

Vegfam, The Sanctuary, Lydford, Oakehampton, Devon, EX20 4AL

Green Deserts Ltd., Rougham, Bury St Edmunds, Suffolk, IP30 9LY

Sunseed Desert Technology, 100 Norfolk Street, Cambridge, CB1 2LF

Harvest Help, Freepost, London N1 2BR

The E numbers list

Compiled with the assistance of Dr Erik Millstone

Recent legislation on food labelling made provision for a list of serial numbers that are still used to identify certain food additives. Numbers approved by the EEC have an 'E' prefix, those without this prefix have only been approved in the UK.

It is generally considered best to try to avoid any foods which contain additives – vegetarians might be especially interested to find out which E number additives are derived from an animal source.

Most additives might have been tested on animals to find out whether they are toxic in high doses.

This list is limited to a description of the sources of additives rather than their safety. For information on these it is advisable to refer to one of the specialised publications (such as *Food Additives –Taking the lid off what we really eat*). With such a variety of sources and processes it is difficult to guarantee the origins of all additives, but the categories below are as accurate as possible.

Additives are listed numerically. The sources of each additive are indicated by the following key:

A	Animal origin	M	Synthetic origin
V	Ovo-lacto vegetarian origin	V*	Vegan origin
U	Unknown origin		

Colourings (E100 - E180)

E100
Curcumin, Turmeric — **V***

E101
Riboflavin, Lactoflavin, Vitamin B_2 — **V* M**

E101a
Riboflavin 5-phosphate — **M**

E102
Tartrazine — **M**

E104
Quinoline yellow — **M**

E107
Yellow 2G — **M**
(No longer permitted on the list)

E110
Sunset yellow, FCF, Orange yellow S — **M**

E120
Cochineal, Carminic acid — **A**

E122
Carmoisine, Azorubine — **M**

E123
Aramanth — **M**

E124
Ponceau 4R, Cochineal red A — **M**

E127
Erythrosine BS — **M**

E128
Red 2G — **M**

E129
Allura Red — **M**

E131
Patent blue — **VM**

E132
Indigo carmine, Indigotine — **M**

E133
Brilliant Blue FCF — **M**

E140
Chlorophyll — **V***

E141
Chlorophyllins — **V* M**

E142
Green S, Acid brilliant green, Lissamine green — **M**

E150
Caramels — **V* M**

E151
Black PN, Brilliant black BN — M

E153
Carbon Black, Vegetable carbon — U

E154
Brown FK, Kipper brown, Food brown — M

E155
Brown HT, Chocolate brown HT — M

E160(a)
Alpha-carotene, Beta-carotene,
Gamma-carotene — M

E160(b)
Annatto, Bixin, Norbixin — V*

E160(c)
Capsanthin, Capsorubin — V*

E160(d)
Lycopene — V*

E160(e)
Beta-apo-8-carotenal, Beta-8-apocarotenal — M

E160(f)
Ethyl ester of E160(e) — M

E161
Xanthophylls — V*

E161(a)
Flaxoxanthin — V*

E161(b)
Lutein — V*

E161(c)
Cryptoxanthin — V*

E161(d)
Rubixanthin — V*

E161(e)
Violaxanthin — V*

E161(f)
Rhodoxanthin — V*

E161(g)
Canthaxanthin — M

E162
Beetroot red, Betanin — V*

E163
Anthocyanins — V*

E163(a)
Cyanidin — V*

E163(b)
Delphinidin — V*

E163(c)
Malvidin — V*

E163(d)
Pelargonidin — V*

E163(e)
Peonidin — V*

E163(f)
Petunidin — V*

E170
Calcium carbonate, Chalk — M

E171
Titanium dioxide — M

E172
Iron oxides, Iron hydroxides — M

E173
Aluminium — M

E174
Silver — M

E175
Gold — M

E180
Pigment rubine, Lithol rubine RK — M

Preservatives (E200 - E297)

E200
Sorbic acid — M

E201
Sodium sorbate — M

E202
Potassium sorbate — M

E203
Calcium sorbate — U

E210
Benzoic acid — M

E211
Sodium benzoate — M

E212
Potassium benzoate — M

E213
Calcium benzoate — U

E214
Ethyl 4-hydroxy-benzoate, Ethyl parahydroxybenzoate — M

E215
Sodium salt of E214 — M

E216
Propyl 4-hydroxy-benzoate,
Propyl parahydroxybenzoate — M

E217
Sodium salt of E216 — M

E218
Methyl 4-hydroxy-benzoate, Methyl parahydroxybenzoate **M**

E219
Sodium salt of E218 **M**

E220
Sulphur dioxide **M**

E221
Sodium sulphite **M**

E222
Sodium hydrogen sulphite, Sodium bisulphite, Acid
sodium sulphite **M**

E223
Sodium metabisulphite, Disodium pyrosulphite **M**

E224
Potassium metabisulphite, Potassium pyrosulphite **M**

E226
Calcium sulphite **M**

E227
Calcium hydrogen sulphite, Calcium bisulphite **U**

E230
Biphenyl, Diphenyl **M**

E231
2-hydroxy-biphenyl, O-phenyl phenol, Orthophenyl
phenol **M**

E232
Sodium biphenyl-2-yl oxide, Sodium orthophenyl phenate,
Sodium orthophenyl phenol **M**

E233
Thiabendazole, 2(thiazol-4-yl) benzimidazole **M**

E234
Nisin **V***

E236
Formic acid *No longer permitted on the list*

E237
Sodium formate *No longer permitted on the list*

E238
Calcium formate *No longer permitted on the list*

E239
Hexamine, Hexamethylene tetramine **M**

E249
Potassium nitrite **M**

E250
Sodium nitrite **M**

E251
Sodium nitrite, Chile saltpetre **M**

E252
Potassium nitrite **M**

E260
Acetic acid **V* M**

E261
Potassium acetate **V* M**

E262
Sodium hydrogen acetate, Sodium diacetate **V* M**

E262
Sodium acetate **V* M**

E263
Calcium acetate **V* M**

E270
Lactic acid **V**

E280
Propionic acid **V* M**

E281
Sodium propionate **V* M**

E282
Calcium propionate **U**

E283
Potassium propionate **V* M**

E290
Carbon dioxide **M**

E296
Dl-malic acid, L-malic acid **V* M**

E297
Fumaric acid **V***

Antioxidants (E300 - E321)

E300
L-ascorbic acid, Vitamin C **V* M**

E301
Sodium l-ascorbate **M**

E302
Calcium l-ascorbate **U**

E304
6-O-Palmitoyl-l-ascorbic acid, Ascorbyl palmitate **M**

E306
Tocopherols, Vitamin E **V* M**

E307
Alpha-tocopherol, Vitamin E **M**

E308
Gamma-tocopherol **M**

E309
Delta-tocopherol **M**

E310
Propyl gallate, Propyl 3,4,5 trihydroxy-benzene **M**

E311
Octylgallate **M**

E312
Dodecyl gallate, Dodecyl 3,4,5 trihydroxy-benzene **M**

E320
Butylated hydroxyanisole, BHA **M**

E321
Butylated hydroxytoluene BHT **M**

Emulsifiers, stabilisers, thickeners

E322
Lecithin **V**

E325
Sodium lactate **V**

E326
Potassium lactate **V**

E327
Calcium lactate **U**

E330
Citric acid **V***

E331
Sodium citrates **V* M**

E331(a)
Sodium dihydrogen citrate **V* M**

E331(b)
Disodium citrate **V* M**

E331(c)
Trisodium citrate **V* M**

E332
Potassium dihydrogen citrate, Monopotassium citrate,
Tripotassium citrate, Potassium citrate **V* M**

E333
Calcium citrate, Monocalcium citrate, Dicalcium
citrate, Tricalcium citrate **U**

E334
L-(+)-tartaric acid **V***
-DL-tartaric acid **V***

E335
Monosodium L-(+)-tartrate, Disodium L-(+)-tartrate
Monosodium DL-tartrate, Disodium DL-tartrate **V* M**

E336
Monopotassium L-(+)-tartrate, Potassium hydrogen
L-tartrate, Potassium acid L-(+)-tartrate, Cream
of tartar, Dipotassium tartrate **V* M**
-Monopotassium DL-tartrate **V* M**
-Dipotassium DL-tartrate **V* M**

E337
Potassium sodium L-(+)-tartrate, Sodium potassium

L-(+)-tartrate, Rochelle salt **V* M**
-Potassium disodium DL-tartrate

E338
Orthophosphoric acid, Phosphoric acid **M**

E339(a)
Sodium dihydrogen orthophosphate **M**

E339(b)
Disodium hydrogen phosphate, Acid sodium phosphate **M**

E339(c)
Trisodium orthophosphate **M**

E340(a)
Potassium dihydrogen orthophosphate, Potassium
orthophosphate, Potassium phosphate monobasic **M**

E340(b)
Dipotassium hydrogen orthophosphate, Potassium
phosphate dibasic **M**

E340(c)
Tripotassium orthophosphate, Potassium phosphate
tribasic **M**

E341(a)
Calcium tetrahydrogen diorthophosphate, Acid calcium
phosphate, ACP **U**

E341(b)
Calcium hydrogen orthophosphate, Calcium phosphate
dibasic **U**

E341(c)
Tricalcium diorthophosphate, Tricalcium phosphate,
TCP **U**
-Ammonium dihydrogen orthophosphate,
Ammonium phosphate monobasic **M**
-Diammonium hydrogen orthophosphate,
Ammonium phosphate dibasic **M**

350
Sodium malate, Sodium hydrogen malate **V* M**

351
Potassium malate **V* M**

352
Calcium malate, Calcium hydrogen malate **V* M**

353
Metatartaric acid **V* M**

355
Adipic acid, Hexanedioic acid **M**

363
Succinic acid **V***

370
1,4-Heptono-lactone **M**

375
Nicotinic acid, Niacin, Nicotinamide **M**

380
Triammonium citrate V*

381
Ammonium ferric citrate, Ferric ammonium citrate,
Ammonium ferric citrate green V*

385
Calcium disodium ethylene diamine-NNN"N"tetra-acetate,
Calcium disodium EDTA M
-Disodium dihydrogen ethylene
diamine-NNN"N"tetra-acetate, Disodium M

E400
Alginic acid V*

E401
Sodium alginate V* M

E402
Potassium alginate V* M

E403
Ammonium alginate V* M

E404
Calcium alginate U

E405
Propane-1,2-diol alginate, Propylene glycol alginate,
Alginate ester V* M

E406
Agar, Agar-agar, Japanese isinglass V*

E407
Carrageenan, Irish moss V*

E408
Furcellaran V

E410
Locust bean gum, Carob gum V*

E412
Guar gum, Jaguar gum, Cluster bean, Guar flour V*

E413
Tragacanth, Gum tragacanth, Gum dragon V*

E414
Gum arabic, Gum acacia, Sudan gum, Gum hashab,
Kordafan
gum V*

E415
Xanthan gum, Corn sugar gum V*

E416
Karaya gum, Sterculia gum V*

E420(i)
Sorbitol M

E420(ii)
Sorbitol syrup M

E421
Mannitol, Manna sugar V*

E422
Glycerol A

E430
Polyoxyethylene (8) stearate, Polyoxyl (8) stearate U

E431
Polyoxyethylene (40) stearate, Polyoxyl (40) stearate U

E432
Polyoxyethylene sorbitan monolaurate, Polysorbate 20,
Tween 20 U

E433
Polyoxyethylene sorbitan mono-oleate, Polysorbate 80,
Tween 80 U

E434
Polyoxyethylene sorbitan monopalmitate, Polysorbate 40,
Tween 40 U

E435
Polyoxyethylene sorbitan monostearate, Polysorbate 60,
Tween 60 U

E436
Polyoxyethylene sorbitan tristearate, Polysorbate 65,
Tween 65 U

E440(a)
Pectin, Ammonium pectate, Potassium pectate, Sodium
pectate V*

E440(b)
Amidated pectin, Pectin extract V* M

E442
Ammonium phosphates, Emulsifier YN M

E450(a)
Disodium dihydrogen diphosphate, Acid sodium
pyrophosphate, Trisodium diphosphate, Tetrasodium
-diphosphate, Tetrasodium pyrophosphate M

E450(b)
Pentasodium triphosphate, Sodium tripolyphosphate,
Pentapotassium triphosphate,
Potassium tripolyphosphate M

E450(c)
Sodium polyphosphates, Potassium polyphosphates M

E460(i)
Microcrystalline cellulose V*

E460(ii)
Alpha-cellulose, Powdered cellulose V*

E461
Methyl cellulose, Methogel, Cologel V* M

E463
Hydroxypropyl cellulose V* M

E464
Hydroxypropyl methyl cellulose, Hypromellose **V* M**

E465
Ethyl methyl cellulose, Methyl ethyl cellulose **V* M**

E466
Carboxymethyl cellulose sodium salt, Carmellose sodium, CMC **V* M**

E470
Salts of fatty acids, Soaps **A**

E471
Glycerides of fatty acids, Glyceryl monostearate, Gylceryl distearate **V* A**

E472(a)
Acetic acid esters of glycerides of fatty acids, Acetoglycerides, Glycerol esters **A**

E472(b)
Lactic acid esters of glycerides of fatty acids, Lactylated glycerides, Lactoglycerides **A**

E472(c)
Citric acid esters of glycerides of fatty acids **A**

E472(d)
Tartaric acid esters of glycerides of fatty acids **A**

E472(e)
Mono and diacetyltartaric acid esters of glycerides of fatty acids **A**

E473
Sucrose esters of fatty acids **A**

E474
Sucroglycerides **A**

E475
Polyglycerol esters of fatty acids **A**

476
Polyglycerol esters of polycondensed fatty acids of castor oil, Polyglycerol polyricinoleate **A**

Polyglycerol esters of demerised fatty acids of soya bean oil **A**

E477
Propylene glycol esters of fatty acids, Propane-1,2-diol esters of fatty acids **A**

E478
Lactylated fatty acid esters of glycerol and propane-1,2-diol **A**

E481
Sodium stearoyl-2-lactylate **U**

E482
Calcium stearoyl-2-lactylate **U**

E483
Stearyl tartrate **U**

E491
Sorbitan monostearate **U**

E492
Sorbitan tristearate, Sapn 65 **U**

E493
Sorbitan monolaurate, Span 20 **M**

E494
Sorbitan mono-oleate, Span 80 **M**

E495
Sorbitan monopalmitate, Span 40 **M**

Acids bases and others (500-529)

500
Sodium carbonate, Sodium hydrogen carbonate, Sodium bicarbonate, Baking soda, Bicarbonate of soda, Sodium sesquicarbonate, Trona **M**

501
Potassium carbonate, Potassium hydrogen carbonate **M**

503
Ammonium carbonate, Ammonium hydrogen carbonate, Ammonium bicarbonate, Hartshorn **M**

504
Magnesium carbonate, Magnesite **M**

507
Hydrochloric acid **M**

508
Potassium chloride **M**

509
Calcium chloride **M**

510
Ammonium chloride **M**

513
Sulphuric acid **M**

514
Sodium sulphate **M**

515
Potassium sulphate **M**

516
Calcium sulphate, Gypsum, Plaster of Paris **M**
Ammonium sulphate **M**

518
Magnesium sulphate **M**

524
Sodium hydroxide **M**

525
Potassium hydroxide — M

527
Ammonium hydroxide — M

528
Magnesium hydroxide — M

529
Calcium oxide — M

Anti-caking agents and others (530-578)

530
Magnesium oxide, Native magnesium, Periclase — M

535
Sodium ferrocyanide, Sodium hexacyanoferrate II — M

536
Potassium ferrocyanide, Potassium hexacyanoferrate II — M

540
Dicalcium diphosphate, Calcium hydrogen phosphate — M

541
Sodium aluminium phosphate acidic, Sodium aluminium phosphate basic — M

542
Edible bone phosphate — A

544
Calcium polyphosphates — M

545
Ammonium polyphosphates — M

551
Silicon dioxide, Silicea, Silica — M

552
Calcium silicate — M

553(a)
Magnesium silicate synthetic, Magnesium trisilicate — M

553(b)
Talc — M

554
Aluminium sodium silicate — M

556
Aluminium calcium silicate, Calcium aluminium silicate — M

558
Bentonite, Bentonitum, Soap clay — M

559
Kaolin heavy, Kaolin light — M

570
Stearic acid — U
-Butyl stearate — M

572
Magnesium stearate — U
-Calcium stearate — U

575
D-glucono-1,5-lactone, Glucono deltalactone — M

576
Sodium gluconate — M

577
Potassium gluconate — M

578
Calcium gluconate — M

Flavour enhancers and sweeteners (620-637)

620
L-glutamic acid — V*

621
Monosodium glutamate, Sodium hydrogen L-glutamate, MSG — V*

622
Potassium hydrogen L-glutamate, Monopotassium glutamate — V*

623
Calcium dihydrogen di-L-glutamate, Calcium glutamate — V*

627
Guanosine 5-disodium phosphate, Sodium guanylate, Disodium guanylate — U

631
Inosine 5-disodium phosphate, Sodium 5-inosinate — U

635
Sodium 5-ribonucleotide — U

636
Maltol — M

637
Ethyl maltol — M

Un-numbered additives

Saccharin	M
Calcium saccharin	M
Sodium saccharin	M
Aspartamame	M
Acesulfame potassium	M
Isomalt	M
Xylitol	M
Hydrogenated glucose syrup	M
Thaumatin	M
Mannitol (E421)	M
Sorbitol (E420)	M
Sorbitol syrup (E420)	M
Glycerol (E422)	M
Sucrose	V*

Sugar	V*
(Dried) glucose (syrup)	V*
Dextrose	V*
Invert sugar	V*
Fructose	V*
Lactose	V*
Maltose	V*

Glazing agents (900-907)

900
Dimethyl polysiloxane, Simethicone, Dimethicone	M

901
Beeswax white, Beeswax yellow	V

903
Carnauba wax	V*

904
Shellac	A

905
Mineral hydrocarbons	M

907
Refined microcrystalline wax	M

Improvers and bleaching agents (920-927)

920
L-cysteine hydrochloride, L-cysteine hydrochloride monohydrate	A

924
Potassium bromide	M

925
Chlorine	M

926
Chlorine dioxide	M

927
Azodicarbonamide, Azoformamide	M

Un-numbered additives

Acesulfame potassium, Asulfame K	M
Aluminium potassium sulphate	M
2-Aminoethanol, Monoethanolamine	M
Aspartame	M
Butylstearate	U
Caffeine	V*
Calcium phytate, Calcium mesoinositolhexaphosphate	V* M
Dichlorodifluoromethane	M
Dichloromethane	M
Diethyl ether, Solvent ether	M
Diocytl sodium sulphosuccinate	M
Disodium Edetate	M
Ethoxyquin	M

Ethyl alcohol, Ethanol	V*
Ethyl acetate	M
Glycerol monoacetate, Monoacetin, Glycerol diacetate, Diacetin, Glycerol triacetate, Triacetin	U
Glycine	U
Sodium hepatone	M
Calcium hepatone	M
Hydrogen	M
Hydrogenated glucose syrup, Hydrogenated high maltose glucose syrup	M
Isomalt	M
Isopropyl alcohol	M
Leucine	A
Nitrogen	M
Nitrous oxide	M
Octadecylammonium acetate, Octadecylamine acetate	M
Oxygen	M
Oxystearin	U
Oxidatively polymerised 1/soya bean oil	V*
Polydextrose	M
Propylene glycol, Propane-1,2-diol	M
Extract of quillaia	V*
Saccharin, Sodium saccharin, Calcium saccharin	M
Spermaceti, Sperm oil	A
Aluminium potassium sulphate, Potassium aluminium sulphate, Potash alum	M
Tannic acid, tannin	V*
Thaumatin	V*
Xylitol	M

INFORMATION

Food Additives –
> *Taking the lid off what we really eat*
> Erik Millstone, Penguin Books

Food Adulteration and how to beat it
> The Food Commission,
> Unwin paperbacks

The Residue Report
> Stephanie Lashford, Thorsons

The Food Scandal
> Caroline Walker & Geoffrey Cannon, Century

The Politics of Food
> Geoffrey Cannon, Century

The New E for Additives,
> Maurice Hanssen, Thorsons.

Food Additives Campaign Team (FACT)
> 25 Horsell Road, London N1 1XL

Food Irradiation Campaign.
> c/o Food Commission, 88 Old Street, London, EC1V 9AR.
> Published a book called
> *Food Irradiation –*
> *the Myth and the Reality*

National Consumer Council
> 20 Grosvenor Square, London, SW1W 0DM

Parents for Safe Food
> Britannia House, 1-11 Glenthorne Road, Hammersmith, London, W6 0LS.

Common food additives

Food additives are substances used during food processing in order to change various characteristics of a food. They are used to prevent deterioration in, and to extend the shelf life of, various foods. They are also used to change the colour and flavour of food. Additives can make otherwise unpalatable foods attractive for sale.

The testing of food additives for safety requires the use of animals in feeding experiments, which raises ethical questions for vegetarians. Some additives are still used whilst data is being collected on safety, and others are exempt from regulations – such things as flavourings, modified starches and enzymes. Absolute safety can never be guaranteed – sensitivity reactions such as asthma, hyperactivity in children, nausea and vomiting, nasal congestion, headaches, rashes, swellings and blurred vision do occur. The number of additives used has increased ten-fold over the last three decades, so it is likely that the incidence of sensitivity is increasing although there are no definite figures.

Natural additives are not necessarily 'better' than synthetic ones. They are often extracted from sources not generally considered foods, or they are processed so that the original components are concentrated.

Additives in the *ingredients* of products do not need to be included on the label; so… the flour bleach used does not have to be listed as an ingredient of the bread. Take-away foods also do not need to declare the use of additives. Additives are listed by name, unless they have a number, in which case (to make things really difficult!) they are listed by name or number.

Additives listed by name The glossary below represents some of the more common additives – or groups of additives – permitted in Britain. They are usually listed by name on packets. Additives are listed here alphabetically with cross references (marked q.v.). The sources of each additive are indicated by the following key,

A	Animal origin	M	Synthetic origin
V	Ovo-lacto vegetarian origin	V*	Vegan origin
U	Unknown origin		

Acetic acid

Acidulant (q.v.) and preservative (q.v.). Used in pickles, sauces and preserves. Can be obtained by synthetic processes, or derived from vinegar. **M or V*.**

Acidulant

Added to give tartness (acidity) to foods ,in order to increase flavour intensity. Used in soft drinks, jellies, jams, preserves, pickles, sauces, confectionery, soups. Includes acetic, ascorbic, citric, fumaric, lactic, malic, phosphoric, succinic and tartaric acids. Mainly derived from industrial fermentations. **M, V*.**

Alginate

Thickener (q.v.) derived from seaweed. Includes alginic acid, algin (sodium alginate) and propylene glycol alginate. Replaces gelatin (q.v). Used in processed cheese, salad dressings, ice cream, frozen desserts, cake mixes, puddings. **M, V*.**

Anticaking agent (or desiccant)

Used to dry out foods to prevent lumping. Used in some powdered foods e.g. salt, some sugars, milk powder, onion and garlic salts. Includes calcium phosphate, magnesium carbonate, calcium or magnesium silicate, silica gel, talc, starch calcium stearate. **M** though calcium stearate may be **A**. *Not necessarily included on labels.*

Antifoaming agent

Used to prevent foaming, eg during the boiling of soups and jellies and the fermentation of wines. Also used in cooking oils. Dimethyl polysiloxane is a typical example. **M**. *Not necessarily included on labels.*

Antioxidant

Used to prevent rancidity or browning in foods, thereby increasing shelf life. Added to fruit and fruit products (mainly as ascorbic acid), oils, fats, potato crisps, biscuits, breakfast cereals, soup mixes, wine, beer. Includes ascorbic acid, butylated hydroxyanisole (BHA), butylated hydroxytoluene (BHT), gallic acid derivatives, lecithin and tocopherols. Usually **M or V***.

Ascorbic acid

Acidulant (q.v.), antioxidant (q.v.) and improving agent (q.v.).

Vitamin C. Extracted from plants or synthesised from glucose. **V* or M.**

Azo dyes

Artificial colourings synthesised from petroleum. **M**

Baking powder

Leavening agent (q.v.) **M** and **V***

Benzoic acid

Preservative (q.v.) used in tea and coffee extracts, pickles, juices and soft drinks. **M.**

Biphenyl (diphenyl)

Preservative (q.v.) used to control mould growth on citrus fruit. Applied to wrappers or to the inside of shipping containers. **M.**

Bleaching agent

Used to accelerate the maturing process in flour and also to produce a uniform colour. Includes nitrogen oxides, chlorine, chlorine dioxide, ammonium persulphate. Used in bread manufacture. **M.** *Not necessarily included on labels.*

Bulking agents

To increase the volume of a food. Used in slimming products e.g. polydextrose. **M.** *Not necessarily included on labels.*

Butylated hydroxyanisole (BHA)

Antioxidant (q.v.). **M.**

Butylated hydroxytoluene (BHT)

Antioxidant (q.v.) **M.**

Calcium chloride

A crisping and firming agent (q.v.) used for preserved fruit and vegetables. **M.**

Calcium phosphate

Anticaking agent (q.v.). Used to fortify bread with calcium. Usually obtained from crushed rocks. **M.**

Caramel

Colouring agent (q.v.) used in sauces, pickles, convenience foods. Manufactured from sugars. **M and V*.**

Carob gum

Stabiliser (q.v.). Naturally occurring gum from the locust bean. Used in ice cream, sauces, salad dressing, pie fillings, bakery products, soft cheeses, infant foods. **V*.**

Casein

The principal protein of cows milk. Casein and its salts are used in many dairy products. **V.**

Cellulose

Used as an emulsifier (q.v.) and a thickener (q.v.). Cellulose and its derivatives are used in ice cream, pie fillings and in slimming foods to reduce the energy concentration. Obtained from plants. **V*.**

Chalk (creta preparata)

Used in bread as a source of calcium. **M.**

Charcoal

Clarifying agent (q.v.) used in the manufacture of soft and alcoholic drinks and sugar. Derived from animal or plant materials. **A** and **V***.

Chelating agents

See Sequestering agents.

Citric acid

Acidulant (q.v.). **V***.

Clarifying agent

Used to remove turbidity from wine, beer, vinegar, fruit juices and soft drinks. Can be obtained from a variety of sources. Examples are tannin **(V*)**, gelatin **(A)**, cellulose **(V)**, albumins (usually from battery eggs, **(V)**, pectinases **(V*)** and fungal proteases **(V*)**. *Not included on labels.*

Coal tar dyes

See Azo dyes.

Colouring agent

Colourings may be natural (e.g. turmeric, annatto), or synthetic (see below). Colours are used in a variety of foods, soft drinks, confectionery, icings, jellies, baked goods, pie fillings, cake mixes, packed fruits, cheese, butter, margarine. Natural colours may be of either plant or animal origin: examples are cochineal **(A)**, chlorophylls **(V*)**, carotenoids **(V*)**, anthocyanins **(V*)**.

Dextrose (glucose)

Sweetener (q.v.) manufactured from starch. **V***.

Emulsifier

Emulsifiers permit oil to be dispersed in water. They produce a smooth and even texture, and they allow the desired body and consistency to be obtained in many food products. They are used in margarine, nut butters, shortenings, salad creams, confectionery, biscuits, cakes, ice cream, frozen desserts. Emulsifiers can be obtained from a variety of sources, eg lecithins from soyabeans **(V*)** or egg white (unlikely to be free-range) **(V)**, vegetable gums such as alginates, carragheen, locust bean gum, pectins, algal celluloses (all **V***), fatty acid derivatives (usually **A**). Synthetic emulsifiers **(M)** are also used.

Enzymes

Biological molecules which break down foods, help to modify or synthesise them. Examples are rennet **(A)**, pepsin **(A)** used to make cheese. Increasingly likely to be genetically engineered. *Enzymes do not need to be specified on labels.*

Excipients

Additive powders used as carriers of other additives, e.g. magnesium silicate **(M)**. *Not necessarily included on labels.*

Firming agents

These are used to impart firmness or to improve texture in processed foods. Calcium and magnesium salts are used in canned tomatoes, potatoes, apples and peas. **M**. *Not necessarily included on labels.*

Flavourings

This is the largest group of food additives, many hundreds of such compounds are available. Many of the flavours used are natural, eg spices, essential oils, clove extract, ginger extract, vanilla extract. Others are synthetic, eg citral for lemon flavour, n-decanol for orange flavour and benzaldehyde for almond flavour. Flavours are used in a variety of foodstuffs, eg soft drinks, confectionery, baked goods, desserts. Usually **M** or **V***. *Flavourings do not need to be specified on food labels.*

Flavour enhancers

These are used to emphasise the flavour of a food. Salt, spices, vinegar and sugar are traditional flavour enhancers. The commonest is monosodium glutamate (MSG) produced by hydrolysis of vegetable materials (e.g. cereals, sugar beet or soya beans). It is used extensively in Chinese cookery. **V** *Not necessarily included on labels.*

Freezant

Can be applied directly to foods to chill and then freeze them. Example – nitrogen **(M)**. *Does not need to be listed on labels.*

Gelatin (gelatine)

Thickener (q.v.) obtained by boiling animal skins, tendons, ligaments, bones etc. with water. Used in confectionery, ice cream, and other dairy products, jellies. **A**.

Gelling agent

To thicken foods or form a gel. Examples gelatin (q.v.) **(A)**, alginic acid **(V*)**.

Glazing agent

To create a surface shine or protective coating. Used in dried fruits, sweets and desserts. Examples are beeswax **(V)**, carnauba wax **(V*)**, shellac **(A)**, mineral hydrocarbons **(M)** and refined crystalline wax **(M)**. *Not necessarily included on labels.*

Glyconolactone

D-glucono-1, 5-lactone is a sequestering agent (q.v.) used in the dairy industry. It is manufactured from glucose. **M**.

Glycerol (glycerine)

This is used as a humectant (q.v.) and as a solvent for other food additives. Glycerol derivatives are used as emulsifiers (q.v.). It can be manufacturd from petroleum **(M)**, by fermentation of sugars **(V*)** or as a by-product in the manufacture of soaps (usually **A**). Glycerol is rarely **V*** unless this is deliberately specified by the manufacturer.

Guar gum

This is used as an emulsifier (q.v.) in salad dressings, soups, ice cream. It is extracted from the seeds of a legume. **V***.

Humectants

Used to absorb or retain moisture. They include glycerol, propylene glycol and sorbitol. They are used in confectionery and dried fruit. *Not necessarily included on labels.*

Hydrolised proteins

Added to soups, processed cheese, packeted foods, flavouring extracts and soya sauce in order to enhance flavour and to increase the nutritional value. **A, V** and **V*** depending on the source of the protein.

Improving agents

Used to improve the dough-making characteristics of bread. They include ascorbic acid, calcium phosphate, ammonium or potassium bromate. **M**. *Not necessarily included on the label.*

Incidental additives

Those whose presence in food is unintentional. They include migrant additives from materials used in packaging (e.g. printing ink, waxes, polyvinyl chloride), residues of materials used transiently during processing (e.g. solvents used during extraction) and residues of agricultural chemicals (e.g. antibiotics, pesticides). *These materials are not regarded as additives and so are not listed on the label.*

Lactic acid

Acidulant (q.v.). Used extensively in pickles and preserves, processed foodstuffs, desserts, confectionery, dairy products. Ordinary or racemic lactic acid (DL-lactic acid) is usually prepared from sour milk or by fermentation of plant materials (e.g. corn starch, potatoes, molasses) or by synthesis. **M, V, V***.

Lactose

Lactose or milk sugar is a by-product of the cheese industry. It is used as a sweetener (q.v.) and also in dairy products. **V**.

Leavening agents

Used to render unfermented dough light and porous. They consist of a source of carbon dioxide gas and an acid or acid-producing substance (to release the gas). Include calcium phosphate, sodium bicarbonate, cream of tartar. **M** and **V***.

Lecithin

Antioxidant (q.v.) and emulsifier (q.v.). Usually obtained from soya beans as a by-product of soya oil extraction. Also obtained from eggs (unlikely to be free-range).Used extensively in the food industry and especially in margarine and chocolate. **V*** or **V**.

Maltol

A flavour enhancer (q.v.) used to impart a 'freshly baked' odour to bread and cakes. It is also used in drinks, jams and confectionery. **M**.

Mineral oil (Petrolatum)

Used for the preservation of dried fruit, as a coating on cheese, and in bakeries for greasing tins and trays. It is obtained during the refining of petroleum. Mineral oil may interfere with the absorption of fat-soluble vitamins during digestion. **M**.

Modified starch

Chemically treated starch. Used as stabiliser (q.v.). **M** and **V***.

Monosodium glutamate (MSG)

Flavour enhancer (q.v.) **V***.

Nutrients

These are added to some foods in order to restore those nutrients lost during processing, e.g. iron, calcium and B vitamins are added to white flour. Vitamins A and D are added to margarine. Some additives have a nutrient function eg ascorbic acid, used as an acid-ulant, is also a vitamin. D_2 is **V***, D_3 is **A**.

Pectin

Used as a setting agent or an emulsifier (q.v.). It is used in jams, confectionery, chocolate, ice cream. It is extracted from apple pulp and orange pith. **V***.

Pepsin

A clotting agent obtained from pigs' stomachs, used with rennet (q.v.) during cheese manufacture. **A**.

Phytic acid

A sequestering agent (q.v.). It is found in bread and cereal grain where it binds calcium and iron, making them unavailable during digestion. Its binding effect is reduced during the leavening process. The body can adapt to phytic acid in the diet by producing an enzyme which destroys it. **V***.

Preservatives

Used to prevent or delay the food spoilage caused by micro-organisms. Smoking, pickling and salting are examples of traditional preservation processes. Sulphur dioxide **(M)** is one of the most widely used preservatives. It is added to beer, wine, cider, fruit juices, jams, tinned and dried vegetables. Other preservatives are benzoic acid **(M)**, propionates **(M)**, benzoates **(M)**, and sorbates **(M)**. Spoilage can also be prevented or delayed by physical means, eg pasteurisation, freezing, drying.

Propellants

Gases that are capable of expelling foods from aerosols. *Not listed on food labels.*

Propylene glycol

Humectant (qv). **M**.

Proteases

Enzymes which aid protein breakdown. They are used in the manufacture of soya sauce, tamari and miso. They are also used in clarifying fruit juices. Most proteases are extracted from plants or micro-organisms. One protease, rennet, used in cheese manufacture, is extracted from the stomach of young calves. **V** or **A**.

Releasing agents

Used to prevent food sticking to packaging, moulds, tins and machinery, e.g. magnesium stearate **(U)**. *Not listed on food labels.*

Rennet

A protease (q.v.) used in the manufacture of hard and cream cheeses. Due to economic reasons, rennet is usually mixed with other enzymes eg pepsin from pigs. Plant rennets, extracted from micro-organisms, are available and are used in the manufacture of 'vegetarian' cheeses. **A**.

Sequestering agents

Used to counteract the effects of metal ions by binding them and thus making them inactive. Metal ions can adversely affect colour, clarity, flavour and stability. Citric acid, phytic acid, tartaric acid and orthophosphate are examples of such additives. They are used in margarine, salad dressings, soft drinks, tinned fruit and vegetables. **M, V***. *They do not need to be included on labels.*

Solvents

To dissolve and help carry other additives, e.g. dichloromethane **(M)**, ethylacetate **(M)**, glycerol salts **(A)**. *Not listed on food labels.*

Sodium carboxy-methylcellulose

A cellulose (q.v.) derivative used as a 'filler' in slimming foods. **V* M**.

Sodium chloride

Or table salt. Used as a flavour enhancer (q.v.) and a preservative (q.v.). **M**.

Sorbic acid

A preservative (q.v.) used in margarines, cheese, sauces, fruit juices and confectionery. **M**.

Sorbitol

Used as a humectant (q.v.) and a sweetener. Used in foods for diabetics. (q.v.). **M**.

Stabilisers

Used to impart a smooth texture to certain foods and to prevent separation of oil-water emulsions. They can be obtained from a variety of sources, e.g. guar gum **(V*)**, carragheen **(V*)**, pectin **(V*)**, agar **(V*)**, celluloses **(V*** and **M)**, gelatin **(A)**. They are used in ice creams and frozen desserts, whipped products, milk products, soft drinks, cake mixes, jam and jellies.

Starch

Starch and modified starches are used as stabilisers (q.v.). **M** and **V***.

Stearates

Fats used as emulsifiers (q.v.). Stearic acid, the parent compound is usually a by-product of the soap industry (usually **A**). Stearates can be manufactured from vegetable oils **(V*, M)**.

Sulphur dioxide

An important preservative (q.v.) **M**.

Synergists

Used to enhance the effect of another substance, e.g. tartaric acid **(V*)**, citric acid **(V*)**.

Sweeteners

Include natural products such as sucrose, fructrose, corn syrup and invert sugar. Saccharine is the most common artificial sweetener (May have been tested on animals). They are used in packeted desserts, puddings, sauces, soft drinks, confectionery, tinned fruit and vegetables. **V*** and **M**.

Texture agents

Include emulsifiers (q.v.), stabilisers (q.v.), and thickeners (q.v.). They are used widely in ice cream and frozen desserts, milk products, soft drinks, margarine, bread and pastry, confectionery. Due to their wide usage they probably constitute the largest class of food additives in terms of the amount consumed.

Thickeners

Added to foods in order to give a smooth, uniform texture. They are similar to emulsifiers (q.v.) and stabilisers (q.v.).

The ϒ Symbol

Guidelines for vegetarian products

1. NO animal flesh (meat, fowl, fish or shellfish).
2. NO meat or bone stock (in soups, sauces or other dishes).
3. NO animal fats (suet, lard, dripping) or ordinary white cooking fats or margarine (some contain fish oil) in pastry, frying, for greasing tins or other cooking.
4. NO gelatine, aspic, block or jelly crystals for glazing, moulding, or other cooking; agar-agar is an acceptable alternative.
5. NO other products with ingredients derived from slaughterhouse by-products.
6. NO battery eggs or intensively produced eggs.

Specific commodities

BUTTER Made from milk fat and so it is acceptable to vegetarians. However, it is high in saturated fat and so many people prefer to use pure vegetable oil margerine.

CHEESE Traditionally rennet, an enzyme extracted from the stomach of a calf, is used to make cheese and and this is not acceptable. Vegetarian cheese can be made using rennet obtained from plant or microbiological sources.

EGGS Eggs can be used but must be free range. To apply for use of the ϒ symbol it is necessary to supply the name and address of the supplier of the free-range eggs. A mixture of soya flour and water can be used as a binding agent.

FATS & OILS Lard, suet, tallow, and fish oils are not acceptable. Vegetarian alternatives are vegetable oil and solid vegetable fat.

GRAVIES & STOCK Cubes and powders which contain meat, chicken or fish extracts are not acceptable. Yeast extract, soy sauce and vegetable stock cubes or pastes are suitable alternatives.

MILK May be used. Soya milks are now widely available. Tofu is a soya product which can be used as a substitute for eggs or soft cheese.

WHEY Whey is a by-product of the cheese-making industry. As here is a strong possibility that this process will have involved the use of animal rennet, whey is not considered acceptable.

WORCESTER SAUCE This product is often made using anchovies. Vegetarian products must not contain anchovies. There are now brands of Worcester sauce which are suitable for vegetarians.

Our ϒ Symbol Liaison Officer, Lesley Wilkinson, will be pleased to help with your enquiries.

Corporate membership was introduced this year by the VSUK to create a relationship with other organisations who may not be in a position to use the ϒ Symbol, but who would benefit from membership of the Society. They receive regular copies of our publications and enjoy all the privileges of normal membership apart from voting rights.

Cosmetics & toiletries authorised to use the Vegetarian Society's ⋎ symbol

House of Bentley

– natural Cleansing Bar

Maxim Pharmeceuticals

– amber soap

Montagne Jeunesse

– avocado cleansing milk
– cucumber cleansing milk
– honey & lemon facial scrub
– avocado & pineapple face mask
– wheatgerm & comfrey face mask
– eye make-up remover
– apricot astringent lotion
– comfrey herbal face lotion
– cucumber facial skin toner
– witch hazel facial skin toner
– aloe vera anti-wrinkle night cream
– cucumber moisturising cream
– melon anti-wrinkle cream
– peach & almond vitamin E cream
– orange lip gloss balm
– eyebright eye gel
– chamomile shampoo
– henna gloss shampoo
– seaweed shampoo
– chamomile conditioner
– henna gloss conditioner
– jojoba conditioner
– chamomile hair gel
– green citrus bath oil
– melon bath oil
– passion fruit bath oil
– orange spice shower gel
– orchid foam bath
– milk & honey foam bath
– rose foam bath
– orange blossom bath crystals
– wild raspberry bath crystals
– goats milk bath powder
– honeysuckle bath milk powder
– cucumber pure glycerine soap
– peach pure glycerine soap
– vitamin E pure glycerine soap
– aloe vera cleansing bar
– blue orchid oil soap
– honey & beeswax soap

– purest vegetable cleansing bar
– aloe vera body moisturising gel
– apricot oil body moisturiser
– evening primrose body moisturiser
– black grape body oil
– white grape massage oil
– aloe vera hand cream
– apricot & almond hand lotion
– coconut & rose hand cream
– cocoa butter hand lotion

Organic Product Company

– orchid cleansing milk
– fragrance-free cleansing lotion
– eye makeup remover
– aloe vera cold cream
– lotus cleanser
– water soluble wash cream
– passion fruit facial scrub
– oatmeal facial scrub
– elderflower toner
– strawberry toner
– grape & honey toner
– rose water
– aloe vera toner
– melon day cream
– melon night cream
– melon moisturising cream
– cucumber moisturising cream
– carrot oil facial cream
– jojoba neck oil
– vitamin E cream
– lip balm, mint, cherry, apple
– rose foaming bath
– deep cleansing foam bath
– coconut milk bath
– cucumber bath essence
– strawberry bath essence
– cherry shower gel
– evening primrose shower gel
– apple shower gel
– aloe vera body lotion
– evening primrose body lotion
– leg & vein gel
– arnica knee & elbow cream
– men's cologne body wash
– after shave balm
– musk massage oil
– apple massage oil

– leg & vein gel
– arnica knee & elbow cream
– men's cologne body wash
– after shave balm
– musk massage oil
– apple massage oil
– coconut sun tan lotion

– coconut after sun lotion
– rose & glycerine hand cream
– avocado moisturising lotion
– rose hand cream
– peach hand cream
– herbal foot soak
– peppermint foot cream

Medicines & remedies authorised to use the Vegetarian Society's ⋎ symbol

Allens & Co

– Coltsfoot Pine & Honey Balsam

Booker Nutritional Products

– Vege Vitamins

Britannia Health Products Ltd

– Efamol Eveing Primrose Oil (but NOT capsules)

Holland & Barrett

– Vegetarian Vitamins & Minerals

Honeyrose Health Products Ltd

– All Mins
– Super Multiplex
– Kiddiplex
– Vitamin B complex with Vitamin C
– Multiplex
– Vitamin C

Jessup Marketing

– Beta Carotene Supplement
– Night Tablets
– Quiet Life
– Water Balance
– Garlic Tablets

Nature's Best

– Ascorbate powder
– Colon care plus

Nature's Own

– Multivitamin
– Vitamin B Complex Plus
– Niacin

– Pantothenic Acid
– Vitamin B_6
– Vitamin C + Bioflavonoids
– Vitamin C
– Children's Formulation Multivitamin and Mineral
– Multivitamin and Mineral Formulation
– Vitamin B Complex plus Vitamin C
– Thiamin
– Pantothenic Acid (Peptiode bound)
– Vitamin B_6 (Peptiode bound)
– Vitamin E
– Multimineral (Orotate formulation)
– Dolomite
– Calcium and Magnesium
– Calcium Orotate
– Chromium Orotate
– Zinc Orotate
– Calcium
– Germanium
– Chromium
– Iron and Molybdenum
– Magnesium
– Selenium
– Zinc and Copper
– Brewers Yeat
– Kelp Plus
– Pangamic Acid
– Rutin
– Siberian Ginseng
– Bromelain
– Biotin
– Calcium and Vitamin D
– Choline
– Inositol
– PABA
– Vitamin B_{12}
– Folic Acid

Medicines and supplements – useful addresses

General

British Holistic Medical Association, 179 Gloucester Place, London, NW1 6DX.

The Natural Medicines Society, Regency House, 97-107 Hagley Road, Edgbaston, Birmingham, B16 8LA.

The Institute for Complementary Medicine, 21 Portland Place, London, W1N 3AF. (071) 636 9543.

British Natural Hygiene Society, Shalimar, First Avenue, Frinton-on-Sea, Essex, CO13 9EY. (02536) 2823

Community Health Foundation, 188-194 Old Street, London, EC1V 9BP. (071) 251 4076

College of Health, 18 Victoria Park Square, Bethnal Green, London, E2 9PF. (081) 980 6263.

Environmental Therapy Research 2a Comeragh Road, London, W14 9HP.

Acupuncture

The Council for Acupuncture, Suite 1, 19a Cavendish Square, London, W1M 9AD. (071) 409 1440

British Acupuncture Association, 34 Alderney Street, London, SW1V 4EU. (071) 834 1012/6229

Register of Traditional Chinese Medicine, 19 Trinity Road, London, N2 8JJ.

Traditional Acupuncture Society, 11 Grange Park, Stratford-upon-Avon, Warwickshire CV37 6XH.

International Register of Oriental Medicine, Green Hedges House, Green Hedges Avenue, East Grinstead, Sussex, RH19 1DZ.

Alexander Technique

The Society of Teachers of the Alexander Technique, 10 London House, 266 Fulham Road, London, SW10 9EL. (071) 351 0828

Feldenkrais Information Centre, 188 Old Street, London, EC1V 9BP.

Allergies

Action Against Allergy, 43 The Downs, London, SW20 8HG.

National Society for Research into Allergy, PO Box 45, Hinckley, Leicestershire, LE10 1JY.

Food Watch, Butts Pond Industrial Estate, Sturminster Newton, Dorset, DT10 1AZ.

Aromatherapy

Association of Tisserand Aromatherapists, PO Box 746, Brighton, East Sussex BN1 3BN.

International Federation of Aromatherapists, 46 Dalkeith Road, London SE21 8LS. (081) 670 5011

Shirley Price Aromatherapy Group, Wesley House, Stockwell Head, Hinckley, Leicestershire, LE10 1RD. (0445) 615 466

Cancer

Cancer Help Centre (Bristol), Grove House, Cornwallis Grove, Clifton, Bristol, BS8 4PG. (0272) 743 216

Cancer Prevention Campaign Association, 13 Laneside, Chislehurst, Kent, BR7 6BP. (081) 467 5761

New Approaches to Cancer, c/o Seekers Trust, Addington Park, Maidstone, Kent ME19 5BL.

Chiropractic

British Chiropractic Association, Premier House, 10 Greycoat Place, London, SW1P 1SB. (071) 222 8866

The Institute of Pure Chiropractic, PO Box 127, Oxford, OX1 1HH. (0865) 246 687

Spiritual Healing

National Federation of Spiritual Healers, Church Street, Sunbury-on-Thames, Middlesex, TW16 6RG. (09327) 83164

Radionic Association, 16a North Bar, Banbury, OXON OX16 0TF. (0925) 3183

Herbalism

National Institute of Medical Herbalists, 41 Hatherley Road, Winchester, Hampshire, SO22 6RR. (0962) 68776

The General Register and Council of Consultant Herbalists, Marlborough House, Swanpool, Falmouth, Cornwall TR11 4HW. (0326) 317 321

School of Herbal Medicine, 148 Forest Road, Tunbridge Wells, Kent. (0892) 30400

Dr Edward Bach Centre, Mount Vernon, Stotwell, Wallingford, Oxon, OX10 0PZ.

Homoeopathy

British Homoeopathics Association, 27a Devonshire Street, London, W1N 1RJ. (071) 935 2163

Hahnemann Society for the Promotion of Homoeopathy, Humane Education Centre, Avenue Lodge, Bounds Green Road, London, N22 4EU. (081) 889 1595

Homoeopathic Development Foundation, Harcourt House, 19a Cavendish Square, London, W1M 9AD. (071) 629 3205

Society of Homoeopaths, 2 Artizan Road, Northampton, NN1 4HU. (0604) 21400

Hypnotherapy

Association of Qualified Curative Hypnotherapists, 10 Balaclava Road, Kings Heath, Birmingham. (021) 444 5435

National Council of Psychotherapists and Hypnotherapy Register, 1 Clovelly Road, Ealing, London W5. (081) 840 3790 or (081) 567 0262

National Register of Hypnotherapists and Psychotherapists, 12 Cross Street, Nelson, Lancashire, BB9 7EN. (0282) 699 378

Iridology

National Council and Register of Iridologists, Lacnunda, 80 Portland Road, Bournemouth, BH9 1NQ. (0202) 529 793

British School of Iridology and British Register of Iridologists, P O Box 205, Cambridge, CB3 0RE. (0954) 51652

Naturopathy

British Naturopathic and Osteopathic Association, 6 Netherall Gardens, London, NW3 5RR. (071) 435 7830

Incorporated Society of Registered Naturopaths, 1 Albemarle Road, The Mount, York, YO2 1EN.

Nutrition

The Institute of Optimum Nutrition, 5 Jerdan Place, London SW6 1BE. (071) 385 7984

Osteopathy

British and European Osteopathic Association, 6 Adelaide Road, Teddington, Middlesex, TW11 0AY. (081) 977 8532

British School of Osteopathy, 1-4 Suffolk Street, London, SW1Y 4HG.

European School of Osteopathy, 104 Tonbridge Road, Maidstone, Kent ME16 8SL.

College of Osteopaths Practitioners Association, 110 Thorkhill Road, Thames Ditton, Surrey, KT7 0UW. (081) 398 3308

London School of Osteopathy, 110 Lower Richmond Road, Putney, London SW15. (081) 785 2267

Natural Therapeutic and Osteopathic Society, 110 Lower Richmond Road, Putney, London SW15. (081) 785 1991

Reflexology

Association of Reflexologists, Slaters, 14 Willow End, London N20 8EP.

British Reflexology Association, Monks Orchard, Whitbourne, Worcester WR6 5RB. (0886) 21207

British Reflexology Association, 12 Pond Road, London, SE3 9JL. (081) 852 6062

The International Institute of Reflexology, 28 Hollyfield Avenue, London N11 3BY. (081) 368 0865

The Bayly School of Reflexology, Monks Orchard, Whitbourne, Worcester, WR6 5RB. (0886) 21207

Yoga

Yoga for Health Foundation, Ickwell Bury, Northill, Biggleswade, Bedfordshire, SG18 9EF. (0767) 27271

Friends of Yoga Society, 'Piriskey' 5 Weston Crescent, Old Sawley, Long Eaton, Nottingham, NG10 3BS. (0602) 735 435

Meditation & Relaxation

Friends of the Western Buddhist Order, 51 Roman Road, London, E2 0HU.

Relaxation for Living, 29 Burwood Park Road, Walton-on-Thames, Surrey KT12 5LH.

New World Cassettes, Freepost, Paradise Farm, Westhall, Halesworth, Suffolk, IP19 8BR.

Schools

The following schools cater specifically for vegetarians, although not necessarily exclusively so:

Oxford House School
2 Lexden Road
Colchester
Essex, CP3 3NE
Tel: (0206) 576686

A co-educational school day school for children aged from two and a half to eleven years. 130 pupils.

St Christopher School
Letchworth, Herts
Tel: (0462) 679301

Co-educational school for children aged two and a half to eighteen years. Boarders and day pupils accepted.

St James Independent Schools
91 Queens Gate
London SW7 5Ab
Tel: (071) 373 5638

Day schools for girls and boys aged from four to eighteen.

The Society of Friends
Friends House
Euston Road
London NW1 2B
Tel: (071) 387 3601

This society publishes a list of schools which are run along the principles or are associated with them. The list is available from this address.

The Steiner Schools Fellowship
Kidbrooks Park
Forest Row
Sussex RH18 5JB
Tel: (0342) 82 2115

Associated with 24 Steiner/Waldorf schools in the UK Pupils follow the Waldorf curriculum throughout their 12 years at school in unstreamed classes.

Victoria House Nursery School
73 Hook Road, Goole
N. Humberside, DN14 5JN
Tel: (0405) 769770

Nursery School

Wycliffe College
Stonehouse
Glos., GL10 2JQ
Tel: (045 382) 2432

Emphasis is on balanced education, embracing high academic standards, wide cultural opportunities and much scope for extramural activities, games and outdoor pursuits.

Homes for elderly vegetarians

Local Social services are responsible for catering in state residential homes and the standard provision varies from area to area. Meals on Wheels offer a vegetarian option, and in some boroughs such as Brent and Barnet the local council has worked closely with the local community to make sure that their meals on wheels service caters for Asian, Afro-carribean and Jewish diets.

The following is a list of private Old Peoples Homes which are interested in making a special effort to cater for vegetarians. Not all of the establishments listed are 100% vegetarian, i.e. they cater for traditional diets too.

Homes For Elderly Vegetarians Ltd
Estra House
Station Approach
Streatham
London, SW16 6EJ

The specialists in this area. They can arrange sheltered accommodation in self-contained flatlets in Sussex and North Wales, and also run a number of strictly vegetarian homes, including:

Quarry Road, 23 Grange Road, The Ridge, Hastings, Sussex

Comptons Glen, 171 Comptons Lane, Horsham, Sussex

Cliffe House, 31 Whitehall Road, Rhos On Sea, Clwyd

The following are private residential homes

Plas Rhosyn, Private Vegetarian Rest Home, Fernbrook Road, Penmaenmawr, Gwynedd LL34 6DD

Stanton Hall, Trinity Road, Darlington DL3 7AZ

Belle Vue Residential Care Home for the Elderly, Pendine, Carmarthen, Dyfed SA33 4PD

Deep Meadows, Perranporth, Nr Newquay, Devon

Beech Holme, Cronwell Parade, Scarborough, N Yorks

Russell's Rest Home, 15 Windlesham Road, Brighton, E Sussex

Freehold Cottage
452 Market Street
Shawforth
Rochdale OL12 8JB

Home for people suffering from psychiatric problems. Qualified staff, theraputic activities, home cooked vegetarian food.

Bethany Vegetarian Nursing and Rest Home
7-9 Oak Park Villas
Dawlish, Devon
EX7 0DE

This is also the Headquarters of The Vegetarian Hospice Association. Exclusively vegetarian/vegan, holistic 24 hour nursing care, some rooms with sea views.

The Beulah Trust
40 Olivers Battery
     Road North
Winchester, SO22 4JB

Aims to set up a spiritually caring home for vegetarians too frail to look after themselves.

The British Nutrition Foundation produce a leaflet called *Nutrition and the Elderly* which may be helpful for people who care for the elderly. It is available from:

The British Nutrition Foundation, 15 Belgrave Square, London SW1X 8PS

Starting your own business

The following is a list of useful contacts, books, courses etc., which may be of help to people interested in starting up a vegetarian business.

Courses

The Vegetarian Society's Foundation Courses offer a good introduction to vegetarian catering; we also run courses for people intending to start a guesthouse or restaurant, and for people who want to be demonstrators and we can also design and prepare a course specifically for your company. For details, contact the Cookery School Co-ordinator at VSUK, Parkdale, Dunham Road, Altrincham, Cheshire, WA14 4QG. Tel: (061) 928 0793.

Plymouth College of Further Education,
Kings Road, Devonport, Plymouth, PL1 5QG.
Tel: (0752) 264750.

Vegetarian courses leading to BTEC National Diploma in Hotel Catering.

Stafford College of Further Education,
Earl Street, Stafford.
Tel: (0785) 42361.

Vegetarian catering course leading to BTEC National Diploma in Hotel Catering.

Halesowen College,
Whittingham Road, Halesowen, West Midlands, B63 3NA.
Tel: (021) 550 1451

City & Guilds in Vegetarian Cookery for the Catering Industry.

Highbury College,
Cosham, Portsmouth, Hampshire, PO6 2SA.
Tel: (0705) 383131.

Vegetarian catering courses leading to BTEC National Diploma in Catering. Also five-day course to give basic knowledge of vegetarian foods.

Tile Hill College,
Coventry.

They run short courses for people wanting to start a bed and breakfast business (not completely vegetarian).

Westminster College,
Battersea Park Road, London, SW11 4JR.
Tel: (071) 720 2121.

BTEC in Food Studies with vegetarian option available.

The National Association of Health Stores,
Bastow House, Queens Road, Nottingham NG2 5AS.
Tel: (0602) 866848.

Runs training courses leading to the NAHS Certificate in Retailing or Diploma in Health Food Retailing.

Hotel Catering & Training Board,
International House, High Street, Ealing, London, W5 5DB.
Tel: (081) 579 2400.

Courses, conferences etc., on various aspects of catering (general, not exclusively vegetarian). Also publish the *Mastercraft* series of books and videos on various aspects of catering.

The Royal Society of Health,
38a St George's Drive,
London, SW1V 4BH.
Tel: (071) 630 1021.

Course in essential food hygiene. 6 hours, £5.00.

Miscellaneous

The Co-Operative Development Agency,
21 Panton Street,
London, SW1Y 4DR.

For advice on forming a co-operative. *Also at,* Holyoake House, Hanover Street, Manchester, M60 OAS.

Scottish Co-operatives Development Committee,
Building 1, 1st Floor,
Templeton Business Centre,
Templeton Street,
Glasgow, G40 1DA

For advice about getting started, including loans from the Venue Capital Fund. Regional offices at: Aberdeen Business Centre, Willowbank House, Willowbank Road, Aberdeen, AB1 2YG. Tel: (0224) 593159. Unit 9, Meadow Mill, West Hendersons Wynd, Dundee, DD1 5BY. Tel: (0382) 202203. Ceres Chambers, 43A High Street, Kirkcaldy, Fife, KY1 1LL. Tel: (0592) 642154. The Resource Centre, Corn Exchange Road, Stirling, FK8 2HU. Tel: (0786) 79616.

Business in the Community,
227a City Road,
London, EC1V 1LZ

For free counselling and practical help for small businesses.

The Small Firms Service

Run by the Department of Employment gives advice to every type of small business on almost any business subject. Dial 100 and ask the operator for **Freephone Enterprise.**

Greenspeak

A 'Green' PR/ Advertising/ Communications Agency. 129 Barlow Moor Road, West Didsbury, Manchester, M20 8PP. Tel: (061) 434 1211. Fax: (061) 434 1898.

Finance

Livewire,
Freepost,
Newcastle-upon-Tyne,
NE1 1BR.

The Livewire Scheme aims to help young people aged between 16–25 to get their new businesses off the ground.

The Prince's Youth Business Trust
4th Floor,
10 Hills Place,
London, W1R 1AF.

Lends money to young people to help get their businesses off the ground.

The Vegetarian Charity,
51 East Budleigh Rd,
Budleigh Salterton,
EX9 6EW

Gives grants to those under-26 to help finance projects that promote vegetarianism. You must be a vegetarian to be eligible.

The Ecology Building Society, 8 Main Street, Cross Hills, Keighley, W.Yorks, BD20 8TB. Tel: (0535) 35933.

Books & trade magazines

How to Start a Guesthouse or B&B Business. £3 from the English Tourist Board, Dept D, 4 Bromells Road, London, SW4 OBJ.

Running a Small Hotel by Joy Lennick, £5.95 from Kogan Page, 120 Pentonville Road, London, N1 9JN.

The Health Food Business (magazine): Best Way Designs Ltd, Premier House, Madeira Road, West Byfleet, Surrey, KT14 6NF. Tel: (0932) 336325.

Natural Food Trader (magazine): Argus Health Publications, Queensway House, 2 Queensway, Redhill, Surrey, RH1 1QS. Tel: (0737) 768611. Fax: (0737) 760425.

Health Food Buyers Guide: Argus Health Publications, see above. Published annually; lists UK products, manufacturers and wholesalers.

Guide for Environmental Entrepreneurs: Available from either the Conservation Foundation, 1 Kensington Gore, London, SW7 2AR. Tel: (071) 823 8842 or The Environment Council, 80 York Way, London, N1 9AG. Tel: (071) 278 4736.

The International Vegetarian Union

The Vegetarian Federal Union was established in 1889 with the aim of bringing together all the vegetarian societies of the world. The first World Vegetarian Congress was held in Chicago, USA, in 1893. At the World Vegetarian Congress in Nice in 1908 it was decided to replace the Vegetarian Federal Union with The International Vegetarian Union, and since that time vegetarians from all over the world have been able to meet at the World Vegetarian Congress meetings which have been held in many different countries. The 1990 World Congress was held in Israel, and the 1992 World Vegetarian Congress is to be held in India.

The major aim of IVU is to publicise and develop interest in the vegetarian cause and to provide opportunities for vegetarians to meet.

To this end it:

- **promotes** both World and Regional Congresses.
- **encourages** the formation of vegetarian organisations and co-operation between them.
- **promotes** research into all aspects of vegetarianism.
- **aims** to publish and encourage the publication of material on all aspects of vegetarianism.
- **represents** the vegetarian cause on appropriate international bodies.
- **acts** as a contact organisation for vegetarians all over the world.

IVU promotes the Manker International Foundation which was begun in memory of Shri J.N. Manker who was a leader of both the Indian and world vegetarian movements. All donations are invested and the interest is used to further vegetarianism. The IVU is a non-profit making organisation.

Vegetarian societies, and groups involved in movements for animal welfare, health or humanitarian issues are invited to join as full or associate members.

For further information contact Mr Maxwell G. Lee BA, MSc, Cert.Ed, FRGS, Honorary General Secretary, IVU, 10 King's Drive, Marple, Stockport, Cheshire, SK6 6NQ, England.

Honorary Regional Secretaries:–

Africa

Mr Jan Beeldman, 82 Darrenwood Village, First Street, Darrenwood, 2194 Randburg, South Africa

Middle East

Mr Philip Pick, 855 Finchley Rd, Golders Green, London NW11 8LX, England

India and the East

Sri Jashu Shah, 114a Mittal Court, Narriman Point, 400 021, India

USA

Mr Keith Akers, IVU, VUNA, 2166 South Cherokee Street, Denver, Colorado, 80206 USA

Europe

Mr Rob Snijders, De Nederlandse Vegetariersbond, Larenseweg 26, 1221 CM Hilversum, Netherlands.

The European Vegetarian Union

The European Vegetarian Union is a subsidiary of the IVU and was founded in 1985. Originally based in Brussels, it is now based at the offices of the Dutch Vegetarian Society in Hilversum.

The aim of the EVU is to encourage better communications between European vegetarian groups, and since 1988 the EVU newsletter has been regularly mailed out to all members. The newsletter is an important forum for the exchange of views and information, and it also contains reports on relevant research projects and announcements from new vegetarian groups.

Secretary **Rob Snijders** writes: "As Europe starts to unite, a united European vegetarian movement becomes more important. The recent developments in Eastern Europe have increased the workload, but we are very glad to be able to help vegetarians in Eastern Europe."

Forthcoming Events

Sylvestertargung

To be held 28 December '90 to 2nd January '91 at the Oberwesel/Rhine youth hostel, Germany. Contact: Vegetarierbund Deutschlands, Christel Scholvien, Eichenweg 6, D7117 Bretzfeld, Germany.

4th European Vegetarian Congress

From 25th to 30th July '91, hosted by the Vegetarian Society of the United Kingdom. Contact: EVU.

European Vegetarian Union, Larenseweg 26, NL 1221 CM Hilversum Tel: 31 35 834 796, Fax: 31 35 836 152

VSUK Registered branches

Bath: Jim Foreman, 21 Abingdon Gardens, Odd Down, Bath, Avon, Tel: 0225 832118.

Birmingham: Brian Jervis, 281 Monmouth Drive, Sutton Coldfield, B73 6JO. Tel: 021 354 9978.

Bradford Vegetarian Society: Atma Trasi, 66 Kirkgate, Shipley, West Yorks, BD18 3EL. Tel: 0274 598455.

Brighton, Hove & District: Andrew Wallace, Flat 5, 11 St Michael's Place, Brighton, East Sussex, BN1 3FT. Tel:0273 736162.

Bristol Vegetarian & Vegan Society: Caryne Pearce-Steedman, 6 Fern Street, St Agnes, Bristol, BS2 9LN. Tel: 0272 555221.

Bournemouth & District: Harry Mather, 6 Hayes Avenue, Bournemouth, BH7 7AD. Tel: 0202 33398.

Cheshire: Changes! Phone Bronwen Humphries at VSUK HQ.

Chichester: Mrs J M Mitton, 38 St Leodegars Way, Hunston, Chichester, W Sussex, PO20 6PF. Tel: Chichester 779558.

Coventry Vegetarians: Heather Evans, 8 Eden Croft, Kenilworth, Warwickshire, CV8 2BG. Tel: 0926 54139.

Croydon & District: Israel Berz, 37 Fitzjames Avenue, Croydon, CRO 5DN. Tel: 081 654 7524.

Cumbria: Kenneth Hodgkinson, 19 Loughrigg Pk, Ambleside, Cumbria, LA22 ODY. Tel: 0539 33901.

East Kent: Maria Bean, 15 Huntswood, Singleton, Ashford.

Edinburgh & SE Scotland: Andy Billett, 60/3 Bryson Road, Polwarth, Edinburgh, EH11 1DR. Tel: 031 346 2876.

Glasgow: Edna Park, 49 Methuen Road, Paisley, PA3 4JU. Tel: 041 889 9370.

Guildford & District: Alan Pearce, 20 Burnet Avenue, Burpham, Guildford, Surrey, GU1 1YD. Tel: 0483 69257.

Leeds: Winifred Brown, 221 Otley Road, West Park, Leeds, LS16 5LQ. Tel: 0532 755526. (temporary contact).

Leicester: Lance Sullen, 68 Copeland Avenue, Leicester, LE3 9EH. Tel: 0533 311557.

Letchworth & District: Rene Coram, 15 Highfield, Letchworth, Herts. Tel: 0462 683694.

Lincolnshire: David Burgin, 33 Park Road, Boston, Lincolnshire, PE21 7JW. Tel: 0205 64532.

North Wales: Judith Rice, Pentrefelin Cottage, Glanwydden, Llandudno Junction, Gwynned, LL31 9SP. Tel: 0492 48307, or J Lewis, 0745 825581.

Oxford Vegetarians: Paul Appleby, 57 Sharland Close, Grove, Wantage, Oxon, OX12 OAF. Tel: 0235 769425.

St Albans: Lynne Chamberlain, 27 Meadow Walk, Harpenden, Herts, AL5 5TF.

Sheffield & District: Ms S Bingham, 21 Moorthorpe Gardens, Owlthorpe, Sheffield, S19 6RY. Tel: 0742 473538.

Tees-side: WC Teasdale, 3 Cumberland Grove, Norton, Stockton-on-Tees, Cleveland, TS20 1NT. Tel: 0642 551871.

York & District: H Leslie Harrison, 1 Albemarle Road, The Mount, York, YO2 1EN. Tel: 0904 623693.

Affiliated Groups

Animal Action: (Leighton Buzzard): PO Box 236, Leighton Buzzard, Bedfordshire, LU7 8EW. Tel: 0525 371235.

Animal Aid: (London) Jane Holgate, PO Box 254, London, E5 8TB. Tel: 071 241 1362.

Animal Concern Today: (Plymouth) PO Box 67, Plymouth, PL1 1TH. Tel: 0752 22098.

Ashford & District: Elaine Forder, 3 Village Way, Ashford, Middlesex, TW15 2LA.

Boston Vegetarian Group: Mrs Sylvia Chamberlain, The Shrubbery, Station Road, Old Leake, Near Boston, Lincs, PE22 9RE. Tel: 0205 871152.

Bradford University Animal Rights Group: Ms M Pearson, University Hall, University of Bradford, W Yorks.

Bromley & Environs Vegetarian Group: Kathleen Dunn, 19 Wellsmoor Gardens, Bickley, Bromley, Kent, BR1 2HT. Tel: 01 467 9568.

Cardiff Vegetarians: Fiona Hackett, 24 Snowden Road, Ely, Cardiff, CF5 4PR.

Cheltenham & District: David Harris, Garden Flat, 36 College Road, Cheltenham, GL53 7HX. Tel: 0242 245820.

East London Vegetarians: Jill Cameron, 38 Stanmore Road, Leytonstone, E11 3BU.

Enfield/Chingford Vegetarian Social Group: Maria Gill, 89 Mandeville Court, Lower Hall Lane, Chingford, London, E4 8JB. Tel: 01 529 9419.

Grampian Vegetarian & Vegan Group: Allison Tavendale, Little Lynturk, Muir of Fowlis, Alford, Aberdeenshire, Scotland, AB3 8HT. Tel: 09755 81359.

Gwent Vegetarian Society: Wayne Rees, 7 Charnwood Road, Newport, Gwent, NP9 7HP. Tel: 0633 216400 or 0873 880390.

Haringey Animal Rights: (applied for affiliation). Mrs M. Sampath, 15 Torrington Gardens, London, N11 2AB.

Hastings & St Leonards Vegetarian Group: Elizabeth Flack, Quarry Wood, 23 Grange Road, Hastings, E Sussex, TN34 2RL. Tel: 0424 751119.

Hillingdon & Ealing Vegetarian Group: Garry Reynolds, 20 Lilac Place, West Drayton, Middlesex. Tel: 0895 444442.

Kirklees & Calderdale Vegetarian Group: Lindis Tadman, 8 Elms Hill, Slaithwaite, Huddersfield, HD7 5HR.

Louth & District Vegetarian Group: John Bateman, No 1 Queen's Court, Stewton Meadows, Louth, Lincolnshire, LN11 8RR. Tel: 0507 606227.

Medway Vegetarian Group: Mrs Linda Wilcock, 14 Cloisterham Road, Rochester, Kent, ME1 2BW. Tel: 0634 402524.

Mid Glamorgan Vegetarians: D M M Davies, 25a Castle Street, Maesteg, Morgannwg, CF34 9YH. Tel: 0656 733685.

Reading Vegetarian Group: Mrs Margaret Steel, 37 Kentwood Close, Tilehurst, Reading, RG3 6DH.

South Bucks Vegetarian Group: Andy Hedges, 6 Coronation Crescent, Lane End, High Wycombe, Bucks, HP14 3DX. Tel: 0494 882496.

Spalding & District Vegetarian Group: Rosemary Jones, Linjoy Nurseries, Damgate, Holbeach nr Spalding, Lincs, PE12 8QL. Tel: 0406 22442.

Stafford Vegetarian & Vegan Society: Patricia Skinner, 68 Kimberley Road, Stoke-On-Trent, ST1 4BZ. Tel: 0782 212979.

Tamar Valley Vegetarian Group: Michael Cook & Alison Fife, The Stannary, Mary Tavy, Tavistock, Devon, PL19 9QB. Tel: 082 281 897.

Wellington Vegetarian Group: Dawn Harries, 17 Foxdown Terrace, Wellington, Somerset, TA21 8BL. Tel: 667517. Fax: 0823 663311.

Information Centres

Belfast: Mrs Beth Gourley, 66 Ravenhill Gardens, Belfast, BT6 8GQ.

Bexhill-on-Sea: Miss J Wild, 14 Queens Court, West Parade, Bexhill-on-Sea, East Sussex, TN39 3HT. Tel: 0424 211731.

Berwick-on-Tweed: Miss Julie Walker, 16 Ladywell Rd, Tweedmouth, TD15 2AG. Tel: 0289 330875

Cleveleys: Kym Best, 4 Sherwood Place, Anchorsholme, Cleveleys, Lancs., FY5 3BS. Tel: 0253 862756.

Colchester: A. White, 21 Laburnum Way, Nayland, Colchester, Essex CO6 4LG. Tel: 0206 263545.

Dumfries: Gerry Dunn, 4 Warrenhill Road, Collin, Dumfries, DG1 4PW. Tel: 038775 619.

Lichfield: Bridget Lally, 22 Garrick Road, Lichfield, Staffs., WS13 7DR. Tel: 0543 251140.

Lochness Vegetarian Information Centre: Maralyn Shine, Lochness Centre, Drumnadrochit, via Inverness. Tel: 04562 496.

London: James Milton, 19 Newlands Quay, London E1 9QZ. Tel: 071 702 3901.

North Cornwall: Vharles Bingham & Gillian Smart, Hilltop Animal Haven, Thurdon, Kilkhampton, Bude, Cornwall EX23 9RZ. Tel: 028882 268.

Rhondda: Huw Parry, 6 Price Street, Pentre, Rhonnda, Mid Glamorgan CF41 7JY. Tel: 0443 430372.

Salisbury: Ronald Boyes, 1 George Street, Salisbury, Wilts., Sp2 7BA. Tel: 0722 331542.

South West Oxfordshire: Jean Booth, 32 Hazells Lane, Shrivenham, near Swindon SN6 8DS. Tel: 0793 783548.

Steyning: Betty Roper, 20 Penfold Way, Steyning, West Sussex BN44 3PG. 0903 812878.

Worsley & District: Janet Lyle, 20 Kingsway, Worsley, Manchester M28 4FD. Tel: 061 790 8767.

Please feel welcome to contact your nearest local group, you do not have to be a member of the VSUK before you can attend local meetings.

No group in your area? If you would like to set one up, please contact the Branch Liaison Officer at Parkdale for a *Start Up* Pack.

Social groups

Natural Friends
15 Benyon Gardens
Culford
Bury St. Edmunds
Suffolk. IP28 6EA
Culford (028 484) 315.

Natural Friends, the contact service if you seek vegetarians, vegans, 'green' thinkers, and those interested in alternative therapies. Stamp for details.

**Vegetarian Cycling
and Athletic Club**
10 Gallow Hill Road
Paisley
Renfrewshire, PA3 4TF
(041) 889 9576.

The century-old club continues to provide evidence of the merits of vegetarianism in athletics. New members, both active and supporting, are always welcome.

**Vegetarian
Matchmakers**
14A Woodlands Road
Isleworth
Middlesex.

Introductions exclusively for those who don't eat animals; VMM also holds occasional social events, etc. aims to provide friendly, efficient service – many happy couples confirm this. (established 1980).

**Vegetarian
Social Club**
Enq. Sec. Mrs E Moore
23 Sutherland House
Marloes Road
Kensington, W8 5LG.

Organises Social Events, Rambles, Concerts, Theatre, Exhibitions etc. S.A.E. Please.

**Young Indian
Vegetarians**
33 Goldwell Road
Thornton Heath, Surrey
(01) 681 8884.

Y.I.V. was formed in 1978 to encourage members of the Indian Community to remain vegetarian and to introduce vegetarians from other communities to Indian food.

Conclusion

The material contained in this book will no doubt require updating in subsequent editions. I would be pleased to have opinions, updates and suggestions. Write to: Jane Bowler, Handbook, The Vegetarian Society UK Ltd., Parkdale, Dunham Road, Altrincham, Cheshire, WA14 4QG.

I regret that I may not be able to answer all letters. If you are interested in purchasing the book in bulk for resale, please contact Pat Bowker at the above address.

Thanks to everybody!